TWISTED

One Drug Addict's Desperate Struggle for Recovery

C. Adam Richmond

The Noble Press
Chicago

Publisher's Note: Hunt's Point Avenue in the south Bronx of New York City is real, as are all the events told in these pages. The opinions expressed herein are in no way intended to reflect the thoughts, philosophies, or policies of any organization or institution, either referred to or imagined. The author is not a spokesperson or a representative for any group of individuals. Names, dates, and locales have been changed.

Printed in the United States of America

Library of Congress Cataloging-in-Publication Data
Richmond, C. Adam, 1958–
        Twisted : one drug addict's desperate struggle for recovery / by
C. Adam Richmond
        p.   cm.
        ISBN: 1–879360–08–X : $11.95
        1. Richmond, C. Adam, 1958–   . 2. Narcotic addicts—United
States—Biography.   3. Narcotic addicts—Rehabilitation—United
States—Case studies.   I. Title
HV5805.R53A3   1992
362.29′3′092—dc20   91–36257
[B]   CIP

10 9 8 7 6 5 4 3 2 1

Noble Press books are available in bulk at discount prices. Single copies are available prepaid direct from the publisher:

Marketing Director
The Noble Press, Inc.
213 W. Institute Place, Suite 508
Chicago, IL 60610

For Anita Lenore and Francis Julian

Purchased With Funds

From A

Vermilion Healthcare

Foundation Grant

CONTENTS

CHAPTER ONE: The Wind in My Hair 1

CHAPTER TWO: And the Needle in My Arm 9

CHAPTER THREE: Bicycle Rides in the Park 17

CHAPTER FOUR: Early Hypotheses, Experiments, and Discoveries 37

CHAPTER FIVE: Doctors, The DEA, and the Black Bear 49

CHAPTER SIX: On the Run 83

CHAPTER SEVEN: Rehabilitation 97

CHAPTER EIGHT: Mental Illness and The Chair 125

CHAPTER NINE: Goodbye, Mom 149

CHAPTER TEN: Tennis Matches and Bartending 159

CHAPTER ELEVEN: Marriage 171

CHAPTER TWELVE: Voices, Graveyards, and Denial 191

CHAPTER THIRTEEN: Going Up the River 203

CHAPTER FOURTEEN: Say Hello to Death 221

CHAPTER FIFTEEN: Suicide Sal, Where Are You Now? 233

CHAPTER SIXTEEN: Delusions and Insanity 249

CHAPTER SEVENTEEN: A Steel Cage and a Hospital Bed 263

CHAPTER EIGHTEEN: A Place for Us 275

ACKNOWLEDGMENTS

More than simply sitting at the word processor and retelling my experiences and what it was like, *Twisted* is the culmination and combined effort of many, many people. My life, and the book you currently hold in your hands, can only be acknowledged as testament to their godlike caring and true unselfishness, their love and patience, their time with me, their understanding, and the wisdom and knowledge they have chosen to share. With profound love and appreciation, I thank them here for the presents they have given:

To Catherine, forever, always and a day, for her love and funny bones and weekends in Gloucester during the almost two years it took to make a go of this project; to the beautiful people out at The Noble Press, who took a chance, who believed, and who patiently listened to my worries, fears, and delusions; *especially* to my editor, Mark, whose critical eye and tempered comments to a first-time author took an undisciplined manuscript and transformed it into a polished book. Thank you.

To Phyllis, Loren, Robert, Demaris and the other brats for beginnings; to Will and Ross and Kevin for their telephones, paper towels, coffee cups, and for taking little boys to the ball park; to Jean, whose cheeseburger, more than anyone else's, gave one dopefiend the courage to give it his best; to Dick and Kathy; to Steven, Bethany, Heather, Aunt Jean, and Uncle Don, for being as silly as they are, always were, and probably always will be; to Rosebud, Brother Jay, Brother Pat, my partner Kevin, Ed Who Thinks He's Unique, Kenny, Mike, Russ, Scott, Jim, Michael and Sheila, Lisa, Judy, Gerry, Carrie, Armondo, Units of Blue, Elizabeth, Deeski, Broccoli Rob, Claudia, Keith, Gertrude, Father Dennis, Alan, Catherine, Bill, Dave, Joe, Let Go Enzo, and Mary, The Lovely Miss Jane and The Man Of Her Dreams (their beautiful new baby, Max, Liam, Bear, and swimming pool inclusive), Terry, Erica, Peggy, Michael The Birdman, Brigette, John, Not Really Doctor Tim and Ann, Don, Marcellus, Bobby, Jason, David, Joyce and Jim, and the rest of my family (many of whose names I've probably forgotten; yes, I'll keep coming, maybe, perhaps, I'll even get better).

To my full-time psychiatrist at the laundromat, Maureen, for her innumerable "sessions"; to Stephanie, Mark, Mercia and all the Thomas sweethearts for their ice cream and cookies; to the Wakeman puppies now and forever; to the doctors at the university and the boys in the laboratory, who, unbeknownst to them, did quite a lot to help in their own inimitable ways; to the VideoManiacs at FilmFest who helped me wait out the long winter months; to Judy, Bill, Ted, Ted, Cathleen, Jamie, Cheryl and Richard for welcoming me; to Rebecca, Wendy, Roy, Joany, Dawn, Kim, Bev and Bob, Lorraine and Bob, Frank, Eric, and John for finally saying, "No!"; to Lenny, Kevin, Tom, and Nick of the NHPD who gave me back some self-respect; and to the Narcotics Chief whose name I don't know and the caring officers whose names I don't know either.

And of course, to Bill Wilson, Bob Smith, and God. Thank you so much.

And with loving memory for my brothers in spirit, Daniel Quinton and Lawrence Davis. This book is more yours than mine.

ONE

THE WIND IN MY HAIR

I rode a Kawasaki 1100, a monster of a motorcycle.

When I was seventeen I owned my first bike, a Honda 350. In college I had a Suzuki 750, and then I got myself the Eleven Hundred. It was an awesome amount of horsepower underneath my groin.

I used to get loaded up on heroin, hop onto my motorcycle, and go joy riding around in the late afternoons. It was the perfect thing to do: kick over the engine, put 1100 ccs between my legs, and cruise along the back country roads in lower New York State, taking in the scenery and the twisting corners high as a kite on morphine. I felt like God Almighty when I was loaded on dope and riding that bike.

One afternoon I was having a good old time cruising down one of those back highways that aren't quite interstates, but, still, you could do about fifty or sixty miles an hour if you really wanted to press the issue. The sun was warm on my face and arms, and the wind was perfect, rushing around my ears and sweeping down the back of my BVD's, making it snap against my back. Nothing bothered me. Nothing mattered. It felt like being inside a cocoon: warm, cozy and safe. I was probably going about seventy.

I had shot a pretty big load of heroin before I had left my hometown that afternoon, maybe six or seven bags. Man! I kicked back my head and let the wind whistle around my Ray Bans, and I could be Marlon Brando in *The Wild Ones* and dream about roads, and highways, and heroin, and long, long journeys to movieland nowhere on my Kawasaki 1100. There was nothing better.

While I was dreaming along, just enjoying the ride, I started to go on the nod. I suppose I had just done too much dope, or maybe the quality was a little better than usual, and I just started to nod out while I was flying down the highway. Maybe it was the sun, or the cocoon, or maybe it was the way the wind seemed to wrap me up in a downy comforter and make everything all right. The morphine was making me fade: in and out, in-...and...aout....Maybe Death wouldn't be so bad after all, if it were anything like this. Besides, who cared? The heroin was there for me.

I was so warm....

So free....

My feet were up on the highway pegs, and I wasn't really concerned with the throttle, or the lane in which I was riding, or the double yellow line on my left or the guardrail on my right, or even the trees and hills that were rushing by me, going faster...and faster...and....

I was in another time. Another space.

The car screaming down the road barked its horn.

I swerved back into my lane, chunks of gravel flying from my rear tire, and I missed going off the side and into the guardrail by inches. I slapped my head around and tried to shake some reality back into my motorcycle ride.

Where the . . .

What the fuck had I been . . .

I didn't fall. I didn't crack up the bike. I made it home safely, to shoot heroin again another day and to go for another joy ride. I was still a punk.

▲ ▼ ▲

Riding a motorcycle high on morphine was incredible. It was the epitome of what it was to get high, the pinnacle of what I was seeking to achieve by using chemicals. In my early years, it was an awesome experience: heroin, sunshine, the summer wind, motorcycle rides, and syringes in my veins, and eleven hundred cubic centimeters nestled sweetly underneath my groin. It seemed the coolest thing a punk like me could do.

But then what usually happens to people who screw around with too much morphine happened to me.

I became a junkie.

I still had the bike. I still wore my sunglasses and my tee shirt, but when I became a junkie, things became different. Dope was no longer a take it or leave it thing. I *had* to have it. Now, I packed a syringe and a cooker down into the sock of my ankle wherever I went. My works had become *a part of me.*

Every time I shifted gears with my left foot, I could feel the little pieces of metal from the Pepsi bottle cap—my cooker—scrape against the skin of my ankle. I could feel the syringe rub against my leg and I'd worry about whether or not it was going to slip out of the sock if I shifted gears too much, so I kept reaching down and tucking it back in. When I drove the motorcycle down into the ghetto to get heroin, I was constantly aware of the small, one hundred-unit insulin syringe and the bottle cap I had tucked into my left sock. It was a gnawing, rubbing away at the skin down there, a chewing, just above the top of my Nikes, held tight against my ankle by a white gym sock.

Gone were the earlier days of buying my heroin and shooting up, doing a little now, saving some for later on, or maybe even for tomorrow, then riding around on my bike for a while and stopping on the side of the road to maybe get a hot dog or a hamburger. Gone were the fine days of cruising at sixty miles an hour on The Old Eleven Hundred, enjoying the sunshine on my face, feeling the wind whip my tee shirt up and down my back. Gone was the downy cocoon, the Marlon Brando smile, the movieland nowhere. It was all gone. The only thing left in its place was heroin. Because heroin had become my god.

▲ ▼ ▲

I bought my dope on a street in my hometown called Edward Hill. My dopefiend friends and I cleverly renamed it "Boot Hill" because we "booted" our heroin—pulling the plunger back and forth while it's in the vein to better mix the heroin and the blood from the arm. It's supposed to be a better high. I never saw that much of a difference. To me, shooting dope is shooting dope.

And now I ride down to Boot Hill and all the boys come running up to me and make their offers: "Yo, man! I got the BEST! Man! Don't buy from him, he's BEAT! You know my shit is GOOD, man! Hey white boy, my dope is ON!" *Yea, yea, yea,* I think. *Just gimmee my fucking dope and let me get the fuck out of here.*

I pay the man eighty dollars for my four dime bags of P-Dope and I stick them down into the front pocket of my blue jeans. I tuck the bags down into the bottom of the pocket where I can feel them against my thigh. I'm all set. I've got my cooker and my set of works in the sock of my left ankle, I pull away on my bike, and I drive around the corner to the nearby gas station. This is the closest place I have to get off. I leave the motorcycle on its kickstand outside the bathroom. The door is unlocked.

The gas station bathroom is my world and what my world has become: water, cookers, syringes, a leather belt, a butane lighter, and my bags of Chinese white heroin. My whole being is centered around getting the heroin into the vein in my forearm and working in my system as fast as I can before I get any sicker from the withdrawal. I'm even coming to get aroused from the smell of the bathroom. The sickish urine smell means I'm going to be high soon. The slick feel of my sneakers on the greasy tile floor means that pretty soon nothing's going to matter anymore. Pretty soon I'm going to get off. The tinted yellow light? The locked door behind me? The hand-printed mirror I see my sickening face in and the bent metal door to the graffiti-filled stall? They're all right. They get me going. Pavlov's Fucking Dog. It's all going to be okay in just a few moments.

I take out my cooker, my syringe, and my lighter, and I lay them on top of the toilet tank. I pull my belt off through the loops in my jeans and lay that on the toilet tank too. Then I get the bags of heroin from the bottom of my pocket.

The bags of heroin are folded over three times. I unfold them and hold the top of each between the thumb and forefinger of my left hand, and flick the bag with the middle finger of my other hand to make sure all the powder drops to the bottom of the small, glassine envelope. I tear open the bag at the last fold and pour the powder into my cooker. I tap out the last of it. Now I begin the ritual.

I hold the syringe with my right hand, sort of like I am holding a pen. Underneath a stream of running tap water, I cup my left palm. I catch the water with my left hand, and with my right, I stick the needle point carefully into the forming pool. With my teeth, I delicately pull up the plunger, drawing water into the syringe.

I watch the water as it comes into the barrel, its level rising against the gradations on the syringe's side. When the barrel is full, I squirt out the water onto the powdered heroin in the cooker. It makes a paste. Or glue maybe. Firing my butane lighter, I heat the paste until it boils, I let it cool down for a few moments, and I draw the now clear solution back into the syringe, filtering it through a small piece of wadded cigarette filter I have dropped into the cooker. My heart is throbbing. I am starting to get an erection. I wrap the belt around the top of my biceps, pulling the tourniquet tight, clenching the end of it between my teeth, and I squeeze out the mother vein in my forearm. It rises like a worm underneath my skin. My love and I are about to become one. I stick the needle tip into the vein, draw the plunger back slightly to make sure I'm *in* the vein—I push the plunger down, the heroin goes into my bloodstream and. . . .

And the end of tourniquet lazily drops out of my mouth. I lean back against the bathroom wall, my soul is wrapped and lolled about on the great, warm heroin ocean, and I pull the syringe out of my vein. I have consummated the Love. It's just like you see in the movies.

But the ritual, you see, takes time and effort. It requires patience and a steady hand. And most of all, it requires a loving *care*.

By the time I became a junkie, I had simply become too sick to jerk off with bathroom rituals. I was too hungry, too close to death. I dispensed with running the tap and cupping my hand underneath the faucet to carefully-draw-up-the-water-for-my-dose bullshit, and I just went straight for the toilet.

I dumped the heroin into the cooker, drew some water out of the bowl, cooked it up, and shot it. Simple. And if I was in a real hurry, I wouldn't bother to flush.

Even simpler.

AND THE NEEDLE IN MY ARM

These were my days as a junkie. These were the days when all I could see in front of my face was the bag of dope, just that little glassine envelope filled with fine, pure, Chinese white heroin.

I booted cocaine in bathrooms, too. Electric wires to my brain synapses underneath the fluorescent lighting. I'd lock myself in the bathroom stall, tie off my arm while I sat on the toilet, and stick a syringe full of cocaine into my vein, shooting my mind right through the fucking ceiling: high octane, power-packed, space shuttle booster fuel—that syringe loaded with cocaine hydrochloride. A hundred thousand volts right up my ever-loving ass.

Sometimes I'd sit there on the toilet, shaking, sweating, and banging my head against the porcelain tiling behind my back because I'd go into a seizure. The bathroom would go white; my mouth would explode in a pungent, medicinal taste at the top of my throat; my ears would ring;

my heart rate and respiration would take off through the ceiling; and I'd ride the locomotive at a hundred and fifty miles an hour, strapped right down to the front of the fucking thing. Sometimes I'd gag, sometimes I'd vomit myself. And when I had stopped shaking from the cocaine injection, I'd whack the heroin. That got me down enough so I could climb onto my motorcycle and ride it home where I could really get high.

When I became a junkie I always went to the bathroom first. Water from the toilet, cook up the dope, and away we go. I had to get it into my system to stave off the withdrawal before I could do anything else. The day took off from there.

Heroin was to function, to keep from getting sick. If I injected cocaine, it was just a boost, just for fun. A little extra money and a hell-delivering rush to my brain cells. Bathroom seizures, just for kicks.

I never shot up in a shooting gallery. Matter of fact, I've never even seen the inside of one. I know what they probably look like from what other junkies have told me about them, but I never had to get high in one. I've gotten off with other junkies, in nice apartments, around kitchen tables with half-eaten, six-month-old bags of Frito's corn chips lying there; I've done my dope in tenement apartments with a bunch of guys I've never seen before, who might or might not slit my throat for their fix; and I've seen more than my share of the choice porcelain tiling that covers the walls of our country's Shell, Mobil, and CitGo toilet stalls.

But I never had to go into a shooting gallery. I never paid anyone to get me off, and I never shared my gimmicks with another person the likes of me. I suppose I just liked my privacy or something.

▲ ▼ ▲

Hunt's Point Avenue is in the south Bronx of New York City. If you're a junkie in lower New England you know The Avenue. Or at least, you know *of* it. You've heard it the same way you've heard of Harlem, or 125th Street, or The Lower East Side. Your mouth drools at the mere sound of the words. Hunt's Point Avenue is one of the largest areas around for the selling, buying, and use of illicit narcotics. Heroin? Cocaine? Crack? Hunt's Point Avenue is a dopefiend's paradise.

When I became a full-time junkie, I went to Hunt's Point Avenue every day. Each morning. Every day. Seven days a week. And if I didn't go, either I'd made a big enough score the day before to tide me over or, unable to scam enough money together, I'd settle for a small amount of crap bought in my hometown in southern Connecticut.

The New England Turnpike begins to *smell* like heroin as soon as you get past the nice white suburbs of Connecticut and into the boroughs of New York City. Not that there isn't heroin in Connecticut, but it's just that you can smell it a little more the further south you go. Driving the car from Connecticut to The Bronx, I could *taste* the heroin in the air as the thruway signs changed from the sweet middle class towns that dot the Connecticut shoreline to the inner-city workings of New York City. It's just a sense that junkies acquire, especially when it rains. I don't know why, but heroin leaves a stronger smell in the air when it rains. It's like another sense. The yellow taxi cabs you see flying around the streets? The car washes and the stereo stores? The markets? The vegetable stands? The Puerto Rican kids hanging on the steps outside the apartment buildings? The pawn shops? They all stink of dope.

The closer you get to Hunt's Point the more the air grows thick with it.

When the sun is out on Hunt's Point Avenue it can give a little warmth to the vacant lots and the abandoned, burned-out buildings that line parts of the street; and maybe, it can take away some of the cramp in your guts you have from being down in this neck of the woods to cop your heroin. It's tight. And it's threatening. You can peel back the tension on Hunt's Point Avenue with the wrong side of a knife.

And junkies can smell other junkies. I can read it in their faces from twenty feet. I can smell it on their swollen hands, where their veins are red and sore from the edema, and I can tell it from their eyes whether they're using, or dealing, or both. I can see it from the way they sniff and rub at their nose, from the way they look into my eyes when I look into theirs, and sometimes, I can tell just by the way they walk. It's something you learn. I don't know how or why it happens, I just know it does.

There's also a tension in the air on Hunt's Point Avenue between junkies and their dealers. There's a look in people's eyes down there that says, *Don't fuck with me. If you do, I'll kill you. . . . And I won't think twice about it.*

Hunt's Point Avenue is busy. There are four lanes of traffic in the street, and the fire trucks and police cars and business people whiz by on the way to their offices, not paying a whole lot of attention to what's going on or to what's being sold in that little Spanish deli over there on the corner. When you drive down The Avenue maybe you lock your car doors, and maybe you don't. Maybe you feel all right about being down here during the daylight hours, maybe you're scared at night. It kind of depends on how intimidated you are by these kinds of neighborhoods. You might wonder if the guys over there on the corner standing around the garbage can are dealing and using drugs; and then again, maybe you wouldn't.

But if you're a junkie, you don't wonder. You know.

I bought my heroin out of a big brick building on the corner of The Avenue. It was a large apartment building (I guess you could call it that; I suppose some people actually lived there) that had a never ending heroin trade coming and going past the large iron gate that stood guard at the building's entrance. I'd sit in my car and wait for my friend to come back with my dope, and I'd watch the people go in and out through that gate: That good-looking white guy in his nice, Girbaud jeans who just got out of the Corvette over there; the black man, with the construction boots and the dirt still in his fingernails; the blonde woman with the tight ass, who looks like someone just poured her into those Spandex pants; and that *kid! Shit!*, I think to myself. *He's not even old enough to fucking shave yet! What's he doing getting heroin in this place?*

And they'd come. One after another. They all came down to Hunt's Point Avenue to get their heroin. Just like me.

I made my trips down to the south Bronx with a black junkie from Connecticut named Ted. I'd pick up Ted from his apartment in the ghetto, and together we'd make the daily trek down to the south Bronx. He would tell his girlfriend we'd be back in a couple of hours and we'd be off.

It took forty-five minutes to make it to Hunt's Point, fifteen minutes for Ted to cop the heroin and cocaine, and within the hour, we were cranking up the tunes in my Firebird and snorting a gram of the stuff up our greedy little noses. That was The Deal: Ted copped my heroin and cocaine for me and helped me not to get beat in The Bronx. In exchange for the favor, we snorted a mess of cocaine on the way back to Connecticut and I gave him a bag of coke for him and his girlfriend. Ted cut up the cocaine on a match book cover and stuck it underneath my nose while I held the wheel. I sniffed. He sniffed. All the way home. It was a paltry price to pay for his favors.

By the time we made it back to Connecticut though about all I wanted to do was drop Ted off at his ghetto apartment and get back to my home, where I could inject a whopping load of heroin and make the heebie-jeebie's from the cocaine go away. At the Connecticut Border, I was already so fucking paranoid from the cocaine, that I thought the State Police were going to pull us over. I thought that everybody in every car knew exactly what we were doing; and I was terrified that Ted and I would get ripped off the second we got back to Connecticut and I dropped him off at his apartment. Which just so happened to sit right at the top of Boot Hill. My "relationship" with Ted lasted two months. Then I dumped him.

And I went down to The Avenue alone.

▲ ▼ ▲

I used the same Man down on Hunt's Point that Ted had been using to make the deal; only now I simply cut out the middle man, namely Ted. I bought my shit from The Man himself. I could give him my four or five hundred dollars, and he'd go into The Heroin Building and bring me back the goods. I could dispense with the time involved in picking up Ted, the cost of buying him a fifty dollar piece of cocaine, and then the hassle of having to drive him home and drop him off at the top of Boot Hill. Ted had simply become a pain in the ass. And I had become a whole lot more selfish with my dope.

I was back to Connecticut with four hundred dollar's worth of heroin, and maybe a hundred or two of cocaine neatly tucked into the inside pocket of my overcoat, next to my wallet containing my American Express Gold Card, my Chase VISA card, and my Master The Fucking Possibilities.

I brought the stuff to my house in Connecticut, after sniffing up just enough heroin so I wouldn't be sick on the ride home; and once there, I could shoot my pretty little brains to smithereens—all in the comfort of my very own living room. Or my bathroom. Or the kitchen. Or maybe up in my attic. But just leave me alone, all right?

Just let me go off into my very own little world of cocaine hydrochloride seizures and morphium nods, okay? *Just leave me be?* Just leave me to my cocaine runs in the attic of my home, all curled up and twisted into a shaking little ball in the corner, squeezing myself between the old clothes and the dusty boxes, because I'm paranoid someone's going to come home and find me. *Just leave me!* trying to inject the dose of cocaine into the vein of my ankle and missing, because the needle tip is clogged, but I have to get *one more hit!* And, oh my God! *The blood!* All the *fucking blood* that's running down my ankle, making sticky puddles around the soles of my feet, oozing from the fucking holes in my *fucking ankles!* But I don't care. My ankle is swelling, the nerves along the bone are becoming traumatized! Already *black and blue!* But I don't fucking care. I can't feel it anymore. I just want one more hit. The syringe won't stay steady! It's hard to hit the vein! I'm shaking! The needle tip keeps jumping and the sweat is pouring off my forehead in a goddamned waterfall! But I'm going to get off again. I know it. My eyes sting! I can't see! Oh, God! This blood is making such a fucking *mess!* But *fuck* the shaking *goddammit!* I *know* I'll find a good vein! *Somehow* I'll get the cocaine back into the fucking cooker, with all the congealed blood and water all mixed together, and I'll filter it back into the syringe once I've unclogged the fucking needle tip! *Fuck!* not being able to put my sneaker on my foot because my foot is so swollen! *It doesn't matter. Just leave me alone! JUST LEAVE ME THE FUCK ALONE!*

Because by this point, I can't even cry about it. I'm twenty-seven years old and this is what my life has become.

What happened to the good old days of riding my motorcycle on a warm summer's day somewhere off in New York State high on morphine? Where's the carefreeness? The freedom? What happened to the wind through my hair and my feet up on the highway pegs of The Old Eleven Hundred, the breeze whipping around my Ray Bans, the wonder of the needle tip in my veins, the power between my legs, and all the rush and excitement and thrill of being a dopefiend? Where the fuck did it all go? How the hell did I wind up on Hunt's Point Avenue in the south Bronx of New York City, with a three hundred dollar a day heroin habit? What in the name of All God That There Is turned me into a curled up ball in the attic of my home, jabbing and stabbing my ankle with a clogged syringe filled with a gram of cocaine hydrochloride? How the hell did everything go so WRONG???

Even though is was more than four years ago, I still see the way my ankle looked that morning. I still see the cooker filled with the congealed blood and cocaine-water solution. I can taste it on my tongue. And I still feel the dread in my testicles, thinking that someone is creeping up the attic steps to come and find me out. I still feel my feet sticking in the blood on the attic floor.

And I still feel the bugs inside my head. Chewing away at my skull. Eating away at my mind.

Making me stick myself over... and over... and over again with the clogged needle. Jab. And jab. And jab. One more hit. Just one more rush. It was all in my life that mattered.

Sweet Jesus, Dear God In Heaven, where the fuck did I go wrong?

THREE

Bicycle Rides in the Park

You might say it wasn't easy for me to become a junkie. It took a lot of time and effort, and it took a whole mess of miserable outside influences, rotten decisions, lousy judgement calls, twisted role modeling, miscellaneous psychic trauma, and maybe—just a real shitty deck of cards to begin with.

For a boy raised in New Hartford County, a fairly well-to-do area in Connecticut; a boy whose father worked hard, six days a week, to provide for the boy's family; a boy whose mother taught him about art and music and theater and books; and a boy who had more than his fair share of toys and clothing and games and abounding Christmases underneath the Christmas Tree, it was hard to grow up to be a junkie. I didn't decide just overnight to tell a video store clerk to give me all the fucking money he had in his pockets—because I needed to get to Hunt's Point Avenue and fix—or I was going to bash his fucking brains into that fucking wall behind his fucking head. It took a whole lot of work. On *everyone's* part.

For almost twenty years I learned. I studied. I listened. I watched. And I learned. I took notes about the important things I had to know, and I was tutored by those who knew much more than I. I desired. I wanted. And I needed. In the end, I needed to be a junkie. It wasn't a question of "choice."

I believe I was destined to this great achievement well before I even picked up my first joint when I was nine years old. Somewhere along the line during those Tender Years, those Formative Years, when one is busy with the task of learning what is Real, and True, and Constant, and What Can Be Counted On and What Can't Be Counted On—I learned that for some ungodly reason, I was different from everyone else. I was a little more askew, a little more twisted. It was as though everyone in my world, everyone with whom I came into contact, lived on Venus. Or Mars. Or Jupiter, maybe. Me? I was on fucking Pluto. It didn't really matter what planet you lived on; what was important is that whatever planet you lived on I lived on a different one. I was alone and I was scared. Nothing made sense.

Much of my childhood is a blank to me now. It's difficult to recall specific years, specific people, and how I felt during specific times. So when I say "nothing made sense" or that "I felt different," I say it because those two things seem to be very much the only constant threads that run through my earliest years. They are all I can remember: being *confused* and feeling *different*. Sorry, but puppy dogs and long summer afternoons playing catch with dad out in the backyard just don't come to mind.

To me, little kid that I was back then, the only understanding I had of family was the one I was born into. It was my *reality*. There was mom and dad, and two older brothers. At the risk of being redundant, I was and still am the Baby. (And to this day, being "the Baby" remains a friendly source of familial torment.)

My father is a good man. He worked hard at his own small business all of his life and gave me most of the things I wanted. I really believe that my dad did the very best he could with me, and although his father was—and this is only an assumption on my part—a *raving* alcoholic (typically, when my father misbehaved as a child, grandpa's remedy for his son's behavior was simple: beat the living shit out of him), my old man never once raised a finger to me. He might have had a drink (or two) when he got home from work at night, but I never saw my old man lose control or go off hog-wild on a bender. Dad remained too much in control for anything like that.

My father was a provider: he went to work, he took care of his responsibilities, he *always* provided for his wife and three children. But things like playing catch and teaching me how to fly a kite just didn't top his list of priorities.

I love my old man. He's a tough nut to crack, but I wouldn't trade him for the world. To this day he maintains the status quo, and things with him are consistently Business As Usual. In response to any question about how he feels, of how things are going, dad's favorite reply remains, "fine."

My mother was a queen. It seemed she always had time to give her three kids all the attention they wanted, and she was usually willing to listen to the crying, bitching, pissing and moaning we seemed so prone to dish out. Mom's sole purpose in life was her three boys. It was as if in some twisted, confusing way, we gave total meaning to her existence.

My two older brothers claimed to love me despite the wretched fact that I was their Little Brother. And what more need be said about sibling rivalry than that?

I grew up in a *good* neighborhood, in a *good* town, where I went to *good* schools and was surrounded by *good* people. Everything *looked* real good. We had and did all the things that good white, middle-class Jewish families from the suburbs are supposed to. Or at least I thought so at the time. I never questioned it. It just was what it was. But in hindsight, something was missing. A piece of the puzzle just fell off the table and got lost somehow.

In reality, there was a chasm between my father and me, and between my two older brothers and me. It was almost as though dad had just used up all his time and energy on my older brothers, and just didn't have anything left by the time he got to me. The fatherly well had simply run dry. My older brothers were taught woodworking, sailing, how to catch a baseball, and how to tie knots and make soapbox derby cars for their Boy Scout troops, and by the time I came around I guess the old man had just run out of steam. I never got past fucking Cub Scouts.

I had my own room, while my two older brothers shared a room, where I could hear them laughing and giggling at night before we all went to sleep. I wanted to be included, to be a part of their fun. But I never was. Literally, there was a wall that separated us. I had only the *sounds* of their laughter. It was like my brothers were an entity, together—and I was another entity, left only to wonder what could possibly be so much fun in that room beyond my bedroom wall. It was lonely where I slept. Frightening.

Being last in line is tough: you're always told that you're not old enough to play with the big kids, that you're still too young and too much of a punk to do what big kids do; and when your father is busy teaching your older brother how to use the power drill and you want to learn too, the usual reply (at least in *my* home) is something on the order of, "Sorry, but I'm too busy now. I'll show you how it works some other time. Why don't you go play in the traffic until we're finished?" The problem was that Dad was *always* too busy.

The other classic example I think of whenever I think about my boyhood is the time I spent washing and waxing my father's car. Dad would leave early on a Saturday morning for work, leaving his car at home in the driveway and taking my mother's. I'd get up early, go outside, and wash his car down, and polish it in the hopes that my old man would really appreciate the work and give me a proverbial pat on the back. I'd go to the neighborhood store and buy some fancy wax, and I'd rub the car till I could see the cavities in the back of my mouth in the car's reflection. *There*, I'd tell myself with eager anticipation, *wait till he comes home and sees this!* And for a good portion of the late afternoon, I'd sit on the front steps of our house and wait for my dad's return. Hoping.

Eventually, dad would come rolling into the driveway, see me sitting on the steps waiting, and know something was up. He would get out of my mother's car, look at his car (all shiny and spit and polish), and he'd smile at me. Then he'd walk around it slowly, admiring, nodding his head up and down, seeming to appreciate the fine job I'd done. Then he'd stop at the back bumper. He crouch down and peer into the chrome. Then he'd stand and look at me. He'd look back at the rear of his car. He'd point his finger at the trunk, and he'd say, "Ya missed a spot!"

And I'd think, yea. I guess I did dad, huh. . . . Shit!

Somehow, I think my mom saw what was going on and decided she'd better take me under her wing. When dad and my two older brothers went off to paint the hull on the family sloop, I stayed home with mom. We watched old movies together on the TV; she taught me how to cook and how to bake. Mom and I sat for hours on end in the den of our house, just talking, or reading, and mostly mom just sharing her dreams and fantasies and how she'd like to go to Paris someday or live long enough for dad to make enough money so they could see the Tower of London.

Mom took wonderful care of me. She taught me about songs and Broadway shows, about art and painting, and about singing and writing music. And she taught me that there were other things in life for young boys besides power drills, and boat hulls and learning how to tie a stupid square knot.

But she couldn't do it all. Not by herself. You see, my mom was pretty sick. She had diabetes. And that hurt to watch. And to see. And live with.

Because in the back of my mind, I grew up with a constant gnawing that at any moment something could happen to her. She could get real sick, have a heart attack, or a stroke, or have her blood sugar go whack-o, and then she'd have to go to that Godawful place people called The Hospital. Mom went there *a lot*. And if mom had to go in there, that meant that she was *really* sick. If my mom went into that place it meant that she was *so* sick...that...she... could. . . .

But in my house, it was normal. It was, what it was. *C'mon you kids, it's time to go up to the hospital and see your mother.*

I remember my mom taking me and a friend to New York City once to see a Broadway show. I can still see her trying to keep up with these two crazy, full of energy, little kids (we were probably ten or eleven at the time), mom trudging down the New York City sidewalk behind us, her purse dangling from her sagging shoulder, just needing to *sit* for a moment (she was terribly overweight), just needing to *rest*, just for a few moments, just to catch her breath, the pain on her face from the strain. Yet at the same time she had a fierce determination in her eyes that *goddammit!* she was gonna do this for her kid and nothing, not even the cigarettes and the excess weight and the goddamned diabetes was gonna stop her! *If nothing else in my life goes right—my body, my diabetes, my goddamned legs—I'm gonna see that my kid gets a decent chance. A decent upbringing.* God! I see now how hard she tried.

But eventually, she had to succumb to her condition, and my friend and I had to stop and wait for her.

It was always like that. Mom just had trouble keeping up.

But you know something? I love my parents. I love my mother and I love my father dearly. They did the best they could raising me, I got a lot more than a lot of other kids I knew. I wouldn't trade my folks for any other set of parents. You could probably take another kid and bring him up the exact same way, with the same set of parents, in the same house, with the same toys, in the same bedroom, with the same wall separating him from his two older brothers—and *that* kid would turn out to be a brain surgeon. Me? I just twisted somewhere along the line and turned out to be a junkie.

In hindsight, it seems utterly absurd to blame *my* becoming a junkie on my childhood or on my family. It seems ridiculous. As if my parents had said, "All right now, Adam. If you don't take that needle full of heroin *right this very minute* and stick in your. . . . " I can't blame anyone else for that. I can't even blame becoming a junkie on the fact that I was sexually molested by three older guys when I was nine years old.

But I will admit it helped.

You wanna know the real reason I wound up being a junkie? The drugs *worked.*

Whatever it was that twisted me up when I was a kid and caused me pain—whether it was the wrong bunch of teachers, or poor role identities within my family, or a messed up set of friends, or getting molested when I was nine, or eat-

ing the wrong food, or the wrong sized underwear I wore!—
the drugs took away that pain. *Wherever* the pain came
from.

Drugs work. And that's really the bottom line.

I liked alcohol, and reefer, and heroin, and cocaine, and
ups and downs, and lefts and rights. If I could eat it, smoke
it, shoot it, swallow it, drink it, or stick it up my ass in a
suppository, I liked it. It took away that feeling of *being different*. Of being *in pain*. With chemicals, I could pretend I
was just like you and that I felt just like you. It was a function of what I didn't want to feel—and of how many, and of
which kind of chemical I had to take—in order not to feel
that way. It was a simple equation.

My mother had an ulceration on her left leg, right on
the front of her shin, a big, red, oozing, wound of a thing,
sitting in plain sight for all the world to see. Sometimes
when mom and I were out together, little kids would turn
to their mothers, frightened, and say, "Mommy! What's
wrong with that lady's leg?" It embarrassed me. I was
ashamed to bring my friends (not that I had all that many)
home for fear that they'd ask questions about it. It was
something from which I always wanted to run and hide.

So I learned how to get rid of the embarrassment.
Smoke a couple of joints, drink a few cans of Bud, and the
embarrassment didn't bother me anymore. Presto.

As a child, I was fat. I wasn't pudgy, I wasn't a little
overweight, and I wasn't Just Chubby For My Age. I was a
fat, fucking kid. A couple of Nembutal, maybe a Benze-
drine or two, and it didn't matter anymore. So what if I had
a couple of extra pounds and my mother always had to take
me into the Husky Department at Sears to buy my clothes?
So what if I hated the summertime because I'd have to take
off my tee shirt and everybody could see how big I *really*
was, all naked and sweating and flabby, with that thing just
above the waistband of my swimming trunks my father

used to tease me about and make fun of, calling it my spare tire? So what? A few hits off the old hash pipe and I couldn't care less what my old man thought. I couldn't give a shit.

If I got teased at school? If girls snickered when my back was turned? If people made fun of the way I looked, or if they laughed at what I was wearing, and if their taunting made my brain ache so damned much it felt like it would burst through the bones of my skull? Fuck it. A couple of tabs of LSD and none of it meant jack shit to me anymore.

The bottom line is this: Alcohol and drugs allowed me to cope. They allowed me to *survive.* However I got my pain, drugs and alcohol let me live with it.

Chemicals even allowed me to shove down all the pain, and all the hurt, and all the shame of sucking some guy off behind the dumpster of the elementary school on a dare when I was nine years old.

▲ ▼ ▲

I don't remember what he looked like. I do remember that the weather was getting warmer—springtime—the afternoons were longer, and I could stay out a little later and ride my bicycle around the park before it got dark and I had to go home for dinner. I wore a gray, baggy sweatshirt, with the sleeves cut off just below the shoulders. I thought it looked cool, and, also, I thought it hid pretty well the fact that I was fat. It was 1968.

I was riding around in the park up the street from my house. All I wanted to do was be cool and be accepted. And all the cool kids hung out at the park.

There were buddies up at the park, guys who palled around together. If you were a juvenile delinquent, or just a nine-year-old punk like me trying to be one, you hung out on the bleachers in the park when school got out. You were cool and had some cool friends. If you owned a mini-bike, if you smoked Marlboros and rolled them up in the sleeve of your tee shirt, if you had a girlfriend who'd let you feel her up, or maybe if you tried sniffing glue or smoking pot—you were cool. You got respect, and you got friends. And that's what I wanted. I was only an elementary school kid, but you, god! if you were in junior high, if you were my brother's age, and if you fought with your old man and he gave you a busted lip just so you could prove it to all the little shits you hung around with—to me you were an icon. I wanted so badly to be like you, to have your acceptance and respect.

I can still feel the explosion against my chest when one of those three guys tossed an M-80 a few feet from where I was standing: the seat of my blue Schwinn Stingray between my legs, and my feet trying like all hell to get my sneakers back onto the damned pedals so I could get the hell out of there before the thing went off and blew my leg apart and. . . .

And when the M-80 exploded, I stood there.

I didn't start to cry. And I didn't ride away like a big baby. My ears rang like Quasimodo's bells, but I took it like a man. God! I wanted to be accepted. So I stood there with the bike at my feet, I looked at the guy who threw it, and I took it. Damned if I'd let them think *I* was a pussy.

These guys knew me, or at least, they knew me as Mike's Kid Brother. I held my ground and acted like it didn't bother me. It was their move.

"Hey kid!" one of them said. He turned out to be Todd Winter: The One Who Did It To Me. "I'll give you five bucks if you give me a blow job."

Wow! I thought. *Five whole dollars? Just for a blow job?*

"Will you get me a *Playboy* with it?" I asked.

"Sure kid," he said. "I'll get you a Playboy. C'mon," he said, grinning.

I left my bicycle parked on its kickstand in the grass and went around to the back of the elementary school with Todd Winter and two other guys, Eddie and Johnathan. We went back into the corner of an alleyway where one of those big, green dumpsters was located. What did I know? I forgot to read the chapter on blow jobs in the Dick And Jane On Cherry Street manual.

Todd backed up against the brick wall and pulled out his penis.

"Now what?" I asked.

"Now you put your mouth on it and you give me a blow job, kid!" Like he thought I knew how to do this sort of thing. Like it was an everyday occurrence for me or something. Like *every* nine-year-old punk knows how to suck off another guy.

The two other guys were standing a little further off in the alley, laughing at what was going on between me and Todd. I looked at their faces and thought of The Cheshire Cat from Alice's Adventures in Wonderland.

"No way!" I yelled at him. "You're gonna piss in my mouth!"

I thought it was the grossest thing anyone had ever suggested, realizing *this* was what he wanted me to do to earn the five dollars.

Piss in my mouth? What a way to get five bucks! Put your mouth on somebody else's dick and have him PISS IN YOUR MOUTH? What does this guy take me for?

"Just do it, kid," Todd said. "I ain't gonna piss in your mouth. I swear! C'mon, kid. You want the five bucks, don't you?"

Well....

He was right. I did want the five bucks. And I did want

these junior high school guys to get me a *Playboy* from the variety store around the corner. The store that had all *those kinds* of magazines on a dusty shelf in back. The shelf by the bathroom. The shelf where I used to stop and look when they let me go back there to take a whiz. Where I'd stop and just stare for a while before the owners yelled, "Get the hell away from there kid! Them magazines ain't for you!"

"Okay," I said to Todd. "But I don't want those guys to watch." I pointed at Eddie and Johnathan. Todd told them to "get outta here!" and they disappeared around the corner of the school. I covered my teeth with my lips like a toothless old man, bent over, and placed my mouth along the shaft of Todd Winter's penis.

"Not like that, asshole!" he screamed.

The other two Cheshire Cats were leaning around the corner and laughing at us. Frik and fucking Frak.

"You gotta suck it. And lick it. Make believe it's a lollipop, kid."

"Naaaa," I said to him. "I don't think so. I don't trust you. You're gonna piss in my mouth."

They all started laughing.

This went on three or four times.

Then Johnathan said, "Forget it, Todd. He ain't gonna do it. He's chicken! I told you he's a fucking chicken!" Then to me, he said: "Fucking pussy!" and he slapped Eddie on the shoulder.

Todd said, "C'mon, kid. Just do it. Just make believe it's a piece of candy."

I told him to make the other two go away.

I put my dentures back along the shaft of Todd Winter's penis.

"Ahhhhh, fuck it! Forget it, kid!" Todd put His Thing back into his Levi's. "Yer fucking chicken!" He turned around to Johnathan and Eddie: "C'mon, guys, let's go. He ain't gonna fucking do it." Then he spit at me, "Fucking pussy!"

And they started to walk away.

"Hey!" I yelled. "What about my five dollars?"

"For that?" They cracked up. "You didn't even do nothin', kid!"

"Did too!" I defended. "And you said you'd gimmee five dollars for it! Now gimmee!"

I think it was Johnathan who said something like, "Awwww, go on, Todd. Give the kid a fucking dollar. Be a sport about it."

Todd walked over, put his hand into his pocket, and pulled out a dollar bill. "Here, kid," he said. "Here's your fucking dollar." And he started cracking up again.

"That's it?!" I screamed. "What about my *Playboy?* What about my 'five dollars'? You guys said you'd get me a *Playboy* if I did it for you!"

"Get your fucking mother to buy it for you, kid," one of them said.

And they walked away.

Laughing.

That was It. That was The Big Blow Job I Gave To Another Kid behind the walls of the elementary school, where I had to go the following day and attend class. It was The Big Thing I Did, when I had no idea what was going on, or what was *supposed* to be going on, inside the head of a nine-year-old kid. That was The Incident. And it was how I earned the salutation from Johnathan the following day of "Hey, 'Top Job'!" I thought he fancied me a toilet bowl cleaner or something.

I didn't understand. I couldn't figure it out. I could make no sense of why, or what, or where I had gone wrong. I only knew, somehow, on some level, I had done something really fucking twisted—that now I was *dirty*. That if I was messed up *before* this, now I was fucked for life. All of the sudden, everything got very, very, cloudy.

Three nights later my brother, Mike, called me into his bedroom saying he wanted to talk to me about something. He had a funny look on his face; I'd never seen him look like that before.

He said, "I heard about how you got that dollar the other day." He sat there on the edge of his bed.

I stood in front of him. *What did I do?*

Oh God! He knows!

He looked at me like I was Just A Stupid Little Kid. He put his head down and he shook it. Then he looked back up at me and managed to force a smile that said, *I just can't believe you were so stupid as to go and do something like this.*

He said, "You're really an asshole, you know?" And he smiled. I think he got up and touched me on my shoulder. Then he looked away again. "That's all I wanted to tell you."

And that was the first place I learned the emotion, Shame.

About a week after that, my father caught up with me after we had finished dinner. He took me lightly by the arm and said, "C'mon, I want to talk to you about something."

Again, somebody wants to Talk To Me About Something! What the fuck did I do? What's going on? How come all of a sudden everybody wants to Talk to Me About Something? What's happening??

He pulled me out onto the front steps of our house.

My father had that same look on his face I'd seen a few nights before on my older brother's. It was a look that said, *You know you really screwed up Big Time with this one. You blew it. You know that, don't you? You really fucked yourself up good this time.*

I looked up at my dad.

Help me?

My dad was so big standing on our front porch, leaning against the black wrought iron railing that led up the steps and bordered the evergreens behind him. The sun was going down behind his back. He reached out an arm and put one enormous hand on my shoulder. He looked like he might have started to cry if that were a possible thing for a dad to do.

He said, "Listen, I heard about what you did and I want you to know that it's okay. I want to tell you it's all right."

WHAT, Dad? *WHAT's* all right? *WHAT DID I DO?* I don't understand!

He said, "We're just gonna forget about the whole thing, okay? We'll just pretend that it never happened. All right?"

Forget *WHAT*, dad??? *WHAT THE FUCK HAP-PENED?*

He stood there looking at me with that same kind of sorry smile I'd seen on my brother's face. I think my dad may have given me a hug or a pat on the shoulder or something, I don't really remember.

We went back into the house together, and again, I was consumed by that feeling of shame. It was as if I had really messed up the whole fucking thing and there wasn't going to be a bloody chance in all hell of my ever changing it or straightening this one out.

And that was the last time my father, and my brother, ever mentioned The Thing I Did When I Was Nine. It became *Something We Didn't Talk About.*

And if there had been a chasm between my father and me, and between my two brothers and me *before* this, now there was a fucking abyss.

▲ ▼ ▲

And in the months following that incident, I received what was probably some of my greatest training in how to eventually get to Hunt's Point Avenue. At age nine, I learned very quickly indeed how to disconnect any feeling, emotion, or thought going on inside of me—be it guilt, shame, pain, goodness, evil, or indifference—and I learned how to present an image for all the world to see that everything was really "Okay." Everything was fine. Nope, no problems here. Business as usual. All was right on fucking schedule.

It was necessary for me to take all the confusion, the guilt, the hurt, the shame and remorse for what I'd done, and stick it way up on the top shelf in the closet of my mind, lock the door, and throw away the key. I had to stuff it all the way in back, behind the boxes and the cartons and the musty books. I had to. I wasn't given any other option.

It became My Secret.

And The Front went up.

I still rode my bicycle up to the park at the top of my street, and I still wore my coolest gray sweatshirt. But now, I wouldn't let anyone know. I wouldn't show anyone what was really going on. I was scared. I was hurt. And I thought, *no one has to know. I'll keep it a secret, no one'll ever find out, and no one will ever be able to bring it up and hurt me like this again.*

Johnathan would be sitting on the wall by the bleachers with some of his cronies, yell out to me, "Hey Top Job!" and smack one of the other guys on the back and laugh. I'd stick out my chest, smile, maybe even wave at them, but I wouldn't show them a fucking thing. I'd keep right on riding down the street. I'd still show them I was cool.

Somehow.

My parents called the juvenile authorities, and I had to leave my fourth grade classroom once in the middle of the day to come home and talk with a detective they sent to our house. He got pretty personal with his line of questioning: Would I be able to identify the kid in a line-up? What did they make me do exactly? Were all three of the boys involved in the incident? Did I actually put my mouth on the other boy's penis? On any other parts? Did they ask me to do any other things? Did the boys do anything else to me? Was I sure? Would I mind coming down to The Juvenile Court and giving them my testimony? Et cetera. Et cetera.

I looked to my mom for some kind of help. She looked like she knew about as much as I, about what you're supposed to say in response to the detective's line of questioning regarding Your Getting Molested Behind The Elementary School Just The Other Day. She looked sad also. She made me a tuna fish sandwich and a bowl of Campbell's soup after the detective had concluded his interrogation and had left. Mom didn't make me go back to school that day.

Some of my classmates from the elementary school heard about The Thing I Did. "Wow!" they said. "What's gonna happen to you? Are you gonna have to go to jail or something?"

"No," I told them quietly. "I just gotta go to juvenile court. I don't know what's gonna happen to me after that."

Mike caught it real bad in the junior high; I think he may have caught it worse than I. My brother, Mike, had to go to class with The Jerk Offs Who Did It. He got into a fight one day with one of the kids in the school hallway. The other kid was teasing him and asking him if he was "as good as your little brother, Top Job?" My brother punched him in the face and then kicked the shit out of him.

My other brother, Ben, was fairly big for his age and I

suppose nobody would mess with him too much. By sheer size alone, he could pretty much fend for himself and demand respect from the other kids. He seemed to have the whole thing fairly well together in his head. Ben had a few close friends, and I just don't remember hearing that any of them gave him a difficult time about it. Maybe they did; I just don't remember anyone bothering to mention it to me. Also, I suppose he kept out of the limelight, so to speak, when it came to things like Your Stupid Little Brother's Blow Job.

I never had to go to juvenile court. I never had to go and testify, and I never had to pick out that scumbag Todd Winter from a line-up. Matter of fact, I have never even seen the son of a bitch since then! He just vanished from the face of the Earth and I never found out what happened to him. The other two, Eddie and Jonathan, hung around town for a few more years to make my life a little bit more miserable. Just when I thought people were beginning to forget about it, there'd be Eddie or Jonathan in my face: *Hi'ya, Top Job! Suck off any good. . . .*

My parents must have read a section in a Dr. Spock book on Childhood Sexual Trauma and decided against making me go through with the juvenile courtroom scene. Either that, or they consulted a shrink. I guess they thought it would send me right over the edge. Or maybe, it would send the family right over the edge. Or *somebody'd* go right over the fucking edge, because I never had to do another thing, legally or otherwise, over What I Had Done With That Kid That Day Behind The Elementary School When I Was Nine.

My mother got in a fight over it with her best friend and their friendship was thusly terminated. Mom's friend crucified mom about What A Screwed Up Kid I Was, and What An Awful Parent She Must Be, and How Could She Ever

Have Allowed Something Like That To Happen To One Of Her Kids, and finally, with Well If That Was One Of My Kids I Can Certainly Assure You That. . . .

You get the picture.

My dad simply wanted to kill The Little Bastards That Did That To His Kid. Dad just wanted to meet The Kid Who Did It. One on one. My old man just wanted to make that kid's face, that Todd Winter Kid's face, a Hershey Bar wrapper on a steamy July sidewalk. That's all my old man wanted to do.

And me? *Shit*. . . .

I was a sitting fucking duck.

I dispensed with My Little Secret That Bothered Me So, *pronto!* I discovered Drugs and Alcohol.

That summer I smoked my first joint and cracked open my first six-pack of Bud with John Durke and Eric Waylon in the park about a month or two after The Incident. After My Little Incident That We Were All Going To Just Forget About And Make Believe Never Happened At All, I started getting stoned and messing myself up even more.

Me?

I was off and running.

FOUR

EARLY HYPOTHESES, EXPERIMENTS, AND DISCOVERIES

Before I go much further, I want to give you an idea about what friendships (and any other relationships for that matter) are like when drugs and alcohol enter the picture. What I want to say about friendships is this, a simple statement of fact: using chemicals negates emotional intimacy.

When a person uses chemicals for any extended period of time, real friendships—where bonds are made, support is exchanged, and both good and bad times are shared, together—become a very difficult thing in which to engage. What you are dealing with when you are involved with a person who abuses chemicals is an emotional cripple. This is not to say friendships don't occur; they do. But for the most part, these friendships have a tendency to be superficial, manipulative, dysfunctional (they *function* but on a twisted level), and they tend to serve the interests of the intoxicated person. That is, for the addicted person, the friendships become a means of getting and using chemicals. Sorry, but what you really wind up with in the final analysis are Get High Partners and Drinking Buddies.

So much for emotional bonding.

For me, adolescence was a period filled with such questions as whose parents were going out of town for the weekend, whose house we could use to get high in, and whose sister was old enough to go to the liquor store and get us a couple of cases of beer. And maybe, a bottle of vodka while she was at it.

I don't know if it was peer pressure, weak ego, boredom or loneliness. As an teenager, I just knew everybody did it (at least everybody *I* hung around with); it was the thing to do at home, at school, at parties, and driving in your car; and I just hopped onto the bandwagon with everyone else. I just went along.

My fellow punks and I experimented with hallucinogens, LSD, THC or any other funny-colored pill that could be laid in the palm of our hands. We smoked marijuana and hashish, and if the reefer were laced with Angel Dust, well, so much the better. We tried Tuinal and Seconal (both barbiturates; my grandfather on my mother's side was a pharmacist and he kept jars of a hundred of those little suckers in his medicine chest), I took Nembutal (a short-acting barbiturate), and I loved to eat Quaalude (a sedative-hypnotic, formerly legal in these United States, now *illegal* because of its high potential for abuse). A couple of 'Ludes and I didn't have a care in the world. I took amphetamine ("speed" to the uninitiated), I tried skin popping cocaine when I was fourteen years old, and I drank booze all the while. I *always* drank. That was just a given. Standard Operating Procedure.

These were my guinea pig days. And in my early teens, I was the guinea pig. These were the weeks, months and years I spent trying this chemical or that, this combination or that one over there, and trying to figure out which ones I liked the best, which ones were just "all right" and which ones I'd only resort to if I found myself in a pinch.

Why? It's simple: People who *don't* use drugs or alcohol don't know exactly how and what they will feel from moment to moment. People *on* drugs do.

People on drugs knows *exactly* how they will experience the world, so long as they have that particular chemical in their systems. It's a Control thing. And drugs are just about the best controller of feelings and emotions you can find. Drugs keep your feelings locked up tight and anesthetized. Just what I needed—I didn't want to feel.

Gradually, I became fascinated by the idea that I could monitor and control all of my emotion through chemical means. By taking this little pill or that, by smoking these or sniffing those, I found I could be master of my feelings and keep my mind in check. By taking drugs and drinking, I could prevent my brain from exploding, and I could keep the pain in my gut (perhaps from My Nine Year Old Trauma? or the ever-deepening emotional abyss between my family and me?) from ripping me apart.

This idea, this fascination with controlling my feelings and emotions, became my obsession. It was my raison d'être.

▲ ▼ ▲

After graduating from high school—and after a rather rudimentary schooling in drug and alcohol abuse that was inherent in going through four years at *my* high school—I went on to a university in a small, upstate Connecticut town and began studying psychology, thinking that perhaps by getting a college education in the understanding of humans and human behavior, I might be better able to understand myself and why I got so twisted up in the first place. And if not that, then at least I could improve my knowledge of chemicals and how they could benefit me until I *did* figure out what was wrong with me.

The college was about seventy-five miles away from my hometown. It was nice to get away from home and act like an independent adult, but at the same time, I could come home on the weekends if I wanted to for things like having mom do my laundry. At eighteen, I had the best of both worlds.

I like to fancy myself a fairly intelligent man. I did well at the university; throughout my almost four years there I maintained a 3.73 grade point average. I never missed classes, I studied diligently, sometimes five and six hours a day, and I worked very hard at attaining near perfect grades. But that's because studying was all I did.

Except for doing drugs and drinking.

I was in classes until noon, came home and studied until the late afternoon, and then I cracked open the bottle just in time for cocktail hour. When I wasn't studying, I was drinking alone in my dorm room or going out to a bar and drinking with whomever was hanging around in the bar. And it didn't matter who was there. The bottle was the only thing that mattered. Sometimes I bought a few drugs to help the liquor along (in college, I went through my barbiturate and amphetamine phases along with my abuse of alcohol), and sometimes I got together with a roommate or an acquaintance from class and drank with him or her. But they weren't important either. The only use I had for any friends or acquaintances at college was how quickly, how cheaply, and how good were the drugs they could get for me.

God! That sounds so ruthless. *True*, but ruthless. . . .

Don't get me wrong—I had friends at school. There were a couple of guys with whom I hung around and we were pretty much good buddies: college-aged, wild, hack-around-and-keep-your-beer-steins-filled buddies. I went out with girls, and at one point I even moved in with one of the girls I was dating. But let's call a spade a spade here: people get in the way of using drugs and drinking. When someone gets too close, the possibility exists that he or she might start asking questions. About your "judgement." *Hey Adam, don't you think you've had enough to drink now?*

And if any of the relationships I was in got *too* close... well... as Snagelpus is always so prone to say, *"Exit! Stage right!"*

This is in hindsight. At the time, I had no idea that this was actually going on. All I knew was that every few months, I sort of woke up and took stock of things and said to myself, *what happened to that guy Joe I used to be friends with?* And the usual retort was something on the order of: *well, he was just an asshole, anyway.*

It's *always* the other person's fault.

Drinking and using drugs became *rewards* at college: The harder you studied, and the better you did on your tests, and the higher your grade point average, the more you could drink. And the more drugs you could take. To sum up my collegiate years (and probably those of most of my fellow eighteen, nineteen, and twenty year olds at that time) being an undergraduate meant going to class and studying, and then medicating ourselves with either alcohol, drugs, or the two combined.

And sometimes (well, to be perfectly honest, for me it was *most* of the time) I went to class stoned. On narcotics. I found school easier that way. It seemed to take away the mental stress and relax me enough so I could concentrate on the lecture.

I made an absolutely brilliant discovery sometime early on in my scholastic career that made taking and getting these drugs easy. I have a bad back. As a matter of fact, I have a *horribly* bad back. I have three ruptured discs, a fracture in the thoracic area, and an arthritic condition in my cervical region somewhat close to that which might be experienced by a person seventy-five years old. At the risk of being rhetorical, it can be extremely painful. And early on in my college days—because of my back pain and because this pain was making it difficult for me to sit in class and study in the library and type my research papers on the living room floor and do other things like walk up a flight of stairs—I discovered a number of doctors more than willing to give me "something to make my condition a little less painful." I other words, I discovered I had a *legit* reason to get drugs. So, when the old college stress got too be to much for Adam here... well... Adam just went to the campus doctor, or the doctor down the street, or the doctor across town, or even the doctor back in his hometown who'd taken care of him since he was a little kid, and Adam told the doc just how much pain he was in, and Adam got his narcotics.

It made studying, writing and researching for long hours not *nearly* so strenuous.

In addition to my scholastic studies, I got a job at the end of my sophomore year as a counselor at the LongAcre Psychiatric Institute, working with psychotics, neurotics, schizophrenics, manic-depressives, obsessive-compulsives, anorexics...

...and drug addicts.

Well, I thought it might be fun!

I wanted to learn more about psychology, human behavior, and I honestly wanted to help people. And who better to help than those with whom I could so easily identify?

I secured a position working the graveyard shift, eleven at night to seven in the morning, watching over the manics who couldn't sleep, the depressives who were too scared to go to sleep, the psychotics whose voices ordered them not to sleep... and some of the dopefiends on the unit just wanted to stay up late, watch "The Honeymooners," and talk a while with the new counselor named Adam, who was fascinated with drugs and what they could do. One of the dopefiends on the unit was a guy named Johnny Mammone.

Johnny Mammone was a heroin addict who taught me about heroin. He taught me how to cook it up in a Coca-Cola bottle top, how to get The Hit (visible blood in the syringe's barrel indicating that you are, in fact, inside the vein), when to loosen the tourniquet, and how to rotate injection sites. He taught me where and from whom to buy it, whose shit was good and whose was just "okay," how much to pay, and how to handle myself in "those" neighborhoods. He taught me how to not get ripped off, and he tried to warn me about the ever present Monkey that would someday crawl up onto my back with every intention of kicking the living shit out of me.

Johnny Mammone taught me everything I needed to know about shooting heroin. And Johnny did a very good job, I should add. Johnny really helped get me going on my way to bigger and better things in the seedy world of illicit drug use. I guess you could say Johnny rather took me under his wing.

But it was my professors at college, the doctors and nurses at LongAcre, the pharmacists, the chemical engineers, and the authors of the *Physician's Desk Reference* who really taught me how to be a junkie. You could say they also took me under their wings.

Illicit drugs, dope inclusive, was one thing. But pharmacology—the understanding of so much diverse chemistry legally available to the human mind and the ability to *use* this understanding to its fullest potential—was another story entirely. That took time. *That* took education.

At college, I took courses in biological psychology, anatomy, physiology, abnormal psychology, chemistry, psychopharmacology, and drugs and behavior. I studied drug effects and side effects, and I learned for what disease and for which symptom a particular drug would be indicated. I learned about things like addiction, dependence, tolerance and withdrawal. I was taught the differences between sedative and barbiturate classes; why a tranquilizer was unlike either of the two; why chronic use of amphetamine and cocaine could lead to something indistinguishable from a paranoid schizophrenic disorder; why it was things like Beta Endorphins, Enkaphalins, and THIQ that made narcotics, barbiturates, tranquilizers, and alcohol so damned good; and why when you were abruptly withdrawn from these chemicals, you felt like you wanted to die. And how sometimes, if you weren't medically supervised, you did.

So it was through my classes at the university and my work at the LongAcre Psychiatric Hospital that my skills at being a dopefiend were honed and refined. And God, was I a diligent student! I learned about synthetic narcotics, semi-synthetic narcotics, and potent morphine derivatives. I learned the names, I learned about their potency, I learned which narcotic would be given to relieve which type of pain, and I thought to myself: *Mmmmmm. That sounds like some pretty interesting stuff. I wonder how I could get my paws on some of that?*

I began by learning about the petty stuff, like Darvon and codeine; and moving on to the pretty good stuff, like Percodan, Tylox and Demerol; and finally, progressing all the way to the super terrific stuff like morphine, Methadone, Dilaudid, and heroin.

I learned that heroin and morphine were the same thing, the only difference being that a molecule of heroin has three acetyl groups that a molecule of morphine doesn't, and that as soon as you inject heroin into your bloodstream, it becomes morphine anyway. (The three acetyl groups just give it that little added "boost.") I learned that ninety percent of the stuff people bought on the streets in the late seventies, when the government *really* began to crack down on the heroin importation, wasn't heroin at all. China White, Pacific Black Tar, Mexican Brown, P-Dope and all those other different kinds of "heroin" were merely Fentanyl analogs. Not heroin. But who cared? Fentanyl was better than heroin, anyway. (Fentanyl is a USDA, Grade A Choice Narcotic, which is used as the prime anesthetic agent in half of all surgical operations in a hospital. And an "analog" is simply a chemist's version of a look alike, or in this case, an "act" alike: Take a little Fentanyl, move a carbon atom from here to there, and *Hey! Look at this! We got some stuff here that's about a thousand times more potent than that Fentanyl we started with! Since real heroin's so hard to get now that the feds are cracking down, let's put this stuff out on the street and call it Black Tar! Huh? Whada'ya think?)*

Better living through science and chemistry.

It was during my first year of college, the first time my back really started hurting, and the very first time I was ever given something for the ensuing pain—both physical *and* emotional—that I believe, I fell in love.

With dope.

Roll over Adam, I have to give you another injection.

No more pain. No more stress. No more anxiety. No more hassles of any kind.

Could I have another one of those shots, nurse? Please?

It was then that The Narcotics became my daily voyage to Disney World and The Magic Kingdom. With them, all of my troubles floated away twenty minutes after ingestion. If I was stressed-out with my studies or rejected by my girlfriend; if my family was causing me undue emotional grief, or even if I were in actual, physical pain—The Narcotics made it all go away. If I were too fat, too ugly, too good, or not good enough; if I were too old, too young, working too hard or not working hard enough, I found I could take a little pill—a little *Narcotic* pill—and my troubles would vanish. Poof! A couple of Percodan and I'll be just fine, thank you very much.

Narcotics took away my aches, my pains, my insecurities and my phobias about the world. I could study better, look better, act smarter and perform better on the job (and better in bed! too). The dope got rid of my stress. With a little Demerol in me—or maybe, a Percodan or two—I was able to get higher grades on tests and give a more exacting lecture to the freshman class on The Biogenic Amine Hypothesis Of Schizophrenia. It was like being bullet proofed. With those Magical Opioids From The East floating around up there in my neurochemical brain synapses, all the world became a little better place to be.

A little softer.

Quieter.

And the things like That Trauma That Happened To Me When I Was Just A Punk didn't bother me so much anymore. It was still there; only now, it didn't have an effect on me. The Narcotics made all the pain disappear, and now—I could be superman.

I fancied myself a modern day Doctor Jekyll. I was enthralled with the control I had over my feelings and emotions. I became obsessed with medicine, with drugs, with chemicals, illnesses and addiction.

I watched "Geraldo Rivera" specials on television about The Wall Street Junkies, who, on their lunch breaks, went down to the Lower East Side to get their daily fix. I cut out from *LIFE* magazine the pictorial essays on the lives of heroin addicts in Harlem, New York, and pasted them on the walls of my bedroom. I talked with junkies in LongAcre, I queried nurses for information, and I snooped around physician's offices when I went in for an examination. I read books from the college library, I studied all the medical texts I could get my greedy little paws on, and I pumped my professors for all I could get. For all they knew about Chemically Altering The Body And The Mind. I was twisting more... and more... and more. And all the while, I was experimenting on myself.

My only problem was what to do about Mr. Hyde.

FIVE

DOCTORS, THE DEA, AND THE BLACK BEAR

By the time I finished my career with drugs and alcohol, I had secured a rather notable position within both the legal community and the medical community of my hometown in Connecticut.

The former—the police officers, the lawyers, the sheriff's deputies, the social workers, the judges, and the probation officers—recognized me and knew me for the two felony narcotics violations I had been lucky enough to add to my gleaming record. The first charge was for impersonating a physician; the second was for possession of narcotics. For the possession charge, I was just lucky enough to be in the right place, at the right time (when there was a sting operation in effect on Boot Hill), and I got pinched one day while buying my cocaine. I was given a room in the county jail for that one.

The latter—the doctors, the nurses, the x-ray technicians, the pharmacists, the walk-in clinic secretaries, and the emergency room personnel—knew my name and face from my various and sundry attempts at getting my supply of legal narcotics through not so legal means: I manipulated doctors.

I started this gimmick in college.

It was during the summer between my junior and senior year. I was pushing twenty-one. To lighten the load a little, I had during the previous semester only carried nine semester hours, instead of the usual fifteen. I was taking life easy, winding down for my last year of undergraduate studies. (Once—I think it was during my third semester—I got the bright idea of carrying eighteen credits in one semester. *Ah, could you please pass the Jack Daniels there buddy?*) I had a nice apartment in the same town as the university, I had received a promotion from the third to the second shift (3:00 P.M. to 11:00 P.M.) at LongAcre, I was seeing a girl who was also majoring in psychology, and I had just that spring got my second motorcycle, the Suzuki 750, my Suzy. For a college student, I was doing all right. Things looked pretty good from where I stood. One more year of this college crap, then on to Grad School, get myself a Ph.D., and then—look out world, cause here I come.

My dependence on chemicals, particularly the narcotics, was just beginning to take hold. My tolerance was starting to grow ever so slightly; my physical *need* for them was no where near what it would someday be. The Monkey on my back was still just a puny chimp. I could still get by for a couple of weeks and still have a whole mess of fun with a script for a little codeine, a few Percodan, or maybe just a touch of the hair of the dog that bit'cha, thank you very much.

I did heroin when I could get it, buying my dope in New Haven when I felt like it (New Haven is a major heroin center for the northeast), and shooting a little cocaine here and there when I could afford it *Hi, Ma? Yea, listen, do you think you could lend me a little cash this month for the rent?*

Yea, I know you just sent me two thousand dollars last week, but I just got behind the eightball again. I came up short, and the tranny on my car is about to shit the bed and. . . .

I drank every night.

To keep myself happy, in a good mood, unstressed and unhampered by the problems of the outside world and the pressures of collegiate life, I took chemicals, which I secured mostly from doctors. I got them by Doctor Shopping in my spare time.

I don't particularly believe there's a law against it. I never heard of anyone being arrested for going to too many doctors and scamming a steady supply of pills. But I don't think it's exactly considered ethical either. I don't think one doctor would appreciate the fact that while he was writing you a prescription for thirty Percodan, you had four *other* doctors in your pocket who were doing the same thing. It's not illegal. It's just a real sneaky way to go about it, that's all.

This act required a different kind of education from the one I was getting at the university. Through trial and error, I had to learn which physical symptom to manifest for the doctor in order to have him write out a prescription for a powerful, Schedule Two narcotic like Percodan, or Tylox, or perhaps even, *please! Please let him see how much this REALLY hurts. . . .*

Dilaudid.

But before we go any further, I should take a moment to explain the law:

The Drug Enforcement Administration (The DEA), a branch of The United States Justice Department, "Schedules" all the controlled substances we take. (And anything that's not a controlled substance isn't worth taking. At least if you're trying to get high, that is. Penicillin is not a controlled substance.)

Schedule One controlled substances, like heroin, are illegal. Heroin and other drugs on the first schedule have no accepted medical use (at least in *these* United States), and their potential for abuse is extremely high. Also on Schedule One are things like LSD, Ecstasy, Peyote, and the analog/designer drugs like China White. They're all against the law.

Schedule Two controlled substances, like morphine, cocaine, Methadone, Percodan, Dilaudid, Tylox, Demerol, and the majority of amphetamines and barbiturates, are legal. (Yes, cocaine is legal when used by doctors for some ear, nose and throat procedures, as well as for eye surgery.) But these substances are extremely difficult to obtain since they're highly addicting and have extreme potential for abuse. For these reasons the DEA keeps a pretty tight rein on their distribution and places them in the second classification of their Controlled Substances Act (Title II of the Comprehensive Drug Abuse Prevention and Control Act of 1970—just in case you were interested—and the amendments of 1984).

The next three schedules—Schedules Three, Four and Five—are also legal but not quite as tightly controlled. The last three schedules include the tranquilizers (Librium, Valium, Xanax, Dalmane); the weaker amphetamines and sedative-hypnotics (Ionamin, for instance, and Doral); some of the less strong, less likely to be abused (or so they think!) narcotics such as codeine and hydrocodone; and the semi-synthetics and combinations like Talwin and Talacin. The last three schedules on the list of controlled substances are so loosely controlled in fact (well, as "loosely" controlled as a controlled substance can be) that unlike Schedule Two controlled substances, for which you need a prescription blank filled out in triplicate in most states, all you have to do to get substances on the last three schedules is to give a verbal order for them. Like over the telephone.

There in a proverbial nutshell is the law regarding licit and illicit drugs.

Tamper with any of it and you risk arrest. Back to the manipulation of medicine. . . .

My earliest attempts at Doctor Shopping were a gamble. It was difficult to know exactly what to say or precisely how to act in order to get the doctor to write out the prescription for what I wanted. In the beginning, I frequently left the doctor's office with a prescription for Tylenol #3 with codeine, when what I had really come in for was something much stronger. I didn't yet know what to tell the doctor. I wasn't able to "work" him—to tell him I was allergic to codeine, that he didn't know how *bad* the pain was, that I'd tried that codeine before and it just didn't have any effect on me—and to have the doctor fill out the blank script with Percodan #30.

The first few times I attempted this scam, I got a prescription for thirty lousy little tablets of codeine. Not a great score by any stretch of the imagination. However, on more than a few occasions during my earliest days I did receive prescriptions for a drug called Talwin. Considered by the pharmaceutical world to be a rather innocuous synthetic narcotic, Talwin, when injected, produces one of the most intense highs and some of the strangest hallucinations I've ever experienced. Talwin was the first narcotic I ever used intravenously. After I had crushed up fifteen of them and injected them into my vein, I screamed at my landlord, who was fixing the kitchen sink at the time, that he simply had to get rid of all the rats that were infesting my apartment! He paused underneath the sink, put down the monkey wrench with which he'd been working, and looked at me like I was a person who was seeing things.

So after a few months of discouraging office visits, receiving virtually worthless prescriptions for codeine pain killers and non-steroidal anti-inflammatory medications, I learned how to say the right thing, how to act the right way, and how to get the doctor to give me a prescription for what I really wanted: A Schedule Two narcotic.

I learned how to walk into the doctor's office like I was crippled with pain. I "ooo'd" and "ouched" my way to the seat in the waiting room, grimaced, making sure the nurse saw me (perhaps even asking her if the good doctor could see me even sooner than my scheduled appointment because of the terrible amount of pain I was in), and made sure that all the people in the office noticed what an incredibly difficult time I was having bending over, sitting down, standing up, walking, or making any sort of movement at all.

I told the physician that I couldn't sleep because of my back pain, that work was utterly out of the question, that it was difficult for me even to go to the bathroom without being in agony, and that for the last week or so, I had been unable even to make love with my girlfriend.

I said I had tried lying down for a couple of days, that I had tried resting, and that I had hoped that would do the trick, but the pain simply hadn't gone away. I had never been sick, I said. I couldn't *remember* the last time I'd needed to stay home from work and lay in bed, and I just couldn't understand why I was in so much distress with my back. I told him I hated being ill, that I didn't like to go to doctors, that I detested taking pills, but I was simply in too much pain. I was forced to succumb and consult with him. And was there anything *please!* that he could do or give me that would take away my misery. Anything! I'd do whatever he said. And my prescription for Percodan was usually right around the corner. To make me *a little more comfortable*, he'd usually say.

This was an easy scam. It was helped along by the fact that once the doctor looked at an x-ray of my spine and saw that the last three lumbar discs were, in reality, herniated, or strangulated, or ruptured, or whichever way he chose to describe it, then it pretty much made sense to him that *well, yea, this guy must really be in a mess of pain after all.*

If the doctor tried to pass off some codeine, I merely told him that I had taken it once when I was young and it made me throw up all night. "I think I might be allergic to that codeine stuff, doc."

Worked almost every time.

If he wanted to take an x-ray or a CAT scan, or poke me, prod me, or shove an eighteen-inch needle into my spinal canal, that was fine with me. Just as long as the nurse had that little white slip for me—the one with the prescription for those thirty lavender Percodan written on it—waiting at the reception desk when I went to pay for the office visit.

I milked my illness. I sucked doctors *dry* for their narcotics with my aches and pains and somatic complaints. Whether in reality my back was actually causing me pain or whether it wasn't didn't matter. What mattered was getting that prescription. I just displayed the specific symptoms and acted like I was in agony. (In the clinical world, this is known as "symptom amplification." I just called it lying to the doctor.) And for the most part, it worked.

Most of the time I could walk into the doctor's office hunched over and twisted up like Quasimodo, let the nurse do an x-ray series, and then have the doctor do a physical exam, prescribe bed rest, heat, ice and some back exercises, and waltz out of the office with my script.

When a CAT scan was ordered, I explained I didn't think I'd be able to get to the hospital before the end of the following week, but would he please just give me A Little Something To Tide Me Over till the results were in and we had our next appointment? If the doctor prescribed physical therapy, I said that would be fine also (I had no intention of keeping either the CAT scan or the physical therapy appointments) and that I hoped it would certainly do the trick, but that right now it hurt so bad! I thought I might need to take something until the therapy began to help. Muscle relaxants were okay, too.

But let me have a narcotic along with it, doc, okay? Just to take the bite out of the pain? Just in case?

Thanks. . . .

A Personal Note: Doctors aren't stupid. And I apologize here for speaking about them in a condescending manner. It's not my intention to paint them as incompetent or ignorant. I have the utmost admiration for anyone who goes through twelve years of schooling, internship, and residency trying to understand and heal human suffering. I think that most physicians are extremely intelligent men and women who are quite adept at diagnosing, treating, and prescribing for almost every illness known to man. They have my greatest respect.

But they just don't know *jack shit* about being a dopefiend or about being scammed by one.

Once I got the hang of this scam and saw how easily I could pull it off, well, I guess I really ran with the ball.

I ran doctors in their offices, I ran them in their clinics, and I ran them in hospital emergency rooms. I conned them with my somatic complaints, and I took them for all the narcotics they would give.

Once, I went to a local emergency room to run my thing on the attending physician. I sat on the stretcher, with the doctor sitting next to me, and I told him what a wicked bad injury I had just sustained to my low back.

"It's killing me, doc!" I told him. "I just bent over to pick something up, and *bango!* I couldn't stand up straight! I tried to lift a box up off the floor, back at my apartment and *boom!* Out it went on me!"

The doctor saw me shaking and sweating and having a pretty rough go of it. He asked, "You're really in a lot of pain, aren't you?" I nodded in agreement and gave him my best Jesus Doc, You Don't Know How Bad It *Really* Is! look. He said, "Go home and lay down. And stay there! I'll give you something for the pain, but you've got to go home and rest!" I thanked him with the sincerity of a man on his death bed.

When he left the examining room, I hopped back into my jeans and went out to the reception area to sign the discharge papers, being careful to continue walking like the Hunchback of Notre Dame. I got to the desk and braced myself up against the nurse's counter and I assured the physician that I would "just go home and rest" as he had instructed. I thanked him for his time.

When I got to my car, I smiled. I thought about the thirty Percodan the good doctor had just signed his name to on the hospital prescription blank. I got into my car and drove around the corner to the pharmacy to have the prescription filled.

That was easy. I wonder why I was shaking so much though? I must be getting pretty bad for him to make a comment about how much I was shaking and sweating.

But it's not pain. It's the withdrawal I'm starting to go through, isn't it?

Uh oh . . .

No matter.

And I filled the script at the corner drugstore.

▲ ▼ ▲

Most doctors would write a prescription for a Schedule Two narcotic if I did the right thing. They might even refill it once or twice. But if I tried to play a doctor for a third or forth refill, he'd get That Look in his eye, the look that said he was catching on. That Look that said: *I think you might just be up to something funny here. . . .*

It was usually at that point that I was out the good doctor's office door and going shopping. For a new physician.

No. Doctors aren't as stupid as I might paint them.

Well. . . .

Dopefeinds are just hungry. That's all.

I did find a Doctor Feelgood or two along the way: the doctor who can't practice medicine for one reason or another and who elects for something a little easier. Something a little less draining. For the right amount of money, maybe Doctor Feelgood will write you a prescription for Quaalude, or Percodan, or Dilaudid even, but you have to pay Doctor Feelgood for his services in cash. And most of the time, quite a large sum of cash.

Hi, ma? Do you think I can borrow. . . .

Doctor Feelgoods are usually surgeons or other specialists who've grown too old or too shaky with their cutting hands to continue their practice the way they did in the good old days. They still want to practice medicine, but now, they settle for writing prescriptions for amphetamine to overweight women, Valium prescriptions to neurotic young stock brokers, or maybe, narcotic orders to withdrawing dopefiends. They're hard to find, and even when you do hear of a doctor willing to write out a prescription for 100 Dilaudid Number Four's, by the time you get to him, the DEA has gotten to him first and probably revoked his narcotic license, and possibly, shut him down all together.

In all the years I ran the doctor scams (and I continued this practice on and off well after I'd left college), I found only one doctor while I was at the university who'd write me a continual prescription for all the Quaalude I could eat because I Had Trouble Falling Asleep, and I found another doctor years later who'd give me codeine derivatives and Percodan for My Deviated Septum And The Pain I Had Because Of It. But they were the only two I honestly ever found on whom I could depend to supply me when my other scams ran tight.

But even they gave me shit about it when I asked too often.

No, for the most part I was left to go from doctor's office to doctor's office, walk-in clinic to walk-in clinic, hospital emergency room to hospital emergency room, and put on My Little Act that I had perfected so well in order to secure a steady supply of pills. It wasn't easy. And my father's insurance company wasn't too keen on the idea, either!

How come you're going to so many doctors up there, Adam? You sick or something?

Shit dad, my back's been killing *me! I think it's the stress of school and I have been wrestling a lot of psychotics lately on the job. They've really been going off, and don't you remember? I had that infected upper. . . .*

Running emergency rooms went the same way: Until the well ran dry, I milked it. I guess in the areas where I lived at the time—including both my hometown and the small town where I was going to college—I ran each and every hospital, on and off, for a period of four years. In total, I must have used ten different hospitals. I used different symptoms, I used different names and addresses, and I ran my scam different ways with different doctors. But I always went for the narcotics.

When one emergency room started catching on, I'd just go to another—and then I wouldn't return to the first for six months or so. I'd go at different times of the day so the nursing staff wouldn't be the same, or I'd wait for the intern staff to turn over, always praying that my name wouldn't show up on the computer print-out from the admissions' office. It took a lot of time and effort to get drugs through the hospital, and I didn't particularly like spending my evenings waiting around in a Johnny either, sitting, while the doctors tended to cases more important than mine.

Come to think of it though, I did run one doctor, a late shift doctor at one of the more suburban hospitals, for six months straight, at three o'clock in the morning, for Percodan prescriptions every couple of weeks. He just kept giving them to me and giving them to me; it was like I'd cracked open a fucking gold mine! He never told me he thought I was up to something funny, and he never asked me any questions as to why I was there so often in the wee hours of the morning complaining of my back pain. He just kept writing prescriptions for twenty and thirty Percodan at a time. I think, perhaps, he just wanted to shut me up and get back to sleep.

I continued my doctor shopping, and I continued my studies on becoming a junkie. I kept my eyes and ears open in the physicians' offices, examining prescription blanks, listening to the doctors and the nurses when they ordered medications over the telephone, and taking note of the Latin words they used to place their orders. I watched, I read, and I listened.

And sometimes, when the doctors went out of the examining room and I was left alone to my own devices, I slipped a prescription pad into the pocket of my coat. Or maybe even a bunch of syringes.

You just never knew when they would come in handy.

▲ ▼ ▲

I remember the first time I forged a prescription. My heart pounded like a jack rabbit's, caught in the headlights of an oncoming Mack Truck. The absolute fear and terror of writing out my own prescription, taking it to the pharmacy and trying to get it filled—the terror, the danger, and the possibility of getting arrested—scared the shit out of me.

And at the same time it was exhilarating.

My girlfriend and I had since broken up. (I told you relationships with dopefiends only last so long; she probably wanted something more than an emotional skeleton anyway.) I had taken a couple of days off from work (telling them that my back was killing me), I was bored, and I wanted to catch a buzz. I didn't have enough cash on hand to run all the way down to New Haven for heroin, and most of the local doctors were getting That Look in their eyes when I went to their offices seeking relief.

I stole a prescription blank from a doctor's office in another state. I went to see the doctor and tried to run my scam, but he wouldn't buy it. He gave me a prescription for some worthless, anti-inflammatory medication and told me to try taking those before he would prescribe "anything stronger."

Jerkoff, I thought. *I'll just write the fucking order myself!*

I sat at my kitchen table and looked at the two prescription blanks, the one on which he had written his order and the one I had stolen. I studied the way he wrote the prescription. I examined how he signed his name. I practiced writing it a few times. I got my *Physician's Desk Reference* down from the shelf, dusted it off, and looked up Vicodin.

Vicodin is a Schedule Three narcotic under the DEA's Controlled Substances Act. It's not quite as potent as Percodan and Percocet, but to a starving dopefiend, it'll do in a pinch. Generically, Vicodin is *hydro*codone, and Percodan is *oxy*codone. And I really couldn't be bothered squabbling about the differences between a "hydro" and an "oxy."

I took note of the indications, the dosages, the administration regimen, how much might be a reasonable amount for a prescription, and whether or not to make the script refillable. This being my first attempt at forging a prescription, I decided against the refill idea. I took my best shot.

I put the blank in front of me, took out my Black Imitation Physician's Pen, and where the prescription blank had lines for the patient's name and address I filled in my name and address. Then underneath I wrote: Vicodin 5 mg. tabs. #28. Sig: T q 4 to 6 hr. p.r.n. severe pain. (Meaning: Fill the prescription bottle with 28 Vicodin tablets and put on the label, "take one tablet every four to six hours, as needed, for severe pain.") I signed the doctor's name to it.

I parked my car outside the local pharmacy and walked in with my forgery. I handed my masterpiece to the little high school girl working behind the pharmaceutics counter. I smiled. My heart was thundering. She handed the prescription to the pharmacist behind the counter. He looked at the prescription and then looked at me.

He said: "This'll take about five or ten minutes to fill, sir."

Eureka! You bought it! That's a forged prescription you've got in your hands, you moron! I just wrote the fucking thing out fifteen minutes ago on the fucking kitchen table in my fucking apartment! You're really gonna fill that for me??? Oh, you stupid fucking sap, you.

"Thank you," I said. "I'll just wait for it."

I stood at the counter while the pharmacist filled my forged prescription. I stood there and waited for my script and looked at all the pretty little bottles on the shelves. I looked at the Valium, and the Librium, and the cough preparations with the codeine in them, the ones marked "Control Three." I looked at the psychotropic medications, the tranquilizers, and I saw where they kept the antibiotics. But mostly, I looked at the bottles with the capital "C" on them and the numeral inside of the letter: Controlled Substances. These were the ones I was most interested in.

This is a great place to get drugs, I thought.

Fifteen minutes later I paid the high school girl for the Vicodin prescription and waltzed out the door with a bogus script for twenty eight little codeine-derivative narcotics that I wrote out with my own greedy little paws.

Jesus, I'm getting pretty good with this bit.

▲ ▼ ▲

Now, who was I to be going around writing my own scripts? Really, I was just a wise-ass college student slash promising young dopefiend who went to work in the afternoons and talked with crazy people in a crazy house.

Sometimes I look back and wonder about myself.

But what the hell. It was fun. I wanted the drugs and this seemed as good a way to get them as any.

I forged only two prescriptions during my career. Hand forged, that is. Two, maybe three.

I forged one of the prescriptions for Vicodin; another time I xeroxed a prescription for Percodan and handed it to the pharmacist after going over the lettering with black ink. The pharmacist recognized the forgery immediately and called The State Pharmacist's Commission. He called the physician, too. It was like being ten years old again and being told I had to go to the principal's office.

They were very angry with my bad behavior. I got a lecture: *If you ever do something like this again, we're gonna....*

For me, hand writing prescription blanks was risky and dangerous. The potential that a pharmacist would recognize the bogus signature, or perhaps notice that the DEA number was off by a digit or two, or that it didn't quite match the DEA code, was an ever-present danger. (A DEA number is a secret identification number seen on the prescription blank as a meaningless series of seven digits and two letters, but when deciphered by either a pharmacist or a doctor or DEA man or a wise-ass dopefiend, it indicates the legitimacy of the prescription.) I could write the dosage out wrong. I could spell the brand name incorrectly. Maybe they don't even make this stuff anymore and everyone knows but me. It was too easy to get caught.

No, hand writing scripts was just too risky. Besides, if I wrote the script, I had to stand there while the pharmacist looked it over.

No. There had to be a better way.

A better... mousetrap?

Instead of writing the script, taking it down, handing it to the pharmacist and then waiting around like a do-do, while he decided whether or not to call the police, I simply called in my prescriptions by telephone.

Pretty smart, huh?

It worked like this: I called in the order and waited a couple of hours before going down to pick it up. Then, when I got to the pharmacy, I scoped out the parking lot for FBI agents or DEA cars (dark colored, Ford LTD Crown Victorias, with Virginia license plates). I looked around inside the store for anyone who seemed the least bit suspicious; and when I was sure the coast was clear, I just went up to the counter and picked up my script, paying for it with my Master The Possibilities Card. What could go wrong? What a system!

Now, the laws vary from state to state, but where I lived

a pharmacy would accept an order for a Schedule Three, Four or Five controlled substance by telephone. Just by a voice on the other side of the fiber optic. You'd better be able to speak Latin! But they'll fill the script for you just the same. (I'd imagine this practice saves the doctor the hassle of seeing a patient in his office for something rather run-of-the-mill when he can just as easily do the prescribing over the telephone. *Sure, I can give you something for your menstrual cramps. Lemme call in a little Tylenol with codeine for you. Which pharmacy do you use . . . ?*) It's done all the time. Accepted business practice. And enter: My Telephone Ordering Escapades.

I tried it first with a re-fill for hydrocodone, like the Vicodin stuff I'd forged on that doctor's stolen prescription pad.

As I said before, generically, Vicodin is hydrocodone bitartrate, and in its pill form—in Vicodin Tablets—it can be rather difficult to obtain from the doctor for pain relief. Doctors don't like to write scripts for it too often. For treating minor aches and pains in a doctor's office, the drug of choice (*The One Favored By More Doctors*) is Tylenol #3. That's Tylenol with a dab of codeine in it. Junk.

But for a cough, it's another matter entirely. For relief of that nagging, persistent, non-productive cough, most doctors usually prescribe something with hydrocodone bitartrate in it (names like Hycodan and Tussionex come to mind). Same stuff as in the Vicodin tablets. In a cough syrup it just tastes like cherries or bananas, that's all.

And I developed a terrible cough and a horrible upper respiratory tract infection. (I smoke about a pack of cigarettes a day, and have done so since I was about twelve.)

I took my new illness to a walk-in medical clinic, the ones where the attending physician looks like he goes home and puts on his turban before dinner. And this was where I met Doctor Mustahf Cosandrias. A kindly Indian doctor, who tried quite desperately to alleviate my fitful coughing and cure me of the nasty congestion that lingered in my aching chest. Doctor Cosandrias' remedy was simple: an antibiotic, like Tetracycline, for the infection in my upper respiratory tract, and a strong, hydrocodone-based cough preparation, to help ease the wrackings. The doctor prescribed Tussionex. Nectar Of The Gods.

Doctor Cosandrias ordered a four ounce bottle. *Now lemme see here: one teaspoon equals one-sixth of an ounce. Four ounces in this bottle here. Four times six is twenty four. No shit! I got twenty four hits of this stuff in one little bottle of cough syrup?*

A week later, I asked the doctor for a re-fill.

"Still coughing?" he asked.

I nodded. (*Cough! Cough!*) "Uh huh!" (*Cough! Cough!*) "Yea."

"All right," he said. "I'll re-fill the cough syrup for you."

And I paid his receptionist thirty-five dollars for the office visit and the re-fill.

I hit Doctor Cosandrias one more time for a re-fill, but to push him any further would have brought about that look of something not quite being kosher with this patient. I left him alone.

I had his DEA number. I had his address, his first and last names, his license number—I had all the necessary information from the *PDR* that I needed to secure authorization for a refill myself. And why shouldn't I?

I gave it a shot.

I called the pharmacy on the telephone, donning my best Doctor From Calcutta Voice, and said, "Yes. Good morning. This is Doctor Mustahf Cosandrias. I would like to order a prescription refill for one of my patients?" The pharmacist asked for the patients name. I told him.

"Okay, doctor. Thank you," he said, and hung up the phone.

WHAT? No DEA number? No license number? You don't want the dosage, or the number, or the strength, or NOTHING? YOU DON'T EVEN WANNA KNOW IF IT'S REALLY ME OR NOT?

I set the phone back down on the cradle. I shook my head.

Wakeman Drugs was down the hill and around the corner from my college apartment. I drove down there, parked the Suzuki, and walked into the store and up to the counter where they kept the ChapSticks, the pink and blue pill boxes, the Protect Yourself From Being Attacked spray cans of mace, and the plastic coiled-up key chains you buy so you don't loose your key ring. I looked around. Nope, nobody suspicious looking in here. I checked the store out for FBI and DEA Agents. Nothing. Just the lady over there picking out a Hallmark Card for her mother-in-law's birthday, and that guy by the condom rack trying to figure out which neck brace is going to fit around his chubby little neck and his three double chins. Nope. Nothing fishy so far.

The pharmacist came to the counter and asked if he could help me.

"Yes," I said. "My name is Adam Richmond. I think my doctor called in a prescription refill for me?"

I kept my eyes peeled.

"Yessir. It's right here." He handed me the bag. "That's eight seventy-five with the tax, sir." I gave him a ten. "Do you need a receipt for your insurance?" I shook my head. "Thank you, sir. Have a nice day."

The pharmacist went back to filling his prescriptions behind the counter.

I went to the parking lot, befuddled.

I went back to my bike, with my little white bag, stapled across the top fold, containing cherry flavored nectar of the pharmaceutical gods. A full, four ounce bottle of hydrocodone bitartrate (a.k.a. Tussinex) all for me and my greedy little Hydrogenated Ketone Of Codeine Addicted Brain Cells.

I twisted off the cap, took a big slug, and gulped down an ounce of the stuff in a shot.

This, I thought, *is cause for celebration.* And I stuffed the bottle into my back pocket.

▲ ▼ ▲

I refilled the prescription four times at Wakeman Drugs. The following two times I called, I had to get more "professional" in the way I reordered the medicine. I had to change around the dosage regimen. Or at least, I thought I did. I just got more creative, that's all.

By the third refill, I assumed the pharmacist might begin to question the professional ethics of this "Doctor Cosandrias," who was lately becoming a little too free in his prescribing of controlled substances. I also thought that the pharmacist might question the validity of such prescriptions. It was getting dangerous, both because of the fact that I might get caught! and also because I was getting rather strung-out on the stuff.

So, I ordered a detoxification regimen (gradually reducing dosages to try and get myself off):

"Yes. Doctor Cosandrias again. Yes. How are you? Yes. For Adam Richmond. Uh huh. But I would like to change the dosage on the prescription. Yes. Tussionex, number four ounce. Dispense one teaspoon q.i.d. for two days. Then sig one teaspoon t.i.d. for two days. Then one teaspoon b.i.d. times two days. Then one teaspoon q.h.s. Yes. That should do it. Uh huh. I want him to stop taking it. Right. He knows. Yes, I've explained this to him, he understands. All right. Thank you again. Good bye."

I got it.

Son of a bitch! I got it.

And I meant to stop! It was getting risky and I was getting strung out! I really wanted to stop!

But I drank the bottle in a couple of days.

I needed more. Again.

My last attempt at a refill backfired.

Two days later, I again called Wakeman Drugs and again, I told them that I wanted to order a refill, but this was definitely the last one. "Yes," I said in my Indian Doctor Voice, "I know. But he's having a difficult time coming off it. I'm going to do this for him *one last time.*"

Right. . . .

As I approached the front door of the pharmacy, the pharmacist (who, incidently, was a pretty decent guy) pulled me aside before I even got in through the front door. He was coming out of the supermarket exit that was adjacent to the pharmacy, and he grabbed me and pulled me into a corner before I even got my hand onto the pharmacy's door. He said: "Look, lemme save you a lot of trouble here. I called the doctor this morning, and. . . . "

I lowered my head. The jack rabbit caught in the proverbial Mack Headlamps.

He continued: "Why don't you do yourself a favor and get some help for yourself?" I agreed. "I'm not going to call the cops on you or anything. The doctor knows all about you now; but maybe you should think about going to a shrink, or a clinic or something, and trying to help yourself before this thing gets worse? Okay?" I nodded again. "Next time," he said, "they might just have you arrested."

I kept my head bowed.

He's right! I thought to myself. *I AM getting messed up on this stuff! And I DO need to get some help!*

"Thanks," I said.

I WILL go home and try to get some help! I WILL try and stop! And if I have to, I'll get some PROFESSIONAL help! It's

TRUE! Everything's getting all screwed up! Shit! that's why I ordered the detox regimen in the FIRST place! I WANNA GET OFF THIS CRAP!

I went home and called my favorite doctor (the one I went to when I really *was* sick) and I told him what was up, that I was having a problem with the cough syrups, that I couldn't get myself off them, and before it got real bad I wanted to talk to someone about it, a counselor, or a shrink perhaps.

He gave me the name of a shrink in a nearby town who he thought could probably help. I told him I'd give the shrink a call. I promised! I *swore!*

Just as soon as I called just one more pharmacy and gave them just one more verbal order for just one more bottle of Tussionex cough syrup I'd give the shrink a call.

▲ ▼ ▲

With my pharmaceutical knowledge of medical abbreviations, Latin terminology, Drug Enforcement Administration numbers and schedules, manufacturing company lingo, and standard nursing dosage, regimen, administration and refill sequence secured, I knew everything I needed to do all my own prescription ordering.

I frequently ordered my elixirs in conjunction with antibiotics like Amoxicillin and Pen-VK. This, I reasoned, would more convince the pharmacist that my prescription was a valid one. A Schedule Three narcotic cough preparation by itself was sometimes difficult to order; but when it was ordered along with an antibiotic to treat the respiratory infection, well, again, it's Standard Medical Practice.

I just threw out the antibiotic.

I substituted the names of acquaintances on the prescription orders, and I used doctor's names from other towns, in other parts of the state. I figured the pharmacist would never bother to pay for the cost of the toll call he would need to verify the prescription. I made up fictitious doctors' names; I dreamt up false patients, concocted phony addresses; and I scrambled up the numbers in the DEA code, switching and altering them ever so slightly. (A DEA Number is simple: The odd digits of the seven number sequence, when subtracted from the evens, equals the last digit in the doctor's Number. The second letter of the preceding two, is the same as the first letter of the doctor's last name. It's not a very complex code to figure out; it's sort of like a telephone number. Besides, any pharmacist or doctor's secretary will divulge the information and tell you how it works after you buy him or her a couple of vodka rocks.)

And when I wasn't busy at the doctor's office or the emergency room, I ran The Pharmacy Scams.

At any given time I used between two and six different pharmacies—an initial order for cough syrup and antibiotics at one, a refill at another, and perhaps a real prescription at a third. I used pharmacies from my college town, I used pharmacies back in my hometown, and I used pharmacies all the way in between. Your guess would be as good as mine as to how many drugstores I ran this bit on during my career.

I might suddenly remember that it had been a long time since I had ordered anything from a certain pharmacy, so I'd call them up, tell them my patient still needed the medication, and I'd travel an hour or so to go down and stock up on another bottle. I had the whole thing all figured out and was having a blast. (Although this practice could, every now and then, become a wee bit time consuming.)

I only used certain drugstores for Schedule Three narcotic-containing cough syrups; some I used only when I scammed ER doctors for Schedule Two narcotics; a few pharmacies were only used for tranquilizers, and still others (like the store my family used back in my hometown fifty miles away) were only for real prescriptions. I had the whole operation down to a science.

Or so I thought.

Till I got pinched, that is.

▲ ▼ ▲

It was stupid. I got sloppy. I *deserved* to get arrested for being so careless. Felony Number One.

I had taken two weeks off from work before the fall semester, and had gone home to my parents' house to chill out before the start of classes. My parents had gone away that month to visit a sick relative down South, and I just thought I'd go down to their house, cool my jets for a couple of weeks, and relax with some pills, some nostrums, and maybe—if I could scrape up the cash—a few syringes full of cocaine hydrochloride or diacetylmorphine (heroin). I had the whole place to myself.

What a mistake *that* decision was going to be.

Along with a fairly good-sized addiction to cough syrups, I had a nice little thing going with tranquilizers, Valium and Xanax in particular. Both do pretty much the same thing when you ingest them: a ten milligram Valium is about the same in strength, duration, and effect as a one milligram Xanax; both are listed with the DEA as a Schedule Four controlled substance; and both are fairly easy to convince your physician into prescribing when you're having Trouble Falling Asleep, or when the Work Load At School And At Your Job Over There At The Psychiatric Hospital is stressing you out. Both these tranquilizers make the world just a little better place to live in.

And *both* are very easy to call into a pharmacy by phone.

(I had oral surgery done at one point a little later on in my career to secure a prescription for narcotics. Lost a molar over that one! And once I'd acquired the dentist's DEA Number, I called a pharmacy in another state and asked them if they would accept an order for a controlled substance, Valium, over the phone. I told the pharmacist that my patient's mother had just passed away, he was suffering from extreme duress, and would they kindly take the telephone order because it was just too much emotional turmoil for my patient to travel to my office to pick up the script in person. I had thirty of those little blue suckers in less than an hour.)

I'd been running the Westfair Pharmacy for a few weeks during the course of August. I called in the original prescription for thirty Valium with a Sig q.i.d. p.r.n. (Dispense four times a day, as needed.) The prescription should have lasted "the patient" a little over a week.

I called in a refill the following week, but for some reason, I had a disquieting feeling when I placed the order. I'm not sure why, but I didn't go down that day and pick up the script. I settled for getting some Xanax from another pharmacy.

A week later, I called the Westfair Pharmacy as "the patient" and asked if they had received a phone call from "my doctor" the previous week refilling my prescription. (This was another safeguard: I ordered the prescription as The Doctor first, and then called later on as The Patient, playing stupid, and asking if The Doctor had phoned in a prescription for me. That way, I figured, if they knew the script was bogus and didn't want to fill it, they'd just say something like, *if you ever call here again, you little asshole. . . .*)

The pharmacist at Westfair Pharmacy said: "Oh yes,

Mr. Richmond; it's right here. Yes sir. The doctor phoned it in for you last week. Tuesday, I think. I have the order right here on the counter in front of me."

Great! I'll just take a cruise over there on the bike and pick up my script.

I strolled into the drugstore and gave them my usual patter about how sorry I was that I didn't come down to pick up the prescription last week. I was so busy, I explained, and I really appreciated that they would still fill it even though it was reordered over a week ago. And yes, the doctor is so nice, isn't he? These little pills sure do the trick, don't they? Yessiree. They sure do help me get a good night's sleep in light of that horrible insomnia which I've been suffering with lately. Miracle drug! this Valium stuff here. Don't you agree? Yessiree, Bob.

"It's going to be a few minutes, Mr. Richmond." The pharmacist smiled. "We didn't know if you'd show up for it this week, so it'll just take me a couple of minutes to fill, okay?"

"Okay," I said.

He turned to his female assistant and nodded.

What was that?

Mmmmmm, probably just a Nervous Pharmacist's Twitch or something.

"Do you need a child resistant cap on the bottle?" he asked.

I laughed. I shook my head.

I wonder why he nodded to that girl? I thought they were supposed to have this stuff ready for me when I came here. Where's my little white bag with the staples across the top?

"Here you are, sir," he said. "Sorry it took us so long." He smiled broadly. "It's ten fifty, please." I paid him. "Thanks very much, have a nice day."

I took my change, said thanks, and walked to the front

door with my white paper bag, looking to hop onto my motorcycle and enjoy one of the finest days in August I'd ever seen.

I'll take a few Valium here, maybe do a little cocaine or something, and just fly around for a few hours on my New Suzy. Now where'd I park my bike? My keys are in my pocket here, and my bike is par. . . .

"Hi!" the officer says. I look up. He asked: "How's it going?"

Shit, he was big.

He was the biggest, bluest cop I'd ever seen! He looked about six-foot-six. The sun shone down behind him, and I thought of one of those huge Alaskan Black Bears. I thought he should have had a fresh salmon dangling out of his mouth. He was a *monster!* And his sidekick wasn't too small either. They were both looking at me. Smiling.

"So?" The Black Bear began, "You wanna tell us what you got in the bag there?" He pointed at my little white bag with the staples across the top. The one with the bogus prescription for Valium in it.

"What? This?" I asked. Like I wasn't exactly sure if he were referring to *my* bag. I tried lamely to smile. "You mean this stuff?" I held the bag up a little. "Oh, I don't know. I'm just picking it up for a friend of mine."

"Oh . . . ," he said slowly. He folded his arms across his chest and nodded carefully. He wanted more than *that.*

"Uh . . . yea . . . ," I stuttered. "My buddy just sent me over here to the drugstore to pick it up for him."

"Oh . . . ," he said again slowly. "Who's your 'buddy'?"

Christ! he's fucking big.

"Uh . . . he's just a guy." *I hope this works.* "He, uh, lives around the corner from me. He calls me on the phone and tells me to go to the drugstore for him and get him a package with his name on it."

"Oh...," said The Black Bear. "Is *that* how 'he' works it?"

"Yea!" I said. "I just get a phone call. I pick up the prescription. And then I put it in his mailbox for him. He leaves me the money for it in the box!"

"I see, " The Black Bear said. He nodded and raised his eyebrows.

He's not buying a word of this, Adam.

"Uh huh," I said.

Please, God? Please? Please don't let this guy arrest my ass?

"What's your 'friend's' name?" he asked.

"Uh...I don't know. Uh...but I know where he lives! Yea! I know which apartment he lives in! I know which mailbox is his! It's right around the corner from me!"

"Lemmee get this straight," The Black Bear began. He took a step back and leaned up against a post, crossing his arms again. "Some 'guy' calls you on the phone? He tells you to pick up his drugs and put the bag in his mailbox? And he leaves you the *money for it?*" I nodded. "You do all this for him, but you don't even know what his name is?" I nodded again. He asked: "So, you wanna show us where he lives?"

"Uh...well...," I started. "Uh...I'm not really sure I could...you see...."

"C'mon," The Black Bear laughed. He lowered his eyes at me from underneath his hat. "You can do better than that, can't you?"

I shook my head. "Naaa...," I said.

I held out my wrists.

"I *almost* bought it," he said, "till you got to the part where you couldn't tell me his name. I almost bought it!"

I almost laughed.

"C'mon," he said finally. "Let's go for a ride. You and me. We're gonna go do some talking down at the station."

Terrific.

▲ ▼ ▲

The police officers took me down to the local precinct in
their cruiser and asked me what I was strung out on. They
seemed a little mad at first, they wanted to know if I was
going to throw up in their car. "You're not going to get sick
on us or anything, are you? You gonna go into withdrawal?
You gonna puke?"

"No," I told them. "I'm not strung out on anything." I
had ordered the Valium, I explained, as an adjunct to the
medication I was taking for my upper respiratory tract infection. "The Valium keeps me from coughing." My physician was out of town for a few weeks, I said, and I just decided to reorder the prescription myself. "I know it was
stupid. It's really dumb of me to try and pull a stunt like
this."

"Uh huh," they said.

They took me into one of the offices at the precinct and
told me to sit in the chair while they took down some information. They asked for my name, address, where I
worked, family names, et cetera—all the vitals—and they
looked me up in their computer to see if I had a previous
record and had ever done anything wrong within the legal
system. I hadn't.

This was my first felony.

The cops were nice. They didn't offer me coffee or
anything, but they took the bracelets off my wrists as soon
as we were into the building, and they let me sit around in
the office while they processed the arrest. They didn't put
me behind bars or try to beat a confession out of me with
their nightsticks. They recorded my fingerprints, took a
Polaroid of my face while I held a bunch of numbers above
my chest and below my chin, and they were actually, for
what I thought at the time, pretty cordial guys for police officers.

When it was all over, I was charged with a Class D felony: Impersonating A Physician and was issued a Promise To Appear In Court, A "PTA" as it's called. I wondered if my mother had to bake the brownies.

They kept my bottle of Valium as evidence, and said that as I had never been arrested before, that they wouldn't hold me and I didn't have to post bail. I was free to go on my own recognizance with the PTA. Three weeks from my arrest date, I should appear in the courtroom of my hometown's superior court and go before the judge there to see what he had to say about the whole matter. They suggested I consult an attorney. They were quite nice about the whole thing.

For cops.

For cops that arrested *my* ass, for getting *my* prescription, that *I* needed, for *my* cough! The pharmacist even took my money for the script! I couldn't figure out why he made me pay for the thing, and then had the audacity to have me arrested! Nor could I understand why the police didn't give me back the Valium. I was going to go back and tell the pharmacist off, give him a piece of my mind about the way he conducted his business practices, tell him where I thought he could stick his fucking. . . .

But I didn't. And I didn't ask the cops for my prescription back, either.

When the police finished processing my arrest and saw clearly that I wasn't a real criminal, they offered to give me a lift back to the pharmacy parking lot where I'd left the Suzuki. They gave me the pink PTA slip, and one of the cops took me outside to his cruiser. We headed over to the pharmacy.

The cop tried to talk to me on the drive over. He told me about a brother-in-law of his who'd recently been in the same sort of trouble. His sister's husband, the cop explained, had gotten himself into a mess with his abuse of alcohol and chemicals, but had gotten some help for the problem. And now, his brother-in-law was a pretty nice guy to be around! The officer said that since his brother-in-law had gotten rid of his Little Chemical Abuse Problem, that he was doing rather well. He didn't use drugs and alcohol anymore, he'd made amends with his wife and family, he'd straightened out most of his legal and financial entanglements—and now he was a pretty happy man.

"You know something, kid?" the cop began. "Maybe you should try and get some help for this problem before it gets really bad for you and you get into more trouble. You're not a bad kid! Why don't you try and find a drug clinic or something? Do like my brother-in-law." I nodded. The cop was right.

He was right, and so was the pharmacist who pulled me aside a few weeks ago. They were both right! I *did* need help! *Fuckin' A!* I thought, *Now I'm even getting arrested for this shit!*

"I think so," I said.

We pulled into the parking lot and I thanked the police officer for his friendly advice. I also thanked him for the lift.

"You're right," I said. "I *will* try and get my shit together with this stuff!" He smiled. He nodded and wished me well.

He said, "You'd better start looking at what you're doing, kid." And he left. *God, he's right!*

I cranked up the Suzy.

Man! It was a beautiful day! The temperature was perfect, high in the seventies, maybe even pushing eighty! There wasn't a cloud in the sky, the sun was nice and hot, still early in the afternoon, and it was just about the best time of the day to enjoy a motorcycle ride on a few back country roads. I had a hundred dollars in my pocket and more than a few Xanax left at home in the top drawer of my bedroom bureau. The day was still salvageable.

Too bad about that little bit of trouble I got myself into with the pharmacy and the police, though. That was almost One Real Big Mess, wasn't it? Whew! Oh well, at least mom and dad are outta town. I'm gonna have to tell'em though. . . . Shit! How'm I gonna explain this one? Ah well, not to worry yet, I still got a few bucks left in my pocket.

I pulled out of the pharmacy's parking lot on my bike and got onto the entranceway of the turnpike heading south. I put my feet up onto the highway pegs of the Suzuki, and I cruised down the freeway taking in the sunshine, the breeze flapping in and out of my raggy tee shirt, and the beautiful temperature of this fine New England summer's day. *What a beaut!* I thought.

I got off at the Downtown Exit and rode up the street to Boot Hill. I bought a gram (only $100) of cocaine. My syringe was at home.

I drove back to my parents' house, wearing my sunglasses and feeling like Marlon Brando. I turned down the street, entered the driveway, and I left the motorcycle parked outside on its kickstand. My testicles went up into my abdomen. I could taste the blow freeze the back of my mouth!

I ran upstairs to my night table, took out the bottle of Xanax, and popped three or four of them into my mouth. Then I got my belt, a glass of water, a spoon from the kitchen drawer downstairs to mix the cocaine and water in, and went back to the upstairs bathroom. I locked the door.

I opened up the closet and took out my syringe from where I'd hidden it in between the folds in a pile of bath towels. I put all the stuff out on the shelf of the sink, and sat down on the toilet. Then I blew my mind onto the floor, the window, the shower door, and the ceiling over my head. I whacked the load of cocaine into my system, and I watched. My brain *screamed.* . . .

And that was just the way I fucking liked it.

It was an all right combination: intravenous cocaine and Xanax. The tranquilizers took the bite out of the cocaine if I injected too much and started to seize. I also didn't shake so bad on the tranqs. It was easier to perform the injections. I didn't miss the vein as often. Boot the coke, pop a tranq.

Boot. And pop. Boot. And. Pop. All afternoon long.

It didn't turn out to be such a bad day after all.

SIX

ON THE RUN

Second only to "fine," my father's favorite ex-pression was "son of a *BITCH!*" Which was precisely his response when he came home from his visit down South and heard the news that I had been arrested for calling in phoney prescriptions and that I was now in need of a lawyer to get me off the charge. My father, exclaiming his favorite expression second only to "fine," sent an ashtray flying across the room with an agile backhand, slammed his fist down on the arm of the brown recliner in which he always sat, and shoved the BarcoLounger to its upright position. He stormed out of the room, muttering, swearing, calling me numerous expletives—all reinforcing what a fucked-up punk I still was despite my accomplish-ments at college, and then he went into the kitchen to fix himself another stiff one. On the way out of the den, he spat at my mother, "*YOU* talk to him!" thus relinquishing his parental responsibilities for his still screwed-up, still-wet-behind-the-ears, who-the-fuck-does-he-think-he-is? kid to his wife.

Dad was not about to accept this one with a mere "fine."

But he would, after some persuasion on my mom's part, secure the services of a lawyer to get me off the charge with only four months' probation.

Thanks, Dad.

Mom offered: "All right. I'll talk to him."

Thanks, Mom.

My mother and I talked in the den. Calmly. About the situation: "I'm sorry, Mom. I know it was a stupid thing to do, but I didn't know what else to do at the time. My doctor was out of town, I needed the meds, and I just didn't think it would be such a bad thing for me to do, to call the prescription in myself. I really fucked up, Mom. I'm sorry."

"Why didn't you just call the family doctor if you needed medicine?" she asked.

"I dunno, Ma. I just didn't think of it, that's all. I've been kinda sick with that respiratory tract infection, I've been under a lot of stress with school and trying to work at the same time, and I guess I just did it without thinking. I'm sorry, Ma. Really. God! I'm sorry to have to tell you both something like this."

She came over to the chair where I sat and stroked the top of my head.

Mom said it was "all right," that she'd "talk to dad" and try to get him to understand, and that I was "not to worry." She urged me to get back to school promptly and continue with my education; she admonished me *never* to try anything so stupid like this again, and she wrote me out a check for two thousand dollars to begin the semester with.

"Don't tell your father I'm giving you this money," she reminded me.

"Okay, Ma, I won't."

And I put the check inside my wallet.

Two days later, I left my parent's house and my two-week vacation, and I traveled the seventy-five miles or so back to college and back to my college apartment to begin my senior year. Dad calmed down, Mom put some more cash into my pocket so I'd have something to tide me over till her check cleared, and they stood at the front door and waved goodbye.

I'd be back on their doorstep in less than two months.

Before I go any further, I need to explain something. I think it will help you understand this story better and make things a little more clear in your mind. And it is this: Dopefiends are consummate liars.

As a class, we are probably some of the most manipulative and deceitful people you are likely to come across in your entire life. (And God forbid! that you come across all that many of us.) We have to be. It's called survival. We *need* our drugs, and we will do anything to meet that need. I have a friend who likes to describe his lying and manipulation by saying, "When I was shooting dope, I could talk a starving dog off a meat truck." And if dogs could speak English, most dopefiends probably could do just that.

So, if you are wondering if my parents suspected something funny was going on with my seeing so many doctors or if they could tell just by looking at me that something was wrong, the answer is no.

No they couldn't tell, and no they didn't think there was something funny about all this, and no they didn't find out anything else was going on. They didn't find out because I didn't tell them. And if they asked I lied. It's that simple: Bags under your eyes and rapid weight loss are due to "college stress." Never because you're hungover, or swallowing too many pills, or screwing around with heroin and cocaine.

When a dopefiend is up against his first felony arrest and needs a lawyer to free him of the charge, he *doesn't* tell his parents that this has been going on for a long time; he *doesn't* tell his parents that this is becoming a regular practice for him at college; and he *doesn't* tell his parents that most of the money they're sending him for tuition, books, car repairs, rent, clothes, food, apartment furniture, and MasterCard bills is going to pay for his extracurricular drug use. He can't.

Because if he told his parents these things, they'd make him go for help and probably, they'd make him stop doing drugs. And that—the cessation of the dopefiend's drug use—is the last thing a dopefiend wants.

So dopefiends lie. They lie, they manipulate, they beat around the bush, they tell only what they need to tell, and they do everything they can to continue using their drugs.

I will say that when I went back to college for that final year I ended my Telephone Ordering Escapades. At least for a while. I took my favorite physician's suggestion to see a counselor, and I met with the counselor for two months. In less than a dozen sessions, he was able to help me understand some basic things about myself, such as my perfectionist tendencies in almost everything I do; my unquenchable need to secure my father's approval, acceptance and love; my difficulty in sustaining meaningful relationships (including those with my family); and the fact that using prescription narcotics was not an answer for my somatic complaints.

My counselor suggested I try not worrying so much about what others thought of me and trying so hard to get their approval, and that I begin to learn how to take care of myself, including learning that I'm only human and that I don't have to try and be superman, that I give up treating my aches and pains and everyday stress of school and work with oral narcotics, and that I examine some other options for dealing with my stress. I did.

I picked up heroin.

Full-time.

How quickly this would be my demise. . . .

▲ ▼ ▲

Since my arrest, I had been doing a bag or two of heroin every day. Two months of classes had gone by, and I was working hard in my courses and doing well, despite my growing chemical use. That is, until my midterm exam in Methods in PsychoBiology. My professor stood behind a table on which lay a cat's brain that had been cut in half. My task was to identify the structures in the cat's brain the professor was pointing to with his scalpel.

"The thalamus," I said. "The cerebellum. Uh . . . the corpus callosum."

He asked me to name the cranial nerves.

Okay. Here we go. On Old Olympus Towering Tops A Fin And German Vied A Hops.

Wait . . . I can remember this . . . Wait . . .

"Olfactory . . . optic . . ."

Wait . . . I just memorized these fucking things last night. . . .

"Oculomotor . . ."

What's WRONG here?

"Uh . . ."

Jesus Christ! What's wrong with me . . .

"Glossofacial . . ."

My professor glared at me (there is no such nerve as the "glossofacial" nerve). He asked if something was wrong. I shook my head "no." He asked me if I was sure, we'd just gone over these a couple of days before in class, he reminded me. I assured him I could remember. *Just gimmee a second.* He kept looking at me strangely. Then he prompted me to continue.

I couldn't.

What the hell's the MATTER with me?

Glasso . . . glasso . . . glasso what the fuck is it?

"Can I come back later and finish this up?" I asked him. "Maybe tomorrow? I don't think I'm feeling too well right now."

He said "sure." He told me I could just call him when I was feeling better and then we could finish the oral exam. He kept looking at me funny.

Whew!

I whacked way too much dope this morning!

I went home to my apartment, called the counselor I'd been seeing for a couple of months, and screamed into the phone, "I can't take it anymore! I'm gonna crack if I have to take one more test, or write one more paper, or listen to one more bleeding depressive whine about their fucking childhood at fucking LongAcre Fucking Psychiatric Hospital! I can't take this shit anymore! *I just wanna fucking quit!*"

My counselor asked me why I didn't do just that?

I smiled. I said nothing of my heroin.

The following day I withdrew from classes.

My psychology professor couldn't understand. He seemed so puzzled when I handed him the white Withdrawal From Classes slip and asked him to sign on the dotted line. In the three years I'd been at school, he and I had developed a close relationship: I was one of his best students. I'd always scored the highest, or almost the highest, on his tests; and I'd helped him out in the laboratory researching The Biogenic Amine Hypothesis Of Schizophrenia and cutting up a dead rat here and there. He was well aware of the position I had secured at LongAcre (he'd written a Knock 'Em Dead letter of reference), he thought my research papers extremely well-written, and he had even allowed me, on occasion, to present the lecture to his freshmen classes. Why did I want to quit now? he wondered. Why did I want to give up when, with my grade point average and my test scores, there was such a good chance of my being accepted into a good doctoral program at a good school? Why quit with only two semesters to go?

"It's personal," I said.

He shook his head and put his signature on the slip of paper. Such a waste, he thought.

I didn't bother telling my professor about the heroin, either.

I showed up in late October on my parents' doorstep, explaining that I'd just withdrawn from college for the time being, that I'd taken a leave of absence from my job at the psychiatric hospital, and that I needed some time to breathe.

I asked them if I could just come home for a couple of months, maybe just until the first of the year. I offered to work at Dad's business during the interim, but I let them know that it was really important to me that I get some time off from school and from working at LongAcre, and that if I didn't just STOP! that I was going to crack and I was afraid something bad was going to happen. Like for instance, that I might lose my mind.

Mom understood my request completely; she didn't necessarily like it, but she understood it; Dad was unable fathom why I just "couldn't take it."

I suppose, "like a man."

I neglected to mention the heroin to my father, also.

I pulled my mother aside in the kitchen later on that evening. It was late, my dad had already gone up to bed, my mother was standing next to the stove fixing a bowl of cereal on the counter. The only light on in the kitchen was the one in the range hood above the stove. The television muttered innocuously far away in the den. If there was one person in the world to whom I could go when I had a problem, it was my mother.

I walked up beside her.

"Ma, I've got to talk to you about something."

"What is it sweetheart, what's wrong?" Immediately, she sensed something, that whatever I was about to tell her, was serious. Fear ran across her face in an instant.

"I've got a problem, Ma. I've got to talk to you about it."

"What is it, darling? Are you sick?"

"Oh shit, Ma. No. I'm not sick. I'm . . . " She took hold of my hand and urged me on. I bowed my head, ashamed: "I'm addicted to morphine, Ma."

She took a step backwards and braced herself against the kitchen counter. It was as though someone, someone invisible, had punched her in the chest. She clapped her hand onto her open mouth. Through her fingers she simply said, "Oh my *God!*"

"It's all right, Ma. I'm gonna be okay. Really. I'm gonna get off this stuff. But I think I need to detox or something."

"What's that?"

"Can you call the doctor and ask him if he'll do it? Can you ask him to put me in the hospital and detox me from this stuff?"

"Of course," my mother said, gathering herself. "Of course I will. I'll call him first thing in the morning. We'll call him on the phone first thing, and we'll find out what to do. Don't worry. We're gonna get you off this stuff." She strained to smile.

She reached out and held my two hands tightly. She gave me a kiss and held me. Then she told me to just go to bed and not to worry about a thing, that everything would be taken care of in the morning.

I went to bed and tried not to worry.

▲ ▼ ▲

The next day I was admitted to a general hospital under the care of the family's physician, who entered me with a diagnosis of bacterial endocarditis. Private physicians are not allowed by law to detoxify heroin addicts—that task is delegated to federally approved agencies only—so private physicians need an admitting diagnosis other than simply, "heroin detoxification." So they use a bacterial endocarditis diagnosis. I was in the hospital five days—five days without dope.

My father wasn't told the real reason for my hospital visit, only that the doctor was "checking for a problem with my heart." The members of my family frequently hid "secrets" from one another and made things up, so my mother was not adverse to helping me with this lie in order to avoid the wrath of my father.

The detox wasn't nearly as bad as I had anticipated the dreaded Cold Turkey to be. The doctors performed their tests to make sure there was nothing else wrong with me, and after five days I left the hospital, went back to my parents' house, and swore to my mother and father (we let Dad in on The Big Secret *after* I came out of the hospital) that I was through with drugs! That I was *never* going to go back on that stuff again! *NEVER! I PROMISED!* And my family gave me a chance to prove myself.

In two days, I said to hell with THAT idea!

Two days! to go from my first hospital stay and really wanting to kick the stuff, from being motivated to stop and knowing something was terribly wrong and leaving school and praying to God Almighty for the strength to kick; *two days!* from thinking that a move back home would surely do the trick and that I'd be far enough away from the dope that I wouldn't be tempted; *two days!* till I found out where they sold the heroin in my hometown, till I bought a couple of bags, till I stuck the needle back into my arm.

Two fucking days.

Actually, I think it took only about fifteen seconds once my brain snapped and I said, fuck it! and went into one of our seedier neighborhoods, talked to the right guy, and sniffed out the heroin. Yea. It only took me a few seconds to find "The Palace."

Two days after I left the general hospital, I did dope. I did dope in my hometown, I did dope from The Palace, and I did dope from The Home Boys. I shot my dope at my parents' house, in the car, in the gas station bathroom, and on the side of the road sitting in a storm drain. I did as much dope as I could get, and I did it as often as I could. That autumn when I left school (and LongAcre for that matter) all the stops came out. I went on my first, official "run."

▲ ▼ ▲

Dopefiends get money to pay for their dope any and every way they can. This includes working for it (which I did, at my father's restaurant whenever I felt like it), using money in the bank to get it (like the money my parents had deposited for my college education), lying to get it (I've got to get a new exhaust system put on the car), manipulating other people to give it to you (God I love you, can I have fifty

bucks? I'll give it back to you later, I swear), hocking your
stuff at pawn shops (like your stereo and that gold chain
from your ex-girlfriend), hocking other people's stuff at
pawn shops (like your mom's silverware and your brother's
camera equipment), writing bad checks (like the ones from
your father's checkbook), stealing (wallets and purses),
robbing (gas stations), and knocking over banks (like Bon-
nie and Clyde). The more dope you do, the more "creative" you get ways to acquire the money to pay for your
dope.

And in the end you get the money you need.

Trust me on this one.

The Palace was short for The Barbecue Palace. It was a
nifty little joint in my hometown up on Boot Hill that sold a
lot of chicken and ribs and fries and burgers and sodas and
stuff I'd never even heard of like pickled pig's feet. The
Palace sold regional items with a southern flare, and they
were known far and wide for their Famous Barbecue Sauce
With Just The Right Touch Of Flavors And Spices.

The Palace was also known far and wide for the heroin
they sold.

"Where can I get some dope around here?" I asked a
guy hanging out on Boot Hill.

"You gotta get it out of The Palace." He pointed across
the street. "Just ask the man inside, he'll serve you."

I looked over at the front door of The Barbecue Palace.
It looked seedy, rundown. *Now that looks like a place where
they'd sell dope.* There were a lot of black men and women
hanging around outside. Some of them seemed to be going
in and not coming out with food or soda or anything. There
was a group of men jiving on the corner, and there was a
cop, swinging his nightstick, about two doors down.

"What about him?" I asked, pointing at the cop.

The guy laughed. "That cop ain't gonna bother you,

bro," he said, and he shook his head saying, in effect, *you white 'homes can be so fucking stupid. . . .*

I walked into The Barbecue Palace, I told the man inside what I was looking for, and after he'd made sure I wasn't an undercover, he sold me two bags of heroin. I walked out of The Palace and back to where I'd parked my car. The guy on the corner was right: the cop outside never even batted an eye. I wonder what that cop said to his wife when he came home at night? *Oh yea, honey, sure were a lot of those stupid, white boy junkies from the burbs coming down today and buying their junk at The Palace. . . Huh? Naa . . . I didn't bust none of them. . . . Had some great barbecued ribs, though. . . .*

I never tried the food from The Barbecue Palace. Only the dope. And the dope was *on*.

I ran at The Palace for six months.

I was just twenty-two, and was still very much a punk with regard to the ways of The Street: the dealing and the selling, the police, the hospitals, the jail cells, and what it meant to be A Chronic Heroin Addict. I was learning—and learning quickly. But I was still too busy being enthralled with the game: the running from the undercovers, the thrill of beating the dealers, the ever-present chance of getting caught by the police, the wheeling, the dealing, and the whole damned adrenalin rush of the game. I didn't understand things like needing to fix, and needing to steal and scam and rob in order to supply my habit. I was young, fresh out of college, on my first big-time run, and I was pretty naive when it came to things like what would happen to me when I didn't get my morning fix. I had an idea about it, but I didn't yet really understand what people were talking about when they said, "dope sick." Dope sick to me just meant missing your dope. Christ! I don't think I'd ever gone long enough without my dope to even vomit!

What did I know? I had plenty of money. I could still rip off my family, or cash a bad check against the savings account deposited in my name (my father usually uttering his second favorite expression when this occurred, *son of a BITCH!*). I could still ask somebody for money and usually have them give it to me. I had no idea what happened to an addict who's strung-out and then one day finds himself without any dope.

But in Rehab, I found out. And quick.

I wanted to get clean. After a while, running with junk reaches a point when you ask yourself: Is this really what I want to do with my life? And then you do a number of things to try and get off the shit.

I knew it was getting bad, that I was messing up my life in a big way; but it's a double edged sword: on one level you know it's bad. You know you're screwing up your life and you think, *God! I really wanna get it together here. But then again . . . maybe. . . .*

I tried a program where you moved in and lived for anywhere up to two years, but I ran away before they even started dinner on my first day. I got anxious without my dope and I was out the door. The place was right down the street from Boot Hill.

I tried detoxifying a couple more times, but there too, I was out the door with the needle back in my arm before the detox was even finished. *Did any one see where that junkie in room 518 went to?*

I even tried to go Cold Turkey a few times at home and that never lasted more than twelve hours.

I tried, and tried, and I just couldn't do it on my own. Hard as I might attempt to quit, as soon as I started feeling even the slightest bit sick and nervous without my heroin, I'd be off and running. Right back to The Bag. I needed something more to stop. I wanted to. My family wanted me to. But I needed something stronger than my own feeble attempts if there was to be any hope of my beating this thing.

Hallmarke Hospital was the answer, an answer supplied by my father.

A Rehabilitation Facility. A Hospital, they called it, for Substance Abusers. A place where they would make me better, where they'd care for me. A Treatment Facility that could get me off the drugs for good and teach me how to lead a normal life.

Mom and Dad were up to *here!* with my stealing anything out of the house that wasn't nailed down. (My two older brothers, who were off and married by this point, weren't too keen on my behaviors, either!) The stolen checks were coming back from my old man's bank, Mom seemed to be misplacing more and more of her treasured, antique sterling silverware. I guess I was just getting tired of scamming people I knew, dealing with The Palace, getting ripped off by The Boys on The Hill, and the growing possibility that my ass was going to wind up in a jail cell before too long.

I just needed to stop.

My year-long run with heroin and cocaine had been long enough. It was getting hard to take. I'd give this Rehabilitation Thing a go.

Mom cried. Dad shook his head. Neither understood a goddamned thing about Their Son's Drug Problem.

But they said: "We'll do anything we can to help. We love you."

Actually, I think it was my mother who said, "We love you." My dad just kept shaking his head.

I don't think he could believe what was happening to his fucking kid.

SEVEN

REHABILITATION

My father took me to the hospital at eleven in the morning. Before I went, I injected a feeble amount of heroin that was left in the cooker from the previous day. It amounted to no more than half a bag, but I figured that they'd give me something as soon as I got to the hospital.

After a brief meeting with the intake counselor who asked me about my problems, my drugs of choice, my frequency of use, my insurance coverage (thanks again, Dad), the counselor gave me a short explanation of the program and what I could expect here at Hallmarke, and I went up to the detox floor.

I was introduced to a Mental Health Worker, who led me to my room, which turned out to be rather nice. It had a closet, a bed, a desk, and from the window I could see a large expanse of lawn and watch the people out there playing tennis and volleyball.

But just coming in off my first big league run, I wasn't really all that concerned with playing volleyball. I wanted some meds, and I wanted them fast.

I wanted my detox medication.

"Detoxification" is a process whereby the addicted person is slowly and gradually given decreasing amounts of the addictive substance in order to wean him or her off the chemical with as little discomfort as possible. And Methadone Hydrochloride is the detoxification drug of choice among physicians looking to wean addicts off narcotics.

When I was in my early twenties, you could get a lot of "meth" when you went to your local hospital and asked to be detoxed. Usual starting dosage was between sixty and a hundred milligrams, depending on how well you could convince the attending physician that your habit was severe. Then, every day or every other day the doctor cut your dose by five milligrams, until your body was completely free of the drug. The first day you were given sixty milligrams, the following day fifty-five, then fifty, forty-five, forty et cetera, et cetera, so on, and so forth. At the end of the detoxification process, the nurse came up to you and said, "You can go home now. Go to a clinic and get some help, but your body's free of the drugs now." And that was how you detoxed. It was fairly comfortable, and you rarely had to deal with things like vomiting, shaking, uncontrollable muscle twitching, an elevated blood pressure, and suicidal ideation, which are all pretty common when you try to kick heroin without the aid of detoxification medication.

Hallmarke Hospital used Methadone. They were going to use it to detoxify my body and get me off the drugs the same way our family physician had done for me at the general hospital.

"We'll start tomorrow," the nursing staff told me. "We don't dispense Methadone on the weekend. You'll have to wait until you're seen by the unit psychiatrist."

Well, that's okay, I figured. I can make it till tomorrow morning.

I sat down in the lounge on the detox floor and tried to make some friends. There were only four of us there on this Sunday afternoon. The others, the ones who were feeling up to it, were outside playing volleyball. We were the newest admissions, and we weren't feeling quite up to volleyball yet.

I made an attempt to talk to one of the guys who was sitting in the lounge watching the baseball game, but he kind of growled at me when I asked him who was playing and what he thought of being at Hallmarke.

"Better leave him alone," advised Nick, the guy sitting next to me. He whispered, "He's a vet. Been to 'Nam. Got a mother fucker of a habit on that Chinese shit they got over there, and he's having a really tough detox."

I looked again at the guy watching the baseball game, the one who'd developed his habit over there "in 'Nam," and no, his detox didn't look like it was going all that smoothly. As a matter of fact, it looked as though at any moment this guy was going to bust apart, like he'd shoot the next person who tried to talk to him or maybe, asked how he was feeling. No. I left this guy alone. I thought he'd pull out an AK-47 assault rifle and cream the whole unit if I tried to get to know him any closer. I thought I might be a little bit better off just leaving him to the doctors and the nurses.

Nick was an Italian junkie, a pro. He'd been at this thing a lot longer than I. Whereas this was my first attempt at rehabilitation, Nick had already been to jail twice, had been in a hospital three times, and had just that morning come from a treatment facility he referred to as A Therapeutic Community. Nick was A Real Junkie.

"See this?" Nick said, pointing to his head and bugging out his eyes. He put his index finger to his Marine-style haircut. "See this shit?!" he yelled.

"Uh huh," I said.

"They did this to me at ReGroup! Shaved my fucking head, man! I used to have long fucking hair!"

"Why'd they do that?" I asked.

"Fuck, man! Everybody gets their head shaved! It's like boot camp, man. They shave your head as part of their indoctrination into the place. I was there two days and they shaved off all my fucking hair!" He rubbed his hand back and forth on the bristles. "It's like some kind of privilege to grow it; it's so they can tell who's new and who's been there for a while." He smacked his head with his hand.

"That's fucked up, man," I observed.

"That's nothin!" he started. "I saw this one guy? Everybody in the place though he was acting like a big baby?" Nick moved a little closer to my face and spoke slowly, choosing his words carefully: "They made him wear diapers and walk around the place in 'em! They made him sleep in a crib, and he had to carry a bottle with him wherever he went! They hung a sign around his neck that said: 'I'M A BABY', and they made him wear it for a week!" Nick shook his head. "Man! I saw that shit, and I split! I called my uncle on the phone and said, 'Get me outta this place NOW!'" He threw up his hands. "So? My uncle picked me up and brought me here."

"That's crazy!" I again observed. I was in complete agreement that trying to rehabilitate heroin addicts by making them wear diapers, carry formula bottles, sleep in cribs, and shave their heads was an inappropriate way to go about it. "So whada'ya think of this place?" I asked.

"It's all right, I guess. I wish I could get some Methadone today, though. I'm starting to feel pretty shitty. But they told me they don't dispense Meth on the weekend." He looked at the nursing station and imitated a bratty little eight year old: "'We don't give out Methadone till you've been seen by the chief psychiatrist'." Nick looked like he wanted to spit. He nodded towards the nurse's station and motioned with his thumb: "You can't even get a fucking aspirin out of that nurse!" He turned to me again: "'LuvLee' she calls herself. That's her name. 'LuvLee'. Can you believe that shit?" I looked over at the nurse to whom Nick had referred.

I failed to get the joke.

"LuvLee" was a huge woman. She was not even remotely attractive (except to her mother, maybe), and she had a permanent scowl, perhaps akin to a Marine Corps drill instructor, plastered to the front of her face. Hildegaard maybe! But not LuvLee. I missed that one.

Nick said: "If you ask me, I think she just needs a vibrator. I think she gets off watching us in withdrawal and not giving us any meth. I think she likes it!"

LuvLee ran the detox unit on the three-to-eleven shift. When Nick started to get sick later that afternoon, LuvLee said to him: "If you vomit, I need to see it. Don't flush the toilet. I need to see if you're *really* sick."

Wonderful job you got there, LuvLee.

Nick and I were informed by LuvLee that medication would be given on weekends, but only if you had serious symptoms. If you were really in a nasty way with your withdrawal, the nursing staff wouldn't want to deal with a sick junkie and they would call the on call physician to get you a medication order. It wasn't easy though. You had to vomit into the toilet for LuvLee. Or come close to it.

Nick vomited.

He stuck his fingers down his throat and barfed into the

toilet. "There!" he said to LuvLee. "There's your puke! Now can I get something?"

He left it floating in the toilet bowl as per LuvLee's instructions; she looked at it, flushed it away to Never Never Land, and called the on call doctor to get Nick a verbal medication order.

"Whad'ya get?" I asked after he'd taken something from a little white paper cup that LuvLee had given him.

"Phenergan," he said. "It's supposed to settle your nerves and help with the nausea. I guess it's the best I'm gonna get on a Sunday, the cheap fucks!" He seemed to want to spit at the nurses.

Mmmmm...didn't I once know a nurse who told me that when she used to steal part of the dose of Demerol from her patients, that she substituted Phenergan in the syringe for the stolen Demerol? Yea. That's right. She told me that Phenergan was a narcotic agonist; that it boosted the power of the Demerol. "It also sedates," she'd said to me. Mmmmm, that's the ticket! I thought: Well, sedation is better than nothing.

I was beginning to feel like dog crap anyway. I decided to take a shot.

I walked up to the nurse's station: "Hey, uh, LuvLee?" I began. She didn't move from the book on her desk. I tried again: "Uh, LuvLee? Uh, I'm not feeling too well right now. I think I'm gonna get sick." She looked up from the desk. She stuck the rubber tip of the pencil she'd been holding in her mouth and glared at me, like she already knew what was coming. I asked: "Uh, is there anything I could maybe take before I get sick?"

"No," she said.

And she went back to writing in her book. *Tute finit!*

"C'mon LuvLee, really," I began again. "I'm gonna get sick. Can't you give me something?"

She glared again and tapped the pencil on the medication order book. "No!" she said. "We don't dispense medications on weekends to new admissions. If you get sick and throw up, leave it in the toilet bowl where I can see it." She went back to her med book. "Now go sit down!" she said.

"Look, LuvLee, I'm really gonna get...."

"No!" she screamed. "YOU look! You junkies are just a bunch of big babies! You get the littlest ache or pain, or you feel the slightest bit sick, and all you can think to do is run for a pill! Or a needle!" Now it was LuvLee who looked like she wanted to spit. "Well, you're not getting anything from me. You got it? The answer is NO! I'm sorry if you're a little uncomfortable, but that falls under the category of Tough Shit! So get used to it. Get used to Life Without Drugs!" she said, sounding like a Grade A advertisement for Partnership For A Drug Free America. She picked up her pencil and started working again. She finished with, "Now go sit down and stop bothering me."

I turned away from her desk and I was going to go back to the lounge area. I was going to just "go sit down" like LuvLee said, but something snapped. I was sick. I wanted some drugs. And someone telling me they weren't going to give me any was, well...

"FUCK YOU!" I screamed. "FUCK YOU, LUVLEE! FUCK *ALL* OF YOU!"

There was a glass of orange juice on the counter of the nurse's station and, like I was watching someone else, my right hand grabbed the glass and heaved it into the wall. SMASH! I slammed my fist on the counter, then swung my arm and knocked over a planter which also was kept on the nurse's station counter. Dirt went flying. I had lost it: "FUCK THIS PLACE! AND *FUCK YOU! LUVLEE, YOU FAT FUCK!*"

For a second, everything froze.

Who the hell was that? That was someone else, right? It was WHO? It was ME?

Time started up again and LuvLee said, "That's it! I'm

calling for a restraint." She picked up the phone and dialed
Them.

*Whad'ya say? Uh. . . . Wait a second here. Restraint? Uh. . . .
I don't think I need a restraint or nothin, now LuvLee. . . . Can't
we just talk about this for a moment?*

"Sorry," I said feebly.

Who the hell was THAT?

I turned from the nurse's station and walked back to the
TV room to cool my jets. I sat quietly in the lounge, with
my hands in my lap, and I didn't make so much as a peep,
so if LuvLee did ask that I be restrained, the orderlies
would come up and see how calm I was, and that, really, I
was going to be no trouble to anyone whatsoever. *Honest,
guys! Really! I ain't gonna cause no more trouble! I swear!*

She never did bother to order the restraint.

Luckily.

*Shit! I just wanted to get some drugs. What the fuck happened
to me over there?*

Nick was snickering. He said, "You're too much, man.
Don't worry though, you'll get something now. You can bet
on it." He continued to laugh about my little tirade over at
the nurse's station. "You did perfect," he said.

I sat on the couch. I didn't move a muscle. I just sat
there.

Five minutes later, the on call physician came up to the
unit. "What's the problem?" he asked.

"I'm sick, doc!" I volunteered. "I just wanted some
medication, that's all. I feel like *squat!*"

He looked at LuvLee. LuvLee looked back at him.

Telepathy, I think.

"What do you want?" the on call asked.

Might as well go for the gold:

"Methadone, doc. I'm really sick . . ."

"We don't give out Methadone until you've been seen by the chief psychiatrist. And she won't be in until tomorrow morning. I can't give you any Methadone tonight."

"Well?" I said, "whad'you give him?" I pointed at Nick.

"Phenergan," the on call said, growing more and more weary of all this whining, begging junkie crap. "You want some Phenergan?" he asked.

"Yea!" I said. "Okay."

The on call looked at LuvLee. "Let him have some Phenergan," he said. LuvLee passed him the medication book, and he wrote the order in it.

LuvLee handed me a little white paper cup with a small pill in it and with her eyes, she told me what a Big Baby Junkie she thought I was.

That's okay LuvLee. Who got this little white pill when he wanted it? Huh? And who didn't get restrained, you fat fuck you!

I went out onto the porch where some of the others were sitting and enjoying the evening.

"Did you get something?" they asked.

"Yup!" I said.

I grinned. I was happy.

Fine evening here. Twenty minutes or so from now, this Phenergan stuff'll kick right in and I'll be feeling A-O-Fucking Kay. Blissful comfort, even on a weekend evening in a drug and alcohol hospital. I'll get Meth in the morning when the shrink comes down, and it'll be smooth sailing from here on in. This is gonna be cake.

I settled into the chair on the porch, closed my eyes, and tried to relax.

I went to bed shortly thereafter. I think it must have been around ten.

I didn't start getting sick till around midnight.

▲ ▼ ▲

I lay in bed and tried to go to sleep. It was quiet enough, most of the other patients on the detox floor were all ready in bed and asleep; the lights on the unit were turned down low, and I could hear a steady babble from the television in the lounge where the night shift nurse was watching it. I lay on that bed in my little detox room and tried to get some shut eye. It wasn't happening. I felt nervous. I rolled over, pounded the pillow a few times but couldn't get comfortable. I tossed. I turned. I rolled over a few more times, and then I flipped back again. I tried masturbating. I jerked off twice. That didn't relieve my anxiety either.

The first thing that happens when you go into withdrawal from narcotics is you give birth to rodents: little baby rats, with pink lids covering their newly formed, watery eyes, and fresh placental fluid all over their slimy little bodies. They're still wet. They're still blind. And they still can't tell exactly what it is they're scraping at with those sharp little claws of theirs. You give birth to these rats in your gut.

It's hard to tell exactly how many of them were crawling around down there, maybe eight or ten, but they were doing their best to chew their way out from my stomach, my chest, and my groin. They had a particular desire to exit my body through my mouth. I tried jerking off a few more times.

Nice try.

By two o'clock in the morning my withdrawal syndrome had progressed to the point where it felt as if leather straps had been applied to my chest, my back, and the backs of my legs—to insure that the rats remained inside. The muscles in my legs and low back tightened up like someone was twisting them with a steel shaft; they snapped taut like a rubber band and didn't let loose for a second. This is why when the nursing staff came in to check on me throughout the course of the night they found me curled up into a shaking, shivering, little ball. The Man With The Steel Shaft just kept twisting tighter...and tighter...and... tighter.

Orgasm can relieve this: beta endorphin, the body's own naturally occurring opiate, floods the system and relieves this tightness. But only for a few moments. The Man With The Steel Shaft eventually returns.

And the sheets get progressively wetter.

Along with ejaculating, I was sweating. I'm not sure exactly why this happens during withdrawal; I only know that at one moment I'd be sweating like a glass of Bud at high noon in July, and in the next, I'd feel like I had just stepped into a walk-in meat freezer. It's like wearing damp pajamas and shopping for the family's frozen foods. In January maybe. It's a physiological roller coaster: Up and down. Sweat and chill. Back and forth. And the whole time the rats keep trying to claw their way out.

I did manage to get a couple of the rodents out during the course of the night, either by puking or by evacuating my insides from the other end. Just lovely, don't you think?

People will say that narcotic withdrawal is just like having a really bad flu. And I suppose it is. You get nauseous, maybe you have to vomit a couple of times, your body and head ache like there's no tomorrow, you get a fever, the chills, and you have about all the energy of someone who's just been run over by an eighteen wheeler. In short, you feel like shit. So with respect to those people, yes, I'd imagine narcotic withdrawal is just like having a really bad flu, or at least, having flu-like symptoms. Sure. They probably are about the same. I know: I've had the flu a couple of times also.

But you don't get rats with a flu.

You don't get rats, and you don't get the leather straps around your chest, back and legs. The straps that are pulled to the last notch. The ones that get tighter and tighter as the night creeps by, the ones that get so tight at times that you can hardly breathe.

But that's the only difference, I guess. Puking is puking.

There was a nurse who worked the eleven-to-seven shift that night, a compassionate one. She understood that what I was going through without my drugs, or without the benefit of any detoxification medicine, was something just short of lying on a bed of hot and cold razor blades. She gave me a kind smile each time I went past the nurse's station on my way to the bathroom.

"Rough, isn't it?" she asked. I nodded. "Well, just lie down and try to bear with it. The doctor'll be in first thing in the morning." She opened up a closet door. "Here," she said, "take another blanket."

I accepted it gratefully. Middle of the summer and I need another fucking blanket. I said "thanks" and tried to go back to my room and rest.

I spent the remaining hours of the morning laying in the bed with The Withdrawal Sisters: Shake, Rattle, and Roll.

Wake-up was 6:00 A.M. I got up out of the fouled bed in which I'd been shaking for the last eight hours, and went into the lounge area to sit with Nick. He took one look at me.

"Man!" he said. "You're really sick! Didn't you do enough dope yesterday?" He was referring to the feeble amount of heroin I'd shot the previous day and was wondering why I hadn't dosed myself more heavily.

"Guess not," I said, shaking.

"Hang on," he told me. "You'll get some medication in

a couple of hours. The doctor's gotta see you first!" He laid a hand on my shoulder.

I thought about the heroin I'd scraped off the sides of the cooker the day before; the dope I'd melted down, cooked up, and shot into my vein in an attempt to get one last little buzz before coming into treatment and giving it all up for good. I thought about how I'd barely felt a thing.

It all seemed so very far away.

The doctor saw two other weekend admissions before she got to me around noon. The interview lasted almost an hour, and I couldn't help but wonder the whole time why she didn't just shove some Methadone down my throat. I was sweating bullets, I had doubled over in the chair by this point, my body was shivering like a jackhammer at full bore, and I was having trouble just opening my mouth to answer her questions without my gag reflex getting in the way.

"I need to get your history first," she said.

The seconds crept by as slowly as tree sap.

And then finally, after the medical assessment, and the forms, the needing to vomit once, and signing all the papers...

Fido Got A Biscuit. A forty milligram biscuit.

The Eli Lilly Corporation, the pharmaceutical manufacturing house, makes dolophine hydrochloride for heroin detoxification and maintenance as Methadone Diskets, USP, forty milligram.

Biscuits. Forty Migs.

The Germans came up with Methadone during World War II when the Allies cut off the supply of morphine from the Axis. The Nazis were even gracious enough to name this stuff after their Fuehrer, A*dolph* Hitler, and to honor him with the generic name for the drug, *doloph*ine hydrochloride. (I've always thought it rather apropos that this drug was developed by the same people who brought us the most heinous Holocaust the world has ever seen. Like they wanted to see how severely people could get addicted to a drug. Methadone is a bitch. It kicks ass a hundred fold more than morphine, and like I said earlier, heroin and morphine are the same thing. Methadone isn't too bad of a drug when it's used for detoxification; but anyone I've ever know who's gotten onto this Methadone Maintenance Thing has but one word to say about it: Don't!)

The Eli Lilly Corporation makes the Disket impossible to inject (due to the particulate matter which they put into the Disket). It has to be dissolved in a cup of water. When you toss the Disket into water (or orange juice or Kool-Aid for that matter) you get one dose of Methadone for the purposes of either detoxification or maintenance of the opiate dependant.

And that is how Fido Gets A Biscuit in rehab.

Twenty minutes later, I caught a wicked buzz. The leather straps came off, the belts were loosened, and I could wipe the sweat from my neck without it returning two seconds later. I could breathe again. The nausea went away. The jackhammer shut down. And the rats, well, the rats just disappeared.

The Methadone makes them all go away.

I wondered as I settled down into a cushy chair in the lounge and watched Elmer Fudd hunt dad waskiwee wabbit Bugs why it had taken me so damn long to come into rehabilitation? Why had I been out on the street, scamming and stealing my way to my daily bags of heroin, when all the time there was this nice little place called Hallmarke Hospital just waiting to take care of me? A nifty treatment facility, where they'll give me rehabilitation, make me better, provide me with three squares a day, a private room, counseling and therapy, and pump me up on US Grade A choice pharmaceutical heroin for a week or so? How come I didn't find out about this kind of place sooner?

Monday morning cartoons and Methadone.

Not too shabby for five hundred dollars a day. Not too shabby.

"Be vewee kwiet!" Elmer Fudd said.

I put my head back into the chair and smiled.

". . . I'm hunting wabbits!"

▲ ▼ ▲

Treatment for alcoholics and drug addicts—whether it be a hospitalization, out-patient therapy, clinics, rehabs, dry-out farms, or a social worker's office—isn't bullshit. I was just full of it at the time, that's all.

Treatment is sound, logical help, for an all too difficult problem. But at twenty-two, in my first rehabilitation hospital, and still not even *close* to being tired of The Drug Addict Bit, I was just still too much of a punk.

In my heart I really wanted to quit drugs. Somewhere deep down, there was a spark inside me that honestly wanted to learn a better way. A drug-free way. A way of life that included honesty, unselfishness, charity and love. I was tired of shooting dope, I knew I had more potential than winding up a worthless dopefiend; I was sick of hurting my family, my friends, and my lovers, and I really thought I could give it my all and beat this thing once and forever. The day I came into Hallmarke Hospital I had every intention of doing just that. Whatever the therapy, whatever the treatment, whatever they told me to do, I'd give it a go. Really.

I was a model patient in Hallmarke. I talked about every problem under the sun I had. In a group therapy session one afternoon, I dumped all the garbage I had been carrying around in my head about The Awful Thing That Happened To Me When I Was Nine. I began to cry and to try to let go of some of those demons that had been gnawing and tormenting me for the last twelve years. I'd been ashamed. I'd been embarrassed. And it had always been My Big Secret that was tucked away, back up in the corner, on the top shelf of my closet. Then finally, with the support of two therapists and seven patients in that hospital, I was able to talk about it, to share it openly, and somehow, to make a beginning at some kind of peace and understanding about The Thing that had been busting me up and making my life miserable for so damn long.

Bobby was another patient in the group that afternoon. He came up to me when the session ended and extended his hand. He said, "That was pretty brave of you to talk about yourself like that, in front of all those people. I don't know if I could've talked about what happened to me the way you just did."

"What," I asked, "you too?"

Bobby smiled. "Yea. When I was about seven or eight. My counselor says it happens to a lot of us when we're kids. He says it's a pretty common thing to happen to a kid." (Statisticians put the mark somewhere around fifty percent. Of chemically dependent males, fifty percent have some history of either sexual abuse, molestation, or incest. Ladies will put their figures even higher.) "Especially kids that turn out to be fuck ups like us," he laughed. "I really respect you, man, for talking about it in there. You got balls." We shook hands and something was sealed.

Bobby and I talked a lot after that day. I didn't feel so alone anymore, I didn't feel so dirty. It still didn't make a whole lot of sense, but at least I wasn't the only one to whom it had ever happened. I had made a friend that summer in Hallmarke Hospital. A *real* friend.

Bobby was a cocaine specialist. He played around with heroin, but his real favorite was whacking a syringe full of cocaine into his arm, getting his ears to ring and his world to spin around his head like a freight train and pumping the shit out of his brain synapses. Bobby was a good looking young man, probably just a hair over twenty at the time. He looked as if he could have had anything he wanted out of life, just for the asking. We sat on the screened-in porch and compared our notes, talking about The Good Old Days and how both of us had nearly blown our brains to smithereens injecting cocaine hydrochloride during the last few years.

The words that came out of our mouths were good. They were words of Recovery, of the terrible things cocaine and heroin had done to us, and of how we were going to stay away from that shit forever! They were words of contempt for what we had done to our families, and they were words of fear If I Ever Go Back On That Shit Again. We talked about wanting to get on the Road To Sobriety and staying there forever, and we made vows to each other that I'm Really Gonna Do It This Time! I *Know* I Can Make It! and I *Swear* I'm Gonna Beat This Thing! But we were so young. . . .

Even as we spoke those words during the long afternoon hours that summer on the screened-in porch that was our favorite place to hang out, there was something going on in the backs of our minds. Something was moving around back there.

For me, it was like a movie screen in the back of my head, and the projector was showing a Best Of collection from a Stephen King Film Festival. The whole time we talked about drugs, about the seizures we'd suffered and the near-death experiences we'd had from shooting up way too much heroin, all I could see was the needle tip being placed on my skin, right above the vein in my left forearm. I could see the teflon-coated tip puncture the skin there, and I could see the little bit of blood—The Hit—enter the barrel as I pulled back on the plunger. I pressed my finger down on it and literally I could *taste* the cocaine in the back of my throat. I could feel it rip the back of my neck off and my heart would start to thunder in my chest just from *talking about it*. Just from *watching* that Stephen King Film Festival in the back of my brain. It scared the piss out of me.

Professionals in the field of chemical dependency have a term for this effect: Euphoric Recall. It's the movie projector. It's the screen in the back of your mind that shows only The Good Times. Only The Rush. It's the thing that kicks in when you're trying to talk about how bad it was for you out there, but on the movie screen, all you see is how *good* it was. It's an incredibly strong and powerful effect with intravenous heroin addiction, and it's even stronger with cocaine.

For needle freaks like Bobby and me, it's so powerful that it leads to relapse, after relapse, after relapse.

Bobby got high again before he even finished his term at Hallmarke. He went home for the weekend on a pass, and when he returned, he told the nursing staff he couldn't produce a urine specimen for their routine drug screening.

"I guess I don't have to go," he maintained.

FOR THREE DAYS, BOBBY?

We lost another female patient the same way. She got high on a pass before she even received an official discharge from the hospital. I guess it's just part and parcel of the rehab business. You've got to expect a few losses along the way.

I saw Bobby about eight years after that at a party some friends of mine were throwing.

"Bobby?" I asked, not really believing that it could possibly be him.

"Adam?"

We grabbed onto each other the same way we had that afternoon of the group therapy session. "Jesus!" I said. "I thought you died or something. How the hell have you been, Bobby?"

He smacked the cane he was holding against the thigh of his left leg. It made a sharp, cracking sound.

He said, "I fucked up, man. I got really drunk one night and totaled out my Harley and my leg." I looked at him and shook my head.

Casualties, I thought to myself. Fucking casualties.

"How long you been sober, man?" I asked.

"Almost a year."

"Yea. Me too."

I looked at his leg again and felt like crying.

Bobby made a jumping movement like he was going to try and dance. "Hey!" he started, "at least I didn't die, huh?"

I smiled and hugged him.

I guess, maybe, that's what it's all about. It was like we'd been through a war together. We'd just done our fighting in different cities, that's all.

I remember my therapist in that first hospital, although today, I couldn't tell you his name. I remember he hyphenated his last name; he shared his wife's maiden name with his own. I thought it was a nice idea. I'd like to do that someday, I told myself.

My therapist was the first person with whom I ever even approached the concept of talking honestly. I told him all my dirty secrets. He was the first person, it seemed, who took the time to listen to what I had to say. Even if it was Just Stupid Shit. He met with me two, sometimes three times a week, each time for an hour or more. Sometimes we sat on the lawn outside underneath a tall maple tree, and other times we just went into his office to talk.

And all we did was talk. Just me, and him. It was the first time I'd ever done such a thing without being chemically intoxicated.

He didn't tell me a lot of profound things. He didn't lecture me. He just listened. He cared. I could see it in his eyes.

I cried at a community meeting the day my therapist informed me that he was being transferred to another hospital to complete his psychology internship.

He said, "I'm sorry I have to leave. I'm going to miss you. You've done a lot of good work here, Adam."

I stood in front of all the patients and the administrators at the community meeting and cried like a baby. I told them how much this man had helped me, how he was the first person in my life who'd ever given a damn about me, how he cared, how he listened to all my shit, how he always had time for me and how badly I felt now because he was being taken away. How could they do that? I asked. How could they just send him off to another hospital and take him from me? I didn't understand!

People came up after the meeting and said they were impressed by my sensitivity. Especially the women. How admirable, they said, for a man to cry like that in a roomful of people.

I didn't think it was a big deal. I was upset that they were taking my therapist from me! My tears were real. They were honest tears of mourning and of loss.

They just didn't last, that's all. I couldn't hold onto them. I wasn't ready.

God! I was so young.

I met a man that summer in Hallmarke, "The Doctor," I called him, who after a fifteen-year addiction to heroin and cocaine, had elected to get himself strung-out on the sedative-hypnotic, Placidyl. I called him The Doctor because by the time he'd reached Hallmarke, he had acquired a Ph.D., worked in a hospital in New York, and had published a thesis on Methadone addiction.

"You're really a doctor?" I asked incredulously.

He showed me his thesis. (He'd brought it with him into rehab for just such disbelief.)

"What are *you* doing here?" I asked.

"I got heavy into Placidyl this time around," he said. "I haven't done heroin in years! I pulled the needle out of my neck a long time ago. For my girlfriend."

My concentration wandered at this point.

IN YOUR NECK? I thought.

The Doctor explained that sometimes junkies blow all the veins in their arms and ankles, and they have to resort to using other injection sites, necks (at the carotid artery) and groins (at the femoral artery) being two of the most commonly chosen.

"They're letting me out early," The Doctor said, after only a week or so of being there. "I've been through all this stuff before. I been hospitalized eight times already. I know what I gotta do. I just gotta *do it* this time."

The Doctor's still sober today. Nine years.

And Nick? You mean Nick? The guy who helped me get that little white Phenergan pill my first night in detox? You mean that nice Italian Junkie who took me under his wing and showed me how to work the ropes and play the game in my first rehabilitation? You mean *that* Nick?

It seems that a couple of days into Nick's detoxification, he began to find it, well, how shall I say this? Nick found his detox "uncomfortable." He thought the dose of Methadone the medical staff was administering to him was insufficient. So, he thought he'd just "augment" it a little.

Nick called his uncle (the one who brought Nick there for help in the first place) and asked him if he wouldn't mind just stopping by Hallmarke, and while he was there, maybe dropping off a couple of bags of heroin for Nick. A couple of fifty dollar bags of heroin. Just to help Nick along, of course.

The nursing staff hit the fucking ceiling.

And so did the patients.

A public lynching was held: *HOW COULD YOU BRING HEROIN ONTO THIS UNIT? ARE YOU CRAZY? PEOPLE ARE TRYING TO GET OFF THAT SHIT IN HERE! HOW DARE YOU! THIS IS A HOSPITAL! AND YOU SMUGGLE HEROIN IN HERE! WHAT'S WRONG WITH YOU?!*

My friend The Doctor jumped onto the bandwagon and said, "Yea, why don't you make him bend over and make him spread his asscheeks? I bet he's got an eyedropper and a needle stuffed up his asshole! Why don't you put your finger up there and *really* give him a search?" The Doctor had seen these things from his numerous trips to the city jail.

Nobody bothered to check Nick's asshole.

Nick confessed to sniffing one of the bags the night before. The other one he "misplaced."

"I lost it," he said. "I can't find it. It's up here somewhere, though."

The nurses and doctors and mental health workers and therapists called an emergency meeting for all involved, and we sat in a big circle with the hospital personnel. The lynching took place. It was a little like being in Tennessee at a Ku Klux Klan rally.

HANG THE NIGGER! SKIN HIM! I WANNA SEE HIM BOUNCE FROM THE END OF THAT FUCKING ROPE!

I felt sorry for Nick. He'd been all right to me. He was just a white-boy junkie who'd gotten too far in over his head. He just needed a little more help I thought, that's all. He didn't need to be hung from the tallest yardarm.

"Well?" LuvLee asked him. "What do you have to say for yourself?"

Nick was dead meat.

He didn't stand a snowball's chance in hell in this kangaroo court.

"Look," he said, "I'm sorry. I didn't want to get nobody else in trouble. I brought it here for me. I didn't ask no one else to get high with me!"

That was a lie. The nursing staff knew it was a lie because the person Nick had asked to get high with him told on Nick.

"I didn't mean to hurt nobody!" he said.

And the staff looked at us and asked whether or not we felt like giving Nick another chance.

"BURN HIM! BURN THE WITCH!" we all cried.

I don't really know if our say had all that much bearing on whether or not Nick was allowed to stay at Hallmarke. I imagine the staff already had their minds made up to ship him off to another hospital and to not let him stay at Hallmarke; but I think they wanted to make us feel as though we had something to say about the whole thing. (I found out in my later years that this type of thing happens quite frequently in rehabilitation facilities. It's not an everyday occurrence but it happens occasionally. In my last hospitalization, one of the women patients sewed Librium into the hem of her dress and passed through the search hospitals perform on new admissions. I guess she too thought the nursing staff dosage might not be quite adequate to get her through the pains of her withdrawal. This woman also got the boot.)

I wonder how come I never tried a stunt like that?

The Powers That Be sent Nick to the state mental hospital. Nick's insurance had run out and there wasn't anything left for another private, in-patient hospitalization. I also think they wanted to get rid of him in a hurry. He left in a grand style—by ambulance.

Nick was the brunt of everybody's joke that evening. We holier-than-thou junkies thought it was such fun that Nick had ruined his chances of a nice cushy Methadone detox at Hallmarke, and had instead elected for the lobotomy type we were sure they were giving him in the state hospital. Like *One Flew Over The Cuckoo's Nest? Oh Nurse Rachet? I don't feel well. Could you give me another shot of one of those nice anti-psychotics like that Thorazine stuff you just gave me? Or maybe some Haldol? This withdrawal is killing me and I sure would like another whopper in my butt so I can turn off my brain and. . . .*

We watched Nick go quietly away with two men in white uniforms to the state hospital. On the way out the door, he said, "If you find that bag be careful! It was really good shit!"

Nobody ever turned up the missing bag of heroin that Nick had smuggled onto the hospital unit. Nor did anyone ever locate the misplaced Methadone tablet the nursing staff lost about a week or so after Nick had left.

It seems the nursing staff came up short one night when they were doing their count of the narcotics at the end of one of the shifts. They couldn't account for one Disket of Methadone.

A whole Disket.

A whole forty milligram Disket!

We had another community meeting over that one and the nursing staff informed us that if anyone should find the missing Disket he or she should give it back to the nurse on duty pronto!

"It could be very dangerous!" they warned. "If one of you were to accidentally ingest it, it could be strong enough to kill you!"

It was like an Easter egg hunt for most of us, but, no, we never found the missing biscuit.

How did things go for me in rehab? I tried. I really did. I tried my best to give it all up. I went to family therapy. I met with my mother and father, and I think even one of my brothers showed up for the sessions with the family therapist. I tried to iron out all those things I had screwed up along the way, all the things I had done wrong and all the things they had goofed up. We tried to come up with alternatives for How Could We Handle It As A Family In The Future? and What Could Be Done In Order For Me Not To Return To A Life Of Drugs And Alcohol. We talked about Opening The Lines Of Communication, about Confronting One Another; we looked at Rules and Boundaries and we tried to Set Up Concrete Limits For One Another's Space. As a family, we really did make a gallant effort.

I took part in all the treatment modalities offered by the hospital. I went to creative therapy, where I drew pictures with crayons of images of my childhood and then I talked about how I felt at the time. I saw the chief psychiatrist, the social worker, and I sat underneath the maple tree with my therapist. I took vocational batteries, psychological profiles, and I got my first crack at that beautiful five hundred and sixty-six word test, The Minnesota Multi-Phasic Personality Inventory, MMPI for short.

I went swimming when they took us to the YMCA and I played volleyball outside when I was feeling up to it. I went to group therapy, in-house meetings, and when they told us all to pile into the van, I went off grounds to those stupid twelve-step spiritual recovery meetings as well.

I worked hard at Hallmarke. I wanted to give up drugs. I talked about all the things I thought had made me start taking them in the first place. I talked about The Blow Job. I talked about school, and sex, and friendships, and my relationships with my brothers and my parents and authority figures in general. I got analyzed, scrutinized, and vocationally counseled, and I suppose I went along with just about everything they suggested.

For a while.

Hallmarke waved goodbye and discharged me with that always faithful rehab expression: Don't Use And Go To Meetings! My parents welcomed me home with open arms after my graduation from the hospital, believing that my sixty-day stay there had done the trick. And for the most part, I gave up hanging around many of the places where I'd gotten into trouble.

I got a decent job as a phlebotomist after I left Hallmarke. I went to the hospital in my hometown and looked up my old nurse friend (yes, the one who'd earlier taught me the Phenergan-Demerol Switcheroo), who got me an interview with the personnel director. A week later I was the new phlebot on main south two. Of course, it was the ultimate irony. A phlebotomist is the person with the needles, tubes, and tourniquet who comes into your room in the hospital to draw your blood. I even started to see one of the girls who worked on Hallmarke's Nursing Staff.

Everything looked pretty good there for a while and things seemed to be going all right. My parents were proud of me, I was going to meetings almost every night, and I sold the Suzuki to repay my father for some of my debts which he had repaid (probably at my mother's urging). That quality that all dopefiends lose the minute people find out about them—trust—was slowly being granted again (mind you, I said slowly), and I really seemed to be getting a handle on my drug and alcohol problem.

But in hindsight, I was still too much of a punk. I was nowhere near ready to give it all up yet.

I lasted two months after I left Hallmarke.

Sixty days.

▲ ▼ ▲

"Hey, where you been, man?" one of the guys on Boot Hill asked me after I'd called in sick to work on Monday morning.

My decision to crank out on a little cocaine and heroin had been made at seven o'clock that morning. There was no turning back.

"I gave it up for a while," I said to him. "I've been in a hospital."

"It's been *too long*, man!" he said. "Good to see you again! What can I do for you, amigo?"

I stepped out over the edge: "How's the D? Can you get me some good dope?" I asked. "I wanna boot some coke, too. Anybody got good blow out here today?"

He smiled. "You just wait here for me in your car, my friend. I get you all hooked up." He started to cross the street and then turned around and said: "We missed you down here, amigo! You shouldn't stay away from us this long!" Then he went to the dealer and got me my shit.

Half an hour later, my testicles were up in my abdomen and all the hair on my body was frozen straight up. I began to dry heave and my eyeballs flipped backward in their sockets, making my world rush and rip through my brain like a fucking blizzard. The needle started to shake in my hand, and the blood trickled from the little hole in my forearm where the cocaine-filled syringe punctured the skin and entered the vein. My chest shook like a broken refrigerator. The sweat came in rivers down my face. My lips and gums and tongue and the back of my throat went medicinal, frozen and anesthetized by the cocaine hydrochloride. My heart rate and respiration shot off like a fucking express train, and I strapped myself onto the front of it for the Hell Ride.

The blood from my forearm dripped onto the floor,

making little stains on the carpeting that covered my bedroom floor. I leaned over. I watched it splotch my new white Nikes.

After fifteen minutes or so, the ringing in my ears stopped and the shaking eased.

My old friend, I thought to myself, as I held the syringe filled with the heroin and water mixture up to the light coming through the bedroom window. The nausea was passing. The shaking slowed. My breath was calming.

I held the syringe up to the light with my left hand and flicked the barrel with the third finger of my right. I tapped up any bubbles in the barrel which could enter my bloodstream and kill me from an embolism. I squirted just a little of the solution out to clear the barrel. I licked the needle tip with the end of my tongue. Mmmmmmmmmmm.

Tap...

Tap...

Tap...

My old friend, I thought.

My *ooooold friend*....

EIGHT

MENTAL ILLNESS AND THE CHAIR

From now on my dope shooting days would be forever dismal. I would go to treatment and be labeled A Drug Addict, and attend a few of those stupid recovery meetings, where people even more messed up than I were now sober and happy and leading good lives, where guys who spilled more dope than I'd ever even thought of sticking into my veins were leading productive, even lucrative lives. The combination of these two realities would forever haunt me. Guilt would be instilled, and I would spend the next eight years of my life trying and failing, and trying and failing again to get off The Stuff.

The merry-go-round had begun.

After Hallmarke's attempt at rehabilitating me and after my ensuing dive, once more, into The Deep End, I got the notion into my head that somewhere out there, somehow, somebody, some *other person* could fix my problem with drugs. That someone could guide me along the right path and help me to talk about the right things, give me the right advice, or have me take the right medicine, and my problem would be solved forever. Surely, I thought, if Hallmarke Hospital had tried and failed, there must be another place, a better place, a more knowledgeable physician that could help me find relief for my problem.

Enter Richard E. Green, Psychiatrist. Healer. Confidant. Understander of all things deviant, abnormal, and misdiagnosed. Knower and resident expert in psychopharmacology, and in those persons suffering from the malady called drug addiction. Doctor Rich, as I came to call him, had spent the past ten years of his life studying, researching, and treating the mentally sick, the suffering, and the chemically dependent. Doctor Richard E. Green, who had seen numerous cases like mine and who had treated them all the same way (with a remarkable rate of success, I might add), was sure! absolutely positive! that I too could be saved from the horrible mental anguish of this terrible sickness called addiction to drugs. I put my life into the warm and caring hands of this magnificent icon of the psychiatric world. Where others had failed, I knew Doctor Rich could save me.

I discovered Doctor Rich from my friend, Ann, the nurse. Two months after my discharge from Hallmarke, I was running again full bore with heroin and cocaine.

It went from bad to worse.

I had tried to hide drug my use from my mother and father; I tried to hide it from the girl I'd been seeing since my departure from Hallmarke—*do I hear Snagelpus and his exiting refrain calling?*—and I tried to hide it from the people who employed me at a nuclear manufacturing plant where I worked after losing my job as a phlebotomist. (The phlebotomy job went out the window three months after I had begun, and two days after I'd talked to my supervisor when I told her I was having trouble with drugs again. She suggested that a career which involved sticking people with needles all day long wasn't such a good idea for me. Perhaps, she suggested, a quiet departure from the hospital's staff for "personal reasons" might be appropriate in light of my "situation.")

So, after six months of my screwing around with The Stuff, I was once again under the microscope and the ever-present eyes of those who were close were once again asking, "Well? Just what do you propose to do about your problem this time?"

The jack rabbit in the headlamps once again.

So, I called my friend, Ann. Ann was the nurse who had originally taught me the Phenergan-Demerol Switcheroo, and she and I had always been able to talk. I knew Ann would understand my problem: she was an former drug addict.

In Ann's early years as a nurse, she stole Demerol from her patients and injected the drug into her own body, doing The Phenergan Routine for the stolen dose. One for you, two for me.

But where she had once been hooked on Demerol to the point of abscessing most of the tissue on her buttocks due to the frequency of her injections, Ann had now been clean for eleven years. She had beaten the monster. Somehow, she had found the cure. I called her on the phone, and she invited me over to explain how she had accomplished this remarkable feat.

"It wasn't easy, Adam," she began. She offered me a soda, and we sat down on her living room sofa. "I had a lot of help."

Ann was a small woman, in her mid-fifties by this point. She cut her grey hair close to her head, and she had eyes and hands that spoke of more than their share of the sick and dying she had helped during her nursing career. Ann

was also a close friend of my mother's. Ann had helped de-
liver my two older brothers, and she wanted nothing more
than to see her good friend's son get that damned monkey
off his back, once and for all. She talked to me with a compassionate heart, one junkie to another.

"I struggled with my addiction for almost twenty years!
Adam," she said. "In the end, I went away for six months
to a psychiatric hospital. When I got out, I continued to see
a psychiatrist for another year and a half!" She smiled at
me.

"Was it hard?" I asked.

She rolled her eyes and shook her head, wondering how
I could ask such a redundant question. "Good Lord!" she
said. "I'd imagine it was the hardest thing I've ever had to
do!" She paused a moment and looked away, lost in her
thoughts. Then she returned. "They put me on lithium
carbonate while I was in the hospital. That helped me a lot
after I left and tried to make it on my own on the outside."

"What's lithium carbonate?" I asked.

She lit a Salem. She blew the smoke out towards the
window. "Lithium is a salt. It's used to treat manic-
depressive disorders. It was really helpful for me at the
time. It took the edge off my insane cravings for narcotics. I
couldn't control my mind!" I nodded in agreement. "The
Lithium made the urges more manageable. It didn't take
them away, but it made them less strong. It made them
have less of an effect on me, so I could get over the hump,
work my problems out with my psychiatrist, and make it on
my own."

This stuff intrigued me. A magic pill, I thought.

"Really?" I asked.

"Really," she said. She stubbed out the cigarette she'd
been smoking. "Maybe your problem is similar to mine.
Maybe you're manic-depressive. Have you ever thought

about that?" she asked. I shrugged my shoulders. She smiled again and said, "You know, there are a lot of us, especially narcotic addicts like you and me, who are affected with manic-depression. We get a little too high on the manic end, the urge comes over us, and we dive into the deep end of the pool. We take drugs!"

No shit, I thought, with a touch of sarcasm.

Ann sat back in the sofa. She was getting comfortable, winding down. "Why don't you go to see a psychiatrist?" she suggested. "Maybe he can help. Maybe, if you are manic-depressive, a psychiatrist can give you some Lithium and you can beat this thing." She took hold of my hand and gave it a squeeze. "Try it, Adam. C'mon, what do you say?"

I smiled and assured her I'd take the suggestion. I gave her a hug.

Maybe I will try this stuff, I considered. *Maybe I just will.*

And after much thought and long deliberation, I became manic-depressive. When I injected heroin, I decided it was simply due to the fact that I was unable to control my mind because of my disorder, my mania, as I'd come to call it. I just got too far off the scale, tipped it over, and then I just couldn't help myself: I shot dope. That's the ticket! I told myself. And I consulted a doctor. A doctor of psychiatry.

I first saw Doctor Richard E. Greene on a Saturday afternoon. He had a beautiful stately home with a long driveway that wound around the side, and a simple sign at the beginning that read RICHARD E. GREENE, M.D. There was a small parking lot at the end of the driveway and another sign that directed me to his OFFICE by means of an arrow. Behind the house was a lake.

I wonder if he ever goes swimming in there?

I entered the waiting room and sat down.

Doctor Greene appeared shortly thereafter with another patient and said goodbye to her with a "See you next Saturday." He put a large paw onto her shoulder. She smiled. He seemed like a nice guy.

Doctor Greene was a large, bearded man. (Are there any psychiatrists without beards?) A bit too young though, I thought, only thirty-five or so, to be having his own private psychiatric practice in his own private house. But then again, what the hell did I know?

Doctor Greene welcomed me into his office and we began the first session.

I explained to him that on occasion, I had been known to use both heroin and cocaine intravenously. This, I indicated, was beginning to fuck up my life.

I told him I had been recently hospitalized for it, and that I managed to stay away from the stuff for only a brief period of time before once again falling prey to the needle. "I just can't control myself when the cravings come!" I said. I told the doctor how I had worked in the hospital as a phlebot and had lost the job shortly after I began using again. I explained that I had landed another job as a clerk in a nuclear manufacturing firm, that I was making OK money for the time being, and that the girl I was currently seeing and I were doing all right. "But when the cravings kick in," I told him, "I just can't help myself!"

I gave the doctor a brief history, including the fact that I'd been using chemicals since I was about nine or ten, but I explained that the only problems I had ever experienced had been recently. It had only been since I'd been screwing around with heroin and cocaine that things had begun to really going wrong.

I told Doctor Greene that I came from a nice family, that I'd been to college for three years, and that although I quit in the beginning of my senior year, at the time of my withdrawal I had maintained a three-point-eight grade point average. "I just don't know what's wrong with me," I said, shaking my head and shrugging my shoulders.

I told Doctor Greene that my whole life was getting messed up, and I couldn't understand why I kept on using this stupid heroin and cocaine. I said I thought I was under an incredible amount of emotional stress. From *what* I wasn't too sure, but I felt the stress like a piano on my back, nevertheless. I thought I had problems that needed to be worked on, to be worked through. I told him I thought psychotherapy would greatly help me straighten out my life once and for all. "But I think I might have a problem," I said.

"And what would that be?" he queried.

"Well...," I started, "Do you think I could have... like... manic-depression or something?"

"Absolutely," said Doctor Rich. "It's a rather common illness with the addicted population. I've seen a number of cases like yours in the addicts I've treated, and the symptoms are always the same. Does your mind race?" he asked. I nodded. "Do your thoughts seem to get confused, and garbled? And you can't help yourself?" Again, I agreed. *This doctor is on to something.*

He explained: "What happens with manic-depressive disorders is that the brain's salt becomes imbalanced. When you're in your manic phase, you become very impulsive and have no control over your thought processes. Some manics go for days on end without sleeping. Others perform compulsive behaviors, like cleaning their apartments all night long, over and over again. And still others, yourself included, seek to medicate their illness with illicit drugs. It's actually a common thing for manic-depressives to seek to medicate themselves." *Thank God! Somebody has the answer!*

"There are drugs we have now to control the illness," he said. *Here it comes.* . . . "Actually, there are several. We have drugs now to curb the racing. To slow it down in your mind. Lithium carbonate is one. Trilafon and some of the other more major tranquilizing agents of that class are also useful."

"Do you think it'll help me, doc?"

"Maybe," he said. "We'll have to see. I've been very successful in treating drug addicts in the past with these medications. It takes a little time for the Lithium to take effect in your system, but after a while the mania becomes manageable. Do you understand?" I nodded. "The Lithium appears to lower the threshold, the mania threshold, but this takes time. Until then, I can give you an antipsychotic agent, like Trilafon, which should blunt your impulses to use drugs."

I must have looked frightened at the prospect of taking a medication designed for crazy people, because he smiled and said, "Don't worry. It won't affect you the same way it would someone suffering with a psychoses. It'll just dull your cravings, blunt them a little." I calmed down. "Would you like to try and see if it works?"

"Yes," I said, "I'll try anything!" My shoulders dropped with relief. Finally! an answer to my troubles: drugs to help me stop taking drugs. "Do you really think you can help me with this, doc? You think this stuff'll work?"

"Yes," he said, "I do." Then he looked at me more sternly than he had so far. He said, "But the pills *alone* aren't going to stop this for you. *You* have to do some of the work yourself. The medicine is only going to curb your cravings to use. *You* have to do the work about why you take the drugs in the first place. *You* have to do the talking. *You* have to do the work in therapy." He emphasized,

"You're going to have to work very hard if you want to overcome this, Adam."

"I really want to, doc!" I said. "I can't keep shooting dope! It's killing me!"

"All right then," he said. He reached over to the table and grabbed his prescription pad. He wrote out a prescription for lithium carbonate and another one for Trilafon. He handed them to me and said, "Let's get to work then."

And that was the origin of my mental illness.

▲ ▼ ▲

I had been diagnosed manic-depressive by a well-educated, highly-trained and state-licensed psychiatrist, and I was well on my way to alleviating my heroin and cocaine addiction by chemical means.

It was going to be simple, Doctor Greene explained. The Lithium levels in my brain were going to be sampled at selected intervals by a blood test and monitored by the hospital out-patient laboratory. I would go down each week to have a sample drawn, and from the sample they would check to see the level of salt in my head. When it came down to (or went up to, I'm not quite sure which way it goes) a reasonable level, Doctor Greene assured me, I'd be that much further away from my trouble with intravenous drug use.

I was to see Doctor Greene twice weekly initially, perhaps attend his Saturday afternoon group therapy sessions with others my age who had problems that were similar to mine. I was to take my medication as prescribed, have my Lithium levels monitored, and in a month or so, determine with the doctor whether or not the cure was taking.

"Until then," Doctor Greene admonished, "try not to do any drugs."

"No, doc, I won't. Jesus!" I said to him, as I was leaving. "Am I glad I found you. I was beginning to think I was hopeless!"

"Well," Doctor Greene said, holding out his palm and indicating that all my troubles weren't over yet. "Let's just see how it goes for a while, all right?" We shook hands on the deal.

I handed him my mother's check for a hundred and fifty dollars, his fee for the fifty-minute session, and he said, "I can't give you any guarantees, but I am good at what I do. I really think we're going to be able to help you here, Adam."

"Thank you, doctor," I said.

And I left his office.

I was excited. I couldn't wait to fill my new prescriptions and get cracking with this stuff. Maybe this would really work! Better living through chemistry.

I have to admit it worked. For a while, anyway. I don't know. Two, maybe three months. But it did work. The Trilafon blunted my impulses to use drugs, the lithium carbonate took the bite out of my mania, and I didn't fall prey to the needle again. I went to individual psychotherapy with Doctor Rich twice a week, and I worked hard at all the things that had happened to me when I was a punk. I talked to him about my feelings, my emotions and my thoughts, my goals and my aspirations, and my dreams and my fears. I attended his Saturday afternoon group therapy sessions, and talked with others who had problems like mine. And I took my medication as prescribed. I had my Lithium levels closely monitored by the hospital laboratory, and for a while, it seemed as though I was really going to make it. It looked like my drug problem was finally coming under control. I was getting better under the warm and humane care of Doctor Richard E. Greene.

The cure was taking. (The only thing I didn't care for was the fact that one of the major side effects of taking lithium carbonate is that it makes one shake like a vibrator in high gear. Nor is Trilafon all that nifty of a drug on which to be medicated. It makes you slow, sort of stoned, but in a queer, off-balanced way. But nevertheless, I was pleased not to be shooting dope.)

But three months later, I shot some dope.

Cocaine too.

I was standing at the xerox machine making copies at work, and the old uncontrollable urge came over me. My heart started to throb, I began to shake uncontrollably (and I *knew* this time it wasn't because of the Lithium), and my mind and thoughts began to race and spin through my head like a Texas cyclone.

It's Show Time. . . .

And the projector in the back of my head lit up with another full color presentation of The Best Of Stephen King's Nightmares.

The nuclear corporation where I was working as a clerk let us go at one o'clock on Friday afternoons. At one fifteen, I was at the bank withdrawing all the money I'd managed to save in the last couple of months. Half an hour later I had copped my drugs, driven home, locked myself behind the bathroom door, and was blasting my brains through the roof on another speedball spree.

I sat in my bedroom with the telephone in my hand, shaking my head and wondering *what the fuck happened?*

"Hello? Doctor Greene? Yea, it's me. You gotta help me, doctor. I got high again."

He saw me the following morning at ten. I suppose he gave me top priority.

"What happened?" he asked me.

"I don't know! I just got high! I don't know what happened! It was like I couldn't stop myself all over again!"

"What do you mean you just couldn't stop yourself?" Doctor Greene was more dumbfounded than I. "I thought the Lithium was working! The Trilafon should have blunted your impulses! What happened? Why didn't you call? Why didn't you talk to me before you got high? What do you MEAN you 'just got high'?"

I looked at him like both of us were in a very bad movie.

"I DON'T KNOW!" I screamed back.

And I didn't.

I had no idea what the fuck had happened. One minute I was going along just fine, with everything working out just the way it was supposed to. I was taking my medication, going to therapy, making it day by day and not shooting dope. And then, Bang-O! The needle was sticking out of my forearm again. Back on Boot Hill. Back with the boys. Right back there once again, locked in the bathroom, with the set of works dangling from the vein in my arm. WHAT THE FUCK HAPPENED TO ME? I wondered. My head spun.

Doctor Greene called An Emergency Meeting Of The Family Security Council. It was held that night in his office. Present were my mother and father, my girlfriend (who'd just about had it with my shit by this point), and myself. Doctor Richard E. Greene presiding:

"Sometimes," he began, "this sort of thing happens." He was trying to give his rationale for my particular case of mental illness to those in attendance. "What we see sometimes is sort of like one step forward and two steps back. Manic-depression, and Adam's inherent use of heroin and cocaine when he's on the manic swing, is not always something the medication clears up immediately." The Council listened in earnest. "Sometimes, a relapse of this kind has to happen. Actually, it can even be good for him."

WHAT?

"It can give him a chance to see things more clearly."

HUH?

Doctor Greene looked in my direction but spoke to The Masses: "I still believe there's hope for him, but we're all going to have to be prepared. He might just have to do this again."

I couldn't believe what I was hearing.

My mother was crying. My girlfriend sat in the over-stuffed chair reserved for visitors, with her arms folded tightly across her chest and her legs crossed, looking at me with that How Come I Always Have to Put Up With Your Shit! look on her face. And my father...

Well, my father just looked like he wanted to kick the living shit out of me.

My dad didn't really want to be here listening to a whining psychiatrist tell him all about his son's manic-depression and the lithium carbonate and all that other psychiatric crapola the head shrinker was trying to feed him. My dad thought it was all just bullshit. His kid was just a lousy fucking junkie that's all! What he needs is just a good old fashioned ass-kicking, like the kind my old man gave me when I was a punk and I did fucked-up crap like this! *Gimme just ten minutes with him. I'll cure him of his fucking drug problem. . . .*

Mom had to hold him back.

Under the direction of Doctor Greene's intelligent and well-informed, well-educated advice, we resigned ourselves to the fact that stupid old me might just have to go out there and fall on my face again. That despite the help of the lithium carbonate and the Trilafon, despite the psychotherapy I was receiving on an individual and group basis, and despite even my high degree of willpower to overcome my dependency on heroin and cocaine, the bottom line on the whole fucking deal was simply that I might just have to go out there and do it again.

So I did.

For a while longer.

And six months later I was sitting on "The Chair" at Renew, a therapeutic community for chronic drug addicts in northern Connecticut. I had just turned twenty-three.

At the therapeutic community I was on The Chair, like the one Nick had told me about the summer previous when we were in Hallmarke Hospital together. I found myself in a place where sometimes they shaved your head, sometimes they made you wear diapers and sleep in a crib, and sometimes, they told you to drink your milk from a formula bottle. I had come in under my own volition (unlike some of the other residents who were ordered there by the courts in lieu of going to the state pen), and I was sitting on a broken-down wooden Chair in the hallway of this Renew place, looking at the peeling paint on the walls and wondering about the things that had brought me here.

I was wondering about them because that's what some little seventeen-year-old shit had told me I had to do for the next few hours before they'd allow me to enter the Renew Program officially.

My mother and father had dropped me off. My mother had cried. My father hadn't even come close.

And they left me here, at this—probably The Last Hope In Hell For Their Little Baby Boy—and I was left to sit on The Chair and think.

▲ ▼ ▲

At four that afternoon they let me off The Chair. They asked me if I had thought about all the things that had brought me to a place like this, and when I said that I had, they told me I could enter the Renew Program, but that I had to stay with my "Brother." My Brother was the kid assigned to teach me the ins and the outs of the Renew Operation, show me the ropes, so to speak. He was a seventeen-year-old Hispanic fellow, who had opted to come to Renew instead of doing twelve to twenty-four in the city jail for armed robbery. He was to show me what my responsibilities as a new resident were. Everyone who came to Renew was assigned a Brother, or a Sister if you were female.

My Brother took me to the dining hall around five-thirty and introduced me to a few of the other inmates, er...uh... *residents*. They weren't of the sort to which I was accustomed and certainly not of the same caliber as those with whom I'd been in treatment the summer before at Hallmarke. *I* wasn't there because it was easier than doing jail time for the bad checks I'd written. *I* didn't carry a gun. *I* didn't call my probation officer by name. And *I* certainly didn't live in the slums where all my cousins, friends, older brothers, younger sisters, and the guy who lived in the apartment next door dealt drugs, and getting caught doing it was just part of the fun. I had merely come in, I maintained, so that I could get a grip on the problem I was having with my heroin and my cocaine.

They got a good chuckle over that one.

Before bed, my Brother took me down into the basement where Renew had converted the room into what they now called "Living Space." Living Space was a large room filled with broken-down couches and chairs that seemed to have been donated to Renew from a downtown sidewalk. The off-red sofas and the olive green arm chairs were placed in a circle around the room, with ample supplies of ashtrays on the arms. Each of the rickety wooden chairs hosted an ashtray on its seat.

"This is where we do confrontation groups," my Brother told me. "Also guilt groups, if you get a slip dropped on you, and sometimes, they give Haircuts down here." (In therapeutic community nomenclature, a Slip was a note about your bad behavior from another inmate, uh, *resident*. A "Haircut," as my Brother informed me, had nothing at all to do with the stuff that grew on the top of your head. A Haircut was a term applied to a one-sided "critique," if you will. More appropriately put, during a Haircut you kept you big mouth shut while four or five of your superiors told you what a piece of shit you were.) "It happens once in a while," my Brother said.

I can hardly wait, I thought.

"You gotta pick up The Attitudes in this room," my Brother said. He pointed to the carpeting remnant that covered the concrete floor.

"I gotta pick up the what?"

"The Attitudes, man." He bent down and pulled from the rug a tiny piece of yellowish lint. He grabbed it between his thumb and forefinger. "This is An Attitude," he said. He held it in front of my face to make sure I understood what he was talking about.

"Oh," I said.

"We keep the whole place Tight." ("Tight" equals "clean" in therapeutic community lingo.) "You can't have no Attitudes on the floor of your duty room or your bedroom. You get a slip if you do."

"Oh," I said again. "Okay."

I proceeded to get down on my hands and knees and pick up The Attitudes that covered the carpeting of Living Space. When I had filled up my left hand with musty dirtballs, little pieces of lint, strands of hair, and tiny specks of God only knows what else, I asked my Brother, "How's that?"

"Good," he said flatly. "I'll show you where you're gonna sleep now."

"Thanks."

I couldn't wait to see what this little surprise held in store.

My bedroom turned out to be just about big enough for two—two very small French poodles maybe, but Renew thought two humans could fare just as well. The room was about twelve feet long and ten feet wide. It contained a bureau, a desk, a stand-up closet, and a bunk bed—all seemingly donated from the same sidewalk sale as the furnishings I'd just seen in Living Space. My cell mate . . . sorry . . . *bunk* mate offer me the top bunk. The one with the twenty degree angle of incline. The one without springs.

Ducky.

I approached one of the other guys I had talked to earlier. I walked out into the hallway and said to him, "Uh, is there anyway I could get another mattress? I got a bad back and sleeping on this one's really gonna fuck me up. You think maybe I could find another one? Or maybe a board or something?"

"Too fucking bad," says he. "I got a bad back too." Cheery guy. "That's the only one we got. Take it or leave it."

I took it.

For a while.

Till Tonight's Feature Presentation started up.

I lay down in the hills and valleys and made an attempt to pack it in for the night. *I'll get used to this place in the morning,* I told myself. I lay down to sleep at ten thirty.

I couldn't do it. My eyes stayed open. Stephen King was showing another Film Festival on my personal movie screen, and I had a season pass for the front row.

I was still awake at twelve. At one and at two. At three o'clock in the morning I got out of bed.

All I was seeing were three cc. syringes brimming with cocaine hydrochloride, needle tips in my veins, and little glassine bags dancing with Chinese white heroin.

I opened the door to the fire escape on the second floor, walked down the stairs outside, and bid a fond fucking farewell to Renew and their slips someone might drop on you when you were bad, their haircuts, and their attitudes on the floor of the duty room. I wished my wonderful Brother the best.

It was three o'clock in the morning. I was in a town a hundred miles or more from where I lived and I had no idea of how the hell to get to the nearest highway. And I had a fucking monkey on my back that was going to make this walk home a pretty long one.

This was a new one on me.

▲ ▼ ▲

I found the highway and tried to hitchhike. Nice try. I walked along the shoulder and stuck out my thumb whenever a car or truck came by, but at four o'clock in the morning who's gonna stop and give an escaped junkie a lift?

I got thirsty at one point and left the road to drink from the water that trickled down onto the rocks they blast away to make more room for the roadway. I put my face up to the side of the cliff. I sucked against the crevices in the rock. The water was clear and cold, icy. A wolf in full moonlight, I fancied.

The walk afforded me a lot of time to be alone and think, to get my bearings on this whole thing. I screwed up with the hospital, I screwed up with the shrink, and now I had screwed up again. With Renew. I was in deep shit.

My problem was simple: How was I going to get my family to let me come home again? How was I going to convince my mother and my father to give me another chance? They'd had it up to here! with the drugs, and the shrink, and the stolen checks, and the lies, the blackened spoons, the missing belts, the time spent locked behind the bathroom door, and blood all over the bedroom floor. This would not be easy. This would not be a simple matter of a few tears and maybe a plea for *please? Just one more time? PLEASE?* No. I would have to come up with something better. I would need a reason to come home.

I continued to walk along the highway thinking about my situation. I mulled over in my mind my predicament again and again. How the hell am I ever going to convin...

Oh, no... Oh, Jesus Christ no....

I stopped.

I leaned over the guardrail at the edge of the highway's shoulder and picked up a piece of broken glass from a bottle someone had tossed from a car window. The edges were quite sharp.

Oh no...

A voice in my head said, *This'll do.*

I stepped behind the guardrail and bent over so that no one driving by would be able to see what I was doing. I undid my pants, put the piece of glass in my right hand, shoved it up against my asshole, and ripped away.

There. That ought'a do it. I reached behind my left shoulder and sliced myself a few times there for good measure.

"Ma?" I said into the telephone receiver. The folks in the all night diner where I stopped to make the call were nice enough to let me use their pay phone, even though I wasn't going to do any eating. I made the call collect. "Ma? Listen. I left. I can't stay there." Dead silence. "I got raped, Ma."

I didn't really care if anyone overheard.

"You *WHAT?!*" she screamed. Mom didn't seem too happy to be getting a collect call from her baby boy at four o'clock in the morning, giving her the news that a couple of the *inmates* in this place that was supposed to be rehabilitating her son had held him down against his will, sliced him up with some sharp object he couldn't really see, and had had a good old time getting their jollies off— at the expense of his rectum!—when all he'd done to deserve this was to get up to take a piss at two o'clock this morning. *"Where are you?!"* she screamed again.

"I dunno, Ma. I think I'm somewhere on Route 10 or something. I'm in a diner." What next? "But don't worry, Ma, okay? Don't worry. I'm all right. I'm just gonna come home. Okay?"

My old man got on the line. I could see him rolling over, his face turning red and the tendons standing out in his neck. I could see his eyes, and I could see him grabbing the phone out of my mother's hand: *Gimme that! Lemme talk to the son of a bitch.*

I told the old man what happened.

"Well I'm sorry," he said, "but you can't come here."

"But..."

"I don't care where you go, but you're not coming back here!"

"But..."

"*NO!*" he yelled.

Plan B: I said, "Dad, put mom back on." I knew if I could get to my mother, there'd be a way in with Dad. But I had to get to my mother first. I took my best shot: "Mom? Listen, I know I can do this thing on my own. I swear! I'll do whatever you want! I'll go to the clinic! I'll go to meetings! I'll get counseling, Ma! But I can't go back to that place! I can't! They fucking raped me in there, Ma!"

The line was dead silent.

One last push: "Please, Ma? Please? I swear to God! I'll straighten out! Please? Just lemme come home? PLEASE???"

Nothing. No response.

Then she said, "I don't know . . ."

Bingo! I was in. Anything but a firm NO! meant I might have to weasel my way around it, through it, over it, or under it; but *I don't know . . .* meant my foot, at least, was in the door.

"I'm coming to pick you up," she said. "Where are you?"

"No, Ma. Don't. I'll be all right. I don't want you driving out here. I'll just hitch. I'll be okay."

"NO!" she started, but I told her again I'd be all right.

I said I'd give her a call when I got close enough to town so it wouldn't be a bother for her to pick me up. I told her to go back to sleep (sure . . .), that I'd call her later on in the morning. I told her I loved her. I always told my mother I loved her.

Then I hung up the phone.

▲ ▼ ▲

I got a ride part of the way from a nice guy driving a pick up truck. I told him I'd just escaped from a drug rehab. I got out at the tolls, called my mother, and waited on the shoulder for her to come and pick me up.

Sitting on the southbound side of The New England Turnpike later that morning, I thought *God . . . This is one, big, fucked-up mess I'm in. I'll go through with this rape bit; but after that—I'm giving this shit up! I can't go ON like this!*

The intern at the hospital where I was examined said, "Maybe. He does have lacerations on his anus and on his shoulder. We don't find evidence of semen, but it is possible he was attacked. Would you like us to notify the police?"

I looked at my mother. She was tired, haggard. She looked older than she was supposed to, that if someone shoved a chair underneath her she would have fallen into it like a rock and just passed out. Mom looked like she'd just missed getting KO'd in a twelve rounder.

"No, Ma," I said, "I don't want any of that shit, okay? I'm tired. I just wanna go home and sleep. All right?" Mom was too exhausted to press the issue.

On the way home she said, "This is it! I don't know how I'm going to convince your father, but I'm warning you: If you don't do it THIS time. . . ."

She didn't have to finish.

Mom, Dad, and I had a powwow that evening. I swore that this was it. This time I was through! I said: "You watch! I'm gonna go to the clinic and you watch! I swear to God! I'm gonna make it!"

The following morning, they gave me a prescription at the hospital for thirty Percodan when I came in through the doors of the emergency room and told them how I had busted my back carrying a 10,000 BTU air conditioner up two flights of stairs helping my mother the other morning.

Well, I *did* carry the air conditioner! And I did hurt my back! And I did fashion a syringe out of a medicine dropper from the pharmacy and a needle tip from one of my mother's used insulin syringes that she'd thrown into the garbage can, because that's the size barrel you need when you crush up thirty Percodan at a time and whack the load into the your vein. And if she hadn't hidden her box of syringes I wouldn't have had to grab it out of the garbage can just to shoot my dope.

But Mom and Dad were right: I was in Deep Shit. I was

in way over my head this time and I had to stop. Plain and simple. My aspiration to become a junkie had to be tossed away. Hospitals? Psychiatrists? Therapeutic communities like Renew? And slicing up my fucking rectum? It was time to stop.

I turned in my syringes and my cookers and my three cc. gimmicks brimming with cocaine hydrochloride and my little glassine bags of Chinese white heroin. I gave up my bathroom stalls and the belt around my biceps and my buddies on Boot Hill and my toilet bowl water and my butane lighter. I gave it all up, and for the next year and a half I went to the out-patient clinic downtown and I got my shit together.

I found a good paying job. I straightened out a lot of things in my personal life. And I gave up all my drugs. Entirely. Every single one.

Being a drug addict had kicked my ass. Heroin and cocaine had reduced me to the point where now I was nothing but a lowlife scumbag who resorted to shit like sticking pieces of broken bottle glass up his ass and claiming to have been raped in a treatment facility so he could get one last chance with his parents. Chemicals had beaten me. Totally. Completely. And to the point where I had nothing left.

The choice was obvious: Give up all my drugs...
Or else.

NINE

GOODBYE, MOM

Using drugs is lonely. No one gets near and no one comes close. Although I moved in and out of situations, although jobs changed and girlfriends came and went, and although I slept in different beds in different apartments in different towns and came into contact with a myriad of people throughout my years, I was still very much alone. Using chemicals is probably the ultimate "me" oriented activity. It's selfish.

When you're using chemicals the people with whom you interact are ghosts. As soon as they move close enough to touch you, to hold you, as soon as they get near enough to really become a part of your life, they pass right through you like specters in a haunted house.

If you can, imagine watching Humphrey Bogart and Lauren Bacall in a 1940s black and white movie with the volume off. A piece of the puzzle simply gets sucked away by the chemicals, and you're left to just go through the motions.

No sound . . .
No feelings . . .
No closeness.

Still, there were two who somehow managed to scale
the wall I had been building for the last fifteen years, to
claw their way (if only a little) through the cocoon with
which I surrounded myself. Only two.

One was my best friend Steven. We had been best
friends since we were twelve. The other was my mother.
(And if you're a man, you already understand. If you're a
female, well, you know it too. Maybe it's just reversed.)

After my fall from grace in college and after the year or
so I spent trying to get it together back home, Steven and I
picked up our friendship from where it had been left off
five years earlier. We'd been apart since the end of high
school, but there was always something between us, something neither time nor distance could tear apart. Steven had
watched me destroy my life with chemicals since I was an
adolescent. He had frequently stopped by my parents'
house when I was away at school to chat with my mother
and ask how I was. He and my mother were always close.

*Oh. Sorry to hear that. Well, maybe he'll come around. Tell
him to gimmee a call when he comes home. I'll talk to him.*

My mother and Steven had seen me get into trouble in
high school, and had seen me go to college and leave before
I was through. Both of them had watched me go to hospitals, rehabs, psychiatrist's offices, and they'd been there
when I had walked out. They had watched me screw up
my life to the point of cutting my rectum with a piece of
broken bottle glass.

My mother and Steven also watched while I went to the
out-patient clinic downtown, worked my butt off in therapy, and conquered the needle. They watched me grow up
that year. They watched the days, and the weeks, and the

months pass by with one drug-free urine specimen after another. They watched me get a full-time job as a bartender, stock pile money in the bank, and gain back at least some of the respect and trust I'd lost from people and institutions because of my drug use. Both of them joined me as we celebrated my first year of being clean and drug free. Happy. Off the junk once and for all, and beginning to rebuild my life. The three of us were inseparable.

And two months after my first anniversary—sixty days after we had gone out to dinner, drank champagne, toasted my good fortune, and celebrated my freedom from the throes of heroin and cocaine addictions—my mother died.

Steven and I were spending the weekend on Cape Cod. Both of us worked in bars. Steven, as the manager and head bartender at Billy's Drinking Emporium, and I as a bartender in another restaurant. Together, we enjoyed a lifestyle common to the trade: fast times and fast cash. I had been clean from drugs for over a year and I had been christened an Ex-Addict by the staff of the out-patient clinic. I was working hard, and Steven and I were taking off a well-earned weekend of rock and roll on Cape Cod.

I called the clinic Monday morning to let them know I was on vacation and that I wouldn't be there for their usual Tuesday night group therapy session. My counselor got on the line.

"Adam, you've got to call your house right away."

"What's wrong?" I asked.

"I think it'd be better if you called home yourself, Adam," he said.

"But what's the matter?"

"Adam! Just call home! All right?"

I hung up and dialed my family's house. *What could be the matter?* I was all right. There weren't any problems with my job or with the clinic. *What could be the matter here?*

It never even dawned on me. . . .

A voice got on the other end of the line and said, "Oh God, Adam. I hate to be the one to tell you this... but. . . ." It was my cousin. *What the hell is she doing over at my house?*

"Nancy, what's the matter?" I asked.

"Oh God, Adam... I'm... I'm sorry. . . ."

"Nancy!" I screamed. "WHAT'S THE FUCKING PROBLEM DOWN THERE?"

And then I knew.

"It's your mother, Adam. . . "

"What, Nancy?"

"Last night... she. . . "

"WHAT?"

"Adam... last night... your mother died."

The receiver went dead. The *world* went dead.

"I'm so sorry to be the one to have to tell y. . . ."

I didn't hear anything that followed.

Steven was standing in the hotel room with his girlfriend and they were looking at me funny. They stared. Steven pushed his girlfriend to one side and came towards me. He *ran* towards me.

"No. . ." I said. "NO! Oh Goddammit NO!" My cousin was saying something over the phone but it didn't make sense. I couldn't hear it. I hung up the line. I looked up.

"She's dead, Steven. My mother's dead! Oh Jesus Christ. . . ."

Steven reached for me. I thought I was going to vomit, like I'd been smashed in the back of the head with a wooden bat. I went outside to the second story deck and sat on the steps. I put my head into my hands and cried. Steven came out a minute later.

"C'mon," he said, "let's get you home."

"It's not supposed to HAPPEN like this! She's not supposed to DIE! Steven! We weren't THROUGH!"

He pulled me to his shoulder and let me sob. "C'mon," he said again. "Let's go. I'll get everything together. Let's just go home." My legs felt like Play-Do.

"Steven?"

"C'mon. It's all right. I'm gonna get you home."

"Oh Christ!" I wailed.

And I fell into The Pit

▲ ▼ ▲

Steven loaded up the car and we left Cape Cod for Connecticut and my mother's funeral. About a mile from the hotel, we stopped at a package store, tossed a case of beer into the back seat and started off on the six-hour ride. We talked about what a good woman my mother was. How she was better off now, and how at least she was done with all her pain and suffering in this world. We talked about how much I'd meant to her, how I'd definitely been her favorite, how wonderful it must have been for her to see me off drugs and into my second drug-free year, and how the only thing that mattered to her was to see me make it before she left this earth.

We talked about the good times. The time Steven had brought over a hot fudge sundae and watched my mother eat the whole thing—even if she was fucking diabetic—and we laughed because if my father had found out he would have murdered the three of us right there on the spot. We joked about the cars Steven and I had wrecked, the girls we'd dated, and we laughed because the whole time my mother had been there with a smile on her face saying, *Well, boys will be boys.*

Even with all the trouble I'd gotten into as a result of using drugs—the stolen checks, the missing silverware, the hospitals, and the law—mom was always there to say, "He'll grow out of it. He's just having a tough go of it right now." She was always there. For me and for Steven. It was as though she'd adopted two stray puppies.

Driving through Rhode Island, I turned to Steven and said: "You know what the last thing I ever said to her was?" He turned from the road and face me.

"What?" he asked.

"'I love you'."

Steven began to cry.

I cried most of the way home, I cried with my family when I got there, and I cried with Steven when he came and stayed with me that night. I cried when the family opened the bottle of Dom Perignon and toasted her passing, and I cried when I fought with my father over who was going to take the garbage out and who was going to feed the goddamned dogs. I cried at the funeral parlor, I cried at the graveside service, and I cried when my father, my brothers, and I lowered her casket into the ground. I cried when I shoveled the goddamned dirt onto her goddamned coffin.

For five days, I woke up and my eyes were filled with tears before they were even open. It was like I was getting pummeled with a two-by-four. I drank non-stop from the time I got the news until the pain eased off five or six days later. I drank and drank, and when the pain came back and tried to grab me again—I drank some more. As soon as I awoke in the morning, I grabbed some Kleenex for my eyes, threw back the covers, went downstairs to the liquor closet and poured myself an eight ounce tumbler of Johnny Walker. When that was done, I had another.

But I didn't take drugs. I was so strong that not even my mother's death would make me go back to that!

Time, slowly, took its course. With the help of my counselor at the clinic and Steven, I worked past the anger, the hurt, and the denial of my mother's passing. I began to work out in a local gym; I picked up my guitar and started writing music and playing in a few nightclubs. Eventually, I teamed up with Steven at Billy's Drinking Emporium and became one of their bartenders. In hindsight, if it had not been for Steven in those months following my mother's death, I don't know whether or not I would have made it. Steven became a friend, the likes of which I had never known. Steven was a godsend.

I continued treatment at the clinic downtown, and I progressed to the point where the director of the clinic asked me to do an interview with a local newspaper about what it was like to be an ex-addict. The counseling staff in the clinic even suggested that I might start thinking about someday becoming a drug counselor myself. I had done it, they told me. I had beaten the needle, the monster. I was a success. And they said it was time to really start making something of my life.

"You beat the monkey," they told me. "You should be quite proud of what you've accomplished, Adam."

And I was.

But for the time being I needed space. I needed time to think about things for a while. I was content to continue tending bar at Billy's, making money hand over fist, going on vacation, playing guitar and singing in a few clubs, and just plain taking it easy. I had been through hell. I had beaten a thirteen-year drug addiction which had almost cost me my life, and I had lost my best friend in the world to a goddamned disease called diabetes. I needed time to make some sense of it all.

I wouldn't let Mom down, I told myself. I'd continue on the straight and narrow path. I'd continue to be successful and earn the respect of my peers. I'd continue to work hard and be an ex-addict. I had beaten the monkey! I was working hard for what was now coming my way, and I would never fall prey to the needle again. Never!

I swore it on my mother's grave!

▲ ▼ ▲

When my mother died in 1983 an era in my life ended. My primary source of comfort and compassion (not to mention my chief enabler) was gone. No longer would I have Mom's arms to come home to and cry and be forgiven. I had to grow up. I wasn't given a choice.

I lived at home, just my father and I, and I continued to work at Billy's Drinking Emporium with Steven, where, on my free time, I began to learn to drink like a proverbial fish. I went to the gym on an almost daily basis, kept singing and writing music, and continued my out-patient therapy at the downtown clinic.

But something was going on in my head.

There was something keeping me afloat, something keeping the monster at bay and preventing me from using drugs. It wasn't simply switching from one thing to another, alcohol for drugs. And it wasn't the work I was doing in therapy, or the good paying job, or the feeling of self-accomplishment I had from overcoming my drug problem. They were certainly part of it, but they weren't the only things holding me up and preventing me from jumping off the spring board.

There was a loathing growing inside me, a self-righteous hatred for anyone who used illicit drugs. I despised drugs and the people who took them. King Arrogance, kept the Beast from Beauty. Arrogance, and a control over one's life like a man clenching a steel fist around it.

I had been through Hell because of things like cocaine, heroin and pills, and in the eighteen months since I'd given them up I'd worked hard indeed to get myself to the point where I had a good job at the bar, respect and admiration from my co-workers, money in my pocket and gold credit cards lining my wallet. I prided myself that single-handedly I had BEAT the needle. No one could take that away.

I refused offers to sniff cocaine at the bar and had no reservations whatsoever telling people exactly why. "Sorry," I'd say, "I don't do that shit. I used to have a problem. I used to be a junkie." I set up rules for my alcohol consumption: I only allowed myself to drink after we'd closed the bar, and only after the money was counted, the place was clean, and we were finished for the night. I would never be a drunken bartender, I told myself.

My clients wondered why I never drank with them. "I have a job to do," I told them. "Besides, the boss doesn't pay me to have a good time. He pays me to work." But when work was over I played. Hard. (It's A Reward System. The little voice in your head says, *"Ahh, go ahead! You worked hard for it! Have a few! On me even! And don't worry, Buck-O—you'd only be having a REAL problem if you were drinking ON the job. You're fiiiiiine....)*

Steven and I worked together, we made money together, we took time off vacationing together, and we drank together. We drank in the Florida Keys, on the Coast of Massachusetts, and we drank at the Mardi Gras in New Orleans. We drank in bars, in restaurants, and in the comfort of our own homes. And why not? We worked hard for it.

More than that, for the first time in my life, for the first time in Steven's life, a friendship was developing. We had both been devastated. We had both felt like someone had beat the crap out of us after my mother passed away, and together, we were trying to make our way through it. We were there for each other.

Less than six months after my mother's death, my father moved to Arizona and left the family house in my care. He thought I was doing well enough on my own, that I was making something of myself this time around, and that he could leave the house in my trust. It had been almost two years since I had put any drugs into my system and it seemed I was becoming a self-made man in my own right. The cure was taking this time. Dad went to Arizona to live and work with one of my brothers, and he left me the family house on a silver platter.

Now, I thought, I'll shoot for the Gold. I went out and bought the Kawasaki Eleven Hundred.

An eight-room house in the suburbs of one of New England's wealthiest communities? A brand new Kawasaki 1100? Six, seven, sometimes eight hundred dollars a week *in cash* from a bartending job I only had to work at four nights a week? American Express Gold Cards? Vacations in Key West? Girlfriends? Cars? And all the respect and admiration I could possibly swallow for single-handedly overcoming one of the most deadly addictions known to man?

I was rock and roll.

I pushed in the clutch and floored the accelerator. I threw the shift into high gear, held onto the wheel with both hands, and man I tell you...

... I was fucking flying.

TEN

TENNIS MATCHES AND BARTENDING

I would last almost two years without drugs.
In addition to therapy and work and making music and generally having a good time, I spent a lot of my free time in the gym and grew healthier, more muscular, and took even better care of my body. I rode the ExerCycle, swam in the pool, pumped my way through three-hour free weight sessions, and relaxed afterwards in the steam, maybe even, treating myself to a forty-five minute session with the masseuse.

One morning in the course of my free weight routine I was pressing a hundred or so pounds over my head in a behind-the-neck maneuver designed for upper back and deltoid conditioning. Maybe I wasn't watching my form, maybe my mind was somewhere else, or maybe I was lifting way beyond my limit (I do have a tendency to take things to the extreme), but something in my neck went *cruuuuunnnnnccchhhh!*

I was in deep shit again. Almost two years.

I waited twenty-four hours before I called my family physician.

"Hi, doctor?" I said reluctantly.

A little voice in my head said, *Shit, you're not really doing this, are you?* And the voice of pain commanded, *SAY IT!*

My neck was on fire and I could barely hold the phone against the side of my head without sending lightening bolts into my brain receptors.

I said, "Hi doctor, thank you for calling me back. Listen doctor... I have a problem." He told me to explain. "I was working out yesterday at the gym and, well, I screwed something up in my neck. Bad. It's killing me, Doctor Goldbloom. I'm really in a lot of pain..."

There was no response.

The voice of pain ordered me to *Say it! Say it! SAY IT!*

"...and I went to see my chiropractor and she said I ripped a muscle. She doesn't think there's disc damage, she just thinks I tore up the muscles pretty bad."

Doctor Goldbloom still wasn't playing ball.

SAY IT!

"The problem right now doctor is the pain. I wasn't able to sleep last night, and today I can barely move my neck. I can't even turn it! I'm calling you to ask you..."

Say it!

"...if there's any way you could possibly..."

And I heard the words come out of my mouth and plop into the receiver like they were from someone else's throat.

What happened to my almost two years?

"...just give me some codeine for the pain for a couple of days? Just a few? Just a couple to see me through for the next couple of days till the pain goes away?"

It was my best serve. The match was on.

"Well..." Doctor Goldbloom began. He lobbed: "I

don't know. I'm very reluctant, Adam, to prescribe anything for you with a narcotic in it given your addiction history."

The ball came over the net into my side of the court: "I
understand that, doctor. I agree. I don't particularly want to
take anything like that either. But it's been almost two
years since I had a problem. I'm doing really well! I
wouldn't call and ask you if I didn't really need something.
I'm really in pain, doctor!"

His volley: "I still don't know . . . "

Backhand: "Doctor. I understand your position. I
wouldn't want to give an ex-addict narcotics either. But I'm
going out of my mind with this pain! I just don't know what
else I can do!" *A little English:* "Look, all I'm asking for is a
small amount—just six maybe—just six Tylenol with codeine to get me over the hump for the next couple of days.
I'll take them as directed, I won't ask you for a refill. But
I've got to take something for this pain! Really, doctor—it's
not like I'm going to start taking Percodan or shooting dope
again from taking six little Tylenol Three's! I promise."

Again, he returned my volley: "Adam, I still don't
know if it's such a good idea." He swung hard: "How about
trying some Motrin first and seeing if that helps?"

I rushed the net: "Doctor, if a Motrin would take care
of this, I'd go to the drugstore and buy a bottle of Advil!
I'm in *pain* here! I need something with a narcotic in it!" I
took one more step and slammed with everything I had.
"Doctor, look. I'm asking you. I'm not scamming Percs or
shooting dope. I'm asking. I'm being straight with you, and
I'm asking you to help me with this pain. I'll take the fixed
amount. I won't mess around with them. And I'll take
them only when I need to. But it hurts like hell, I'm really
in a lot of pain, and I'm asking you for a small amount of a

mild narcotic to help see me through. *Please doctor,* I swear I'm not going to screw around with it. I learned my lesson two years ago."

"Well..." he started.

The ball went over the line to his side of the court.

"All right," he said. "I'll call in a prescription of six for you."

I began to smile.

He asked, "Which pharmacy do you use?"

Point. Game. Set.

And fucking match.

▲ ▼ ▲

Doctor Goldbloom telephoned in the prescription for six Tylenol Number Three to relieve my cervical pain, which I took as directed, one at a time, every four to six hours as needed. When I was through, I tossed the bottle away. No problem.

I took a couple of days off from work to make sure I didn't do further damage to my neck by tossing beer kegs around. I continued to see my chiropractor and to take it easy, and three days after the initial injury I went back to Billy's and back to the gym. Good as new, I thought. I feel a hundred percent better.

There, I'm not sticking needles in my veins again. I'm not scamming Percs and writing up my own prescriptions. See? What the hell is everybody so worried about? It's only codeine! What are you all getting so upset for?

I thought about those die-hard ex-junkies who told me I'd never again be able to take anything with a narcotic in it. I thought about how they said I shouldn't even *try.*

"Watch your drinking," they cautioned, "and don't

even *think* about taking anything like tranquilizers or narcotics. Mess with that stuff than you'll be shooting dope again before you even know what hit you."

There was one woman at the gym who told me that all I was doing by not taking drugs and continuing to drink was substituting one addiction for another. She said, "You can't do it. No one can. It's just a matter of time, Adam. Watch. You'll get high again."

What the fuck did she know? I had beat the needle! Why were they all so worried about drinking? I never drank before I went to work and I never drank during work. All I ever do is have a couple at the end of my shift! What's wrong with a couple of drinks? What's all this righteous ex-junkie stuff for? Shit, it had been so long since I had stuck a needle into my arm, that now I could even safely consume an innocuous little narcotic like codeine! I could have a legitimate injury, treat the pain AS DIRECTED, and then be done with it! No problem. What the hell was everybody getting so scared for?

I didn't get it. I just shook my head.

A month after that cervical injury, I sustained some trauma to a muscle group in my groin. I did this while exercising on the Leg Abductor/Adducer Machine. I couldn't believe I was so stupid and careless as to hurt myself again, but once more I treated the injury with a little rest, a couple of days off from the gym . . .

. . . and a little acetaminophen with codeine. And again, I didn't have a problem with them. No needles. *See?*

One morning, I was having lunch with my former counselor in a restaurant next to the gym and across the street from the clinic. We weren't in a therapeutic relationship at the time, but we still worked out in the gym together and every few weeks we'd meet for lunch or coffee or we'd go out for a couple of drinks. It seemed a nice way for us to stay in touch and remain close.

In the middle of my cheeseburger, the director of the clinic, whom I also worked out with, popped his head in and asked me why he hadn't seen me in the free weight room this morning.

"Ahh, I ripped a couple of muscles in my groin the other day, Geraldo. Leg work." I pointed at the area just below my abdomen. "Hurts like a mother. I just need a couple of days off, that's all. I'll be back when the pain eases up."

The director smiled. The look on his face told me what a wimp he thought I was.

"What are you doing for it?" he asked.

"Just taking it easy," I said. "The doctor gave me some codeine for it when the pain gets real bad."

The director squinted his eyes like I was speaking Latin. "What are *you* doing taking codeine?" He folded his arms across his chest. "I don't know if that's such a good idea for you!"

I rolled my eyes at my counselor with whom I was sharing the cheeseburger. I turned back to the director of the clinic and said, "Jesus Geraldo! It's only codeine! It's not like a fucking Percodan or anything." I looked at him wondering why he would even question my judgement. "What would you suggest I do?"

He shook his head. "Well, I don't know," he said. "I just know you shouldn't be messing around with codeine!"

"I'm all right with it," I said to him.

Now, it was his turn to roll his eyes. "Suit yourself," he offered. He shook his head and looked at my counselor friend and me like both of us should know better. "It's your ass . . ." he said as he walked out of the restaurant.

I turned to my counselor friend and asked him, "Do you believe that?" He shrugged his shoulders. "Do you think it's not a good idea for me to take this stuff? Even though the doctor prescribed it? Even if I really am in pain?"

My counselor friend sat back in the chair and looked as though even he wasn't sure of the right answer. He offered, "I think sometimes we have a need for medication when we're sick and in pain. Sometimes, that means taking something that contains a narcotic." He sat forward just above his cheeseburger and French fries. "You just have to be real careful when you take stuff like that." He asked, "You're in pain, right?" I nodded. "So?"

So?

So I watched myself. I stayed "careful."

Shortly after the sprain in my groin, I had to have a thrombosed hemorrhoid removed from my asshole. (Perhaps left over from the night I decided to walk home from Renew?) I explained to the surgeon that I was an ex-addict and that I preferred he didn't give me anything for the pain. But after some persuasion on his part and an explanation that the recovery was going to be extremely painful, I accepted his prescription for twenty Tylenol Number Three.

Soon thereafter, I developed an absolutely horrible septal infection from spraying my nose five and six times a day with Afrin nasal decongestant. My ear, nose and throat doctor treated it with a topical cortisone spray to alleviate the swelling, a systemic corticosteroid to reduce the inflammation...and codeine, for the terrible pain I assured the doctor the infection was causing.

I had a hole drilled in one of my molars as part of a root canal for which I received thirty Tylenol Three. And then my back went out. The doctor at the Walk-Right-In-And-Pay-Us-In-Cash-Or-With-Your-Gold-American-Express-Card clinic gave me a prescription for Vicodin. Five milligram tablets. Thirty pills.

And three refills.

▲ ▼ ▲

It was about two months later and I was staining the redwood deck adjacent to the screened-in porch of my house one glorious summer's afternoon. The deck hadn't had a coat of stain applied in probably four or five years, and the run of beautiful weather we'd been having made it the perfect time to go out there, get some rays on my back, and work up a sweat doing some of the things around the yard that had been neglected. I reached the brush into the corner of the flooring, and I wondered to myself how long had it been since I'd gone a full day without taking some codeine, or a Darvon, or a Vicodin, or some other silly little innocuous narcotic? *Now, how long had it been? A few weeks? A month? A couple of months?*

I really couldn't remember.

I stuck the brush back into the corner and tidied up the edge of the plank to which I'd just applied a coat of stain. *Hmmm . . . I really couldn't tell you when the last day was.*

I put down the brush on the side of the railing and went inside to the kitchen. I wiped the sweat from my neck with a paper towel and reached into the fridge to grab an ice cold can of Budweiser. *Now how long has it been? I wondered.* I thought about it one more time and then dismissed the question from my mind entirely. *Not to worry,* I told myself, *it's not like you're shooting dope or anything, is it?*

I popped open the can of Bud and cooled myself off.

▲ ▼ ▲

Back at the bar, the owner of Billy's—Billy himself—fired me one night after I'd worked for him for almost two years. He shitcanned me for failing to promote the ladies' drink special. He and the day manager called it Insubordination. I called it not getting any from your wife the previous night and being in a rotten mood!

No matter though. I walked around the corner to Luigi's Cafe, asked the owner if he needed any help behind the bar, and he hired me on the spot.

The move was upscale. The clientele was more sophisticated, not as loud, and not nearly as demanding as the crowd back over at Billy's. When a customer at Luigi's Cafe finished his drinks, he left me a nice, fat tip on the mahogany bar. I got stiffed all the time over at Billy's.

I met Suzanne, my wife-to-be, in Luigi's. We had a lot in common. She liked to work out in the gym, ride around on motorcycles, go out to dinner, drink fine wine and good champagne, and vacation around the Northeast Coast.

I also met another woman in Luigi's Cafe. She was like me in a lot of ways, too: we were both ex-junkies. And like me also, she suffered with a bad back.

"So, wha'da you do for it?" I asked her, leaning over the bar and lighting her Marlboro.

"I exercise a little," she said. "When the pain gets really bad, sometimes I'll take a Percodan."

It was Friday night. Late. Close to midnight, I think. *A Percodan, huh?*

I had been on my feet for nine hours already, and I was having a rough night. I had come in early to relieve the day bartender, who had gone home sick at three. I had been through a busy Happy Hour, a business party, the dinner crowd before and after the theater, and it was taking just about everything I had to remain cordial to the customers and not punch out the next person who asked me for drink. *A vodka martini, extra dry there Adam. If you don't mind, please.* I wanted nothing more than to sit down, smoke a cigarette, put my feet up on a chair and call it quits for the night.

She asked, "You wanna couple of Percs?"

I looked at her forearms. Nope. No track marks there.

Didn't she say she used to be a junkie? And now she takes Percodan? Wait a second here. She's an ex-junkie, she's got a bad back, and she takes Percodan?

I tossed the question around in my mind. *The codeine hasn't done me in. I've been taking that stuff for a while here and I don't have needles hanging out of my arms. What's wrong with taking a Perc?*

"Yea," I said to her. "That'd be cool. Thanks."

As I held that one little lavender Percodan in the palm of my hand, another voice in my head went off. It said, *Whooooaaaaaaa! Hold on a minute here. That's some pretty powerful shit you're holding in your little bartending paws there, Buck-O! You sure you wanna screw around with this stuff, you little ex-addict you?"*

I filled a tumbler with Coca-Cola.

Yea. I was sure.

Twenty minutes later, my whole being fell underneath that giant, blue, lolling wave. The warmth and just the slightest touch of nausea came back to my stomach like it had never been away. The freedom, the ease, the carefreeness, the no job too big or too tough or too demanding, and the loss of all worries in the world came floating back to me and wrapped me up again in its soft, fluffy comforter.

My schmooze became effortless as I talked with and worked the customers sitting at the bar. No one disgusted me. Nobody pissed me off. No one offended me because he was sniffing cocaine in the bathroom or because he was dealing it outside in the parking lot. It ceased to matter how late the boss was going to make me stay, and I didn't care how much shit I had to mop up from the floor after we'd locked the front door for the night. The money in my tip jar didn't matter as much, the owner's eyes weren't as scrutinizing.

As I floated there behind the dark mahogany bar with the overflowing ashtrays, the spilled rye and gingers, the bar rags that stank from too much head poured into the glass, I wondered why it had taken me so damn long to figure out that this was the only way to tend bar. That all the pain in my back, all the pressure to perform, all the stress of managing the owners' money and mine, and all the intolerance I had for the drunken clientele I had to serve and be slave to could all be made to go away. It could all just simply be removed by swallowing one little lavender Percodan.

ELEVEN

MARRIAGE

Two words about the woman who in two years would become my wife: big mistake. Not mine—hers.

Suzanne was from a small Minnesota town who came to the East Coast to pursue a career in finance and computing, and she was just lucky enough to hook up with a dirtball like me. Suzanne had a Master's in business administration, and had a fine job for a small, local computing firm where she oversaw about thirty employees. We met at a happy hour at Billy's when I was tending bar, fell in love (whatever the hell *that* is), and decided to get married. In the final analysis though, it was one big, bad move.

She had no idea what she was getting into.

I lost the job at Luigi's Cafe when they closed six months later; I went to the cafe for my regular Friday afternoon shift, the place was locked up tight, all the lights were off, and the handwritten sign on the door read, CLOSED INDEFINITELY.

No matter. I made another move up the bartending ladder to a better establishment, Pembrooke.

Pembrooke was small, and the was clientele young, wealthy, and fast. Where my job at Billy's consisted of cracking open upwards of five hundred to a thousand long neck bottles of Bud on any given night, dealing with half that many screaming college students, breaking up fist fights and mopping up vomit from the top of the bar, at Pembrooke I dressed in tuxedo shirt, tie and cummerbund. I served the clientele Maryland soft shell crab in lemon and caper, Stolichnya on ice with a lemon twist, and I talked to the young and upwardly mobile customers about the newest album on the sound system, the latest New York fashions, or where to invest a few extra thousand dollars.

Pembrooke was a pinnacle of achievement. I came home my first night with two hundred and seventy-five dollars in my pocket. Suzanne, who was living with me by this point, was overjoyed. Pembrooke would become my family.

We were happy now, Suzanne and I. The money rolled in—and plenty of it—and the good times flowed. Life became one, big party for Suzanne, my best friend Steven, and me. But there was also one, big problem.

How then was I to maintain my image as a clean and drug-free ex-addict—hard working, responsible, earning tons of money, and putting his life back in order—and at the same time continue my little fetish for prescription pain killers like Percodan and my ever-developing love for blended Scotch whiskeys? (Professionals have terms like "denial," "rationalization," "manipulation," and "intellectualization" to describe what I was doing in order to maintain that image. Personally, I think the term "bullshit" is more apt.)

I was honest with Suzanne, as I was with everyone else

who knew me by this point in my career. I told her that at one time in my life I had suffered from a horrible addiction to heroin and cocaine. I was completely straight with her about everything I'd been through. She knew about the hospitals, the shrinks, the clinic; she knew about the rectum maneuver I had pulled that night when I left Renew. She knew the history straight up. But the rest of what Suzanne got was bullshit. And everyone else got the same.

You see, I had an image to uphold during those years. People saw a man who had once suffered terribly from the throes of drug addiction and who now was an ex-addict. They saw a man who had once been at the lowest point of human suffering (or so he thought at the time), and now they looked at a man who worked out his body and tried to be the best bartender he could be, a man who made plenty of money and who planned to marry the woman of his dreams. They saw a man who vehemently opposed the use of any illegal drugs, a man who had no tolerance for it whatsoever. To the world around me, I was the consummate actor.

I could have gotten an Academy Award.

I'm sorry for the way I treated people back then, the way I lied, the way I presented such a false exterior. I am especially sorry for Suzanne. She was completely innocent. She thought she was getting a fair bill of goods, and today, I look back at those years and realize that Suzanne was really victimized. But it just gets back to what I said earlier: dopefiends are consummate liars. But that doesn't take away the pain those lies can inflict.

I'm sorry Suzanne.

So I could, with relative safety, tell Suzanne or my employers or Steven or my friends at the bar, that I had worked out so hard at the gym last week that I strained the muscles in my lower back. Or I could say that I'd put in a particularly strenuous day at Pembrooke, lifting and stacking kegs of beer. And because of this, I needed the aid of a legitimate, doctor-prescribed pain reliever. With very little danger of being confronted or being asked just a few questions about my behavior, I could leave a bottle of cough syrup on the back bar behind me and take a teaspoon of it every now and again to ease my cigarette hack—also, physician-prescribed. No one questioned my drinking at the end of the night, and no one bothered to hassle me about one little Percodan just to ease the pain. It was all within the bounds of the image.

But what I *couldn't* show the admiring crowd (or Suzanne or Steven for that matter), was that, although I kept a bottle of cough syrup on the back bar and only took one teaspoon every four to six hours as prescribed by the doctor, outside in my car were two *more* bottles underneath the passenger's seat, and that every time I went to my car to get something I forgot to bring in earlier, I drank half of one of those bottles in a slug. Nor could I show that every time I took only one Percodan to help with the pain or excused myself to go to the bathroom, I pulled a bottle of thirty more Percodan from my pants pocket and swallowed another half a dozen.

No. That I could never show anyone.

▲ ▼ ▲

When one drinks enough and takes enough chemicals for a long enough period of time, Voices begin to speak. They're very quiet. They're subtle. And really, they're quite soothing. I might imagine it's rather akin to a psychotic meltdown. The Voices are extremely reassuring. "Ssssshhhh," They say. "Be quiet. Listen to Us. . . ."

At the same time I was taking ten and twenty Percodan

and working the bar at Pembrooke, a little Voice slowly began to speak in my head. It was calm. It was rational. And it was very, very comforting. The Voice said, *"It's all right, Adam. You've got the whole thing under control. You just work too hard, you're too stressed. All you need is a little extra help here. Really, there's no problem at all. Everything's going to be, just, fiiiiiine."*

And when I left the bar at two o'clock in the morning and got into my car to drive home with the glass of Scotch between my legs, the Voice said, *"It's okay, buddy. I'm here. There's no need to be alone anymore. Go home and have a couple more. You worked hard, and you deserve it. Go ahead. And if you really need it, take a couple of slugs off that little bottle of Hycodan you've got underneath the seat over there. You'll stop coughing as soon as you quit those nasty cigarettes. But for now? Go ahead, it won't hurt you. Or how 'bout a couple more Percs, Buck-O? Not like it's heroin or anything now, is it pal?"* And the vials and the bottles clacked and rattled together each time I drove over a bump or a pothole. Click...click...click...like teeth in a skeleton's jaw banging together.

▲ ▼ ▲

It had been eighteen years since that day in the park with John Durke and Eric Waylon, and the maggots that had begun to eat away at my mind that day, the maggots that had continued over the years to chew and to gnaw and to tear away at the things that were supposed to make me human, the dirty little worms that fed on me, were slowly devouring me. But they were so very subtle, so silent, so quiet in their work that I never heard a sound from them. But all the same, they were now beginning to overtake me. And the more the maggots tried to take from me the harder I tried to make everything seem all right.

The more the bugs took the more hours I worked. The more the worms raped me the more clothes I bought, the higher I pressed for my credit rating, the more stock I purchased, and the more desperately I sought to win the favors and approval of my employers, my clients, and my friends. The maggots were stealing my mind and I wouldn't let anyone see.

Least of all, myself.

Suzanne received a promotion at her job, and between the two of us it looked as though we'd never want again. We frequently went up the north coast for weekend getaways, we flew to Arizona twice to visit my father; and at Christmas time, for two years in a row, we traveled to Minnesota and spent a week with her family.

We were in love. We cherished our time together—of which there was very little, as Suzanne worked days and I worked nights--but Suzanne frequently managed to come by Pembrooke's in the evening after she'd gone to the gym and worked out, or after she'd stayed late at the office to catch up on her work. She came by just so we could get in a little time with each other. Early evenings were slow at Pembrooke and the two of us could talk and catch up on each other's day. Suzanne would have dinner at the bar and hang around for a while with some of the other clients. Suzanne was good at making friends like that. People liked her, and Pembrooke treated her like family. God! it all looked so nice on the outside.

One year after taking the position at Pembrooke, Suzanne and I were married. I was twenty-seven years old. The ceremony was performed by a justice of the peace in my cousin's living room and the reception was held in his den. I bought the chef, who catered the affair at a nominal cost because of our friendship, a case of Stolichnya vodka as a tip. For our sixty guests, I purchased two cases of Dom

Perignon. For the wedding party, I bought six bottles of Louis Roderer Crystal. For myself, I got a script of thirty Percodan. I swallowed six before I said, " I do."

A month before we married, I explained to Suzanne that I had resorted to sniffing a bag of heroin one night when I couldn't get any prescription narcotics to relieve my back pain. I told her it was late, that I was all stressed-out from the long hours (her parents' visit hadn't helped things all that much) and that I'd only done it as a last resort. But still, I said it was scaring me.

I sought out my old counselor-turned-friend from the clinic. I went to a couple of sessions, explained that things were getting confusing for me, and told him I was losing my control with pain killers. The heroin, I said, was just the coup de grace. He told me to just stop like I had done before.

I did.

For a couple of days. And then I went back to the races.

The marriage went on as scheduled.

Suzanne and I flew to the Virgin Islands for our two-week honeymoon. When we arrived and went to our hotel room on the beach, Suzanne told me she didn't feel well from all the wedding hoopla and that she wanted to take a nap.

"Sure," I said to her. "I'll just go and scope out the town."

I found a pharmacy down the street, paid the pharmacist the two hundred dollars he explained it would cost me without a prescription, and secured an ample supply of narcotics for the honeymoon. I didn't need the two hundred dollars anyway.

When we came back to the mainland, I noticed my wisdom teeth were bothering me. I consulted a dentist and on his suggestion I elected to have all four of them removed.

"What will you give me for the pain, doc?"

He said not to worry. I'd be in minimal discomfort after the procedure with the prescription for Demerol he'd write. I went to the stereo store and bought a color television so I'd be all the more comfortable during my recuperation. I paid the doctor three hundred of the seven hundred and fifty dollar price of the procedure, and promised to pay him the rest, monthly, after that. I never did. Once fat in Demerol City, I didn't really give a fuck about the doctor's bill.

When I woke up from the dentist's anesthetic, I looked around the recovery room and saw Suzanne.

"Did he give you the script?" I asked. She nodded and pulled it from her handbag. "Let's go," I said.

She filled the Demerol and I settled in for a few days off from work. I lay down on the couch, turned on my new color television that I'd thrown on the old Amex Card, and I was finally able to relax. For a while. . . .

Three weeks later I broke the big toe on my left foot. In two places. On purpose.

Pembrooke was getting more and more difficult to tolerate—the people sniffing drugs, the loud partying, the demands to make their drinks and get their food and light their fucking cigarettes, and my goddamned bartending duty to stand there and talk to them, listening to their whining and moaning, and to give their bleeding hearts my bleeding bartending psychiatry. It was driving me fucking crazy.

I broke my toe because I didn't want to go to work, and I did it because I was lonely. I wasn't able to spend time with Suzanne because our schedules were in such conflict, and it just seemed there was nothing left for our marriage. I missed her. I also did it because I was running out of narcotics and my supply was nil.

A broken bone would be just fine, thank you much.

I had converted an upstairs bedroom into a home work-out area. I was quite happy doing my routine at home now instead of wasting my valuable time going to the gym downtown and doing it there, and it was nicer this way: I didn't have to listen to any one else's shit. There was a weight lifting bench in the room at home, a compliment of barbells and weights, a mirror, and a couple of dumbbells.

And one day my brain began to snap. Everything around me started to spin with Things I Had To Do and What People Expected Of Me and What Was I Going To Do About The Mess My Life Was Becoming With These Drugs and Who Is This Person I'm Supposed To Be Married To? I couldn't seem to see anything clearly.

It was all going around, and around, and around my head at far too great a speed.

And then it stopped.

I lifted a twenty-five pound weight off the barbell rack, held it over my left foot, closed my eyes, let go, and it stopped.

All of it. It just *stopped*.

Now I can get my bearings.

Suzanne rushed up the stairs when she heard the weight smash on the floor, and she stood in the doorway staring at me and my bleeding foot.

"It slipped," I said. "I think something's broken."

She offered to take me to the emergency room. Before we left I swallowed six, one milligram Xanax tablets so I'd make it through the x-ray, the exam, and the waiting for the results I'd come to expect from hospital ER visits. I bandaged my foot as best I could, and Suzanne dropped me off at the ER.

"I'll be all right," I told her. She asked if I wanted her to stay. "No," I said. "I'll call you when I'm finished."

The physician ordered an x-ray (I could have told him I had broken the fucking thing!), and it showed the bone broken in not one, but two places. A little bit better than I'd thought.

"There's not much we can do for a break of this nature," the resident informed me. "You just have to stay off it for a few days and let it heal. I'll give you something for the pain; there's not much else I can do though. Sorry."

I wasn't "sorry" when he wrote the script for thirty Tylox! (Tylox is the same thing as Percocet. For edification, the former is made by McNeil Pharmaceutics, the latter, by DuPont. But generically, they're the same.) No sirree, Bob. I wasn't sorry in the least! (Perhaps some doctors shy away from prescribing Percodan and Percocet because of their high degree of addiction and their likelihood for being abused. Smart doctors. But I guess this resident didn't know I was an avid reader of the *Physician's Desk Reference* and that I knew they were the same drug anyway. Or did he? It doesn't matter.)

When I awoke the following morning the pain in my toe was excruciating. I called the doctor to whom the emergency room resident had referred me, and the doctor met me in the ER half an hour later.

"You're just going to have to let it heal by itself," the doctor to whom I had been referred to said. "Do you have anything to take for pain?"

"Yes," I answered. "They gave me a few Tylox, but I only have one or two left." The doctor wrote an order for thirty more. Suzanne helped me hobble back into her car, and we drove around the corner to the family drugstore.

"I won't fill it for you," my family pharmacist said. "You're taking far too much of this stuff and you're going to get addicted to it." He handed the prescription blank back to me. And we went to another pharmacy.

▲ ▼ ▲

I returned to Pembrooke after a couple of weeks of eating Tylox, but it was never quite the same: I was tired of the customers. I found the entire bar scene intolerable. The owners, I thought, were running me into the ground. I missed my new wife—there seemed to be no time left at all for us. The late hours were too strenuous. It was time to move on again. One more time.

I left Pembrooke through their back door, sneaking away and telling them I couldn't work because of all the back pain from which I was suffering. I don't think they minded. They were pretty fed up anyway with the bartender they'd hired almost two years ago, the bartender who'd once been dependable, friendly, diligent, and a real asset to their business, but who now was turning sour. Something had happened to that bartender along the line. Now he was sick more than he was at work and getting injured left and right. And those little bottles of Percodan he kept behind the bar—when he did bother to come to work!—seemed to be appearing more and more and in greater quantity. *His new wife is okay, but what the hell she sees in him we'll never know.*

But the Voices told me I was still all right. *"Just a little bit of trouble here, Buck-O. Here, have a couple of these. You're still the best bartender I know! C'mon, we'll find you another job where they'll appreciate you, where the bosses and the customers won't be such fucking jerks. It was a rotten job, anyway. C'mon, let's go. And here, take a couple more of these Percodan."*

My next bartending job was back in my hometown working the day shift. I thought I would have more time to spend at home with Suzanne. I thought the daytime hours might be less draining, take less of a toll, and I thought a new job would be better for the two of us. But I just couldn't last. I went out with a knee injury less than a month after I started, which would also require surgery—orthoscopic knee surgery.

I had gone a few years now taking Schedule Two and Schedule Three Oral Narcotics, maybe a few tranquilizers here and there, and drinking Scotch in my free time. Money wasn't much of a problem yet (although I do have to admit the doctor's and the clinic's bills were piling up on the dining room table!) and I still thought I could do it. I still thought I'd get myself out of it sooner or later, that I'd somehow be able to give it up, get my control back, and somehow find a way to remain the ex-addict I knew I really was deep down.

But I was getting strung out again.

Wicked bad.

I took four Xanax and drank half a bottle of cough medicine before I went into the hospital to have surgery on my injured knee. When I awoke from the operation, the nurse gave me seventy-five milligrams of Demerol IM (and an intramuscular injection of 75mg of Demerol is a fairly stiff dose!) and it didn't do jack shit. I couldn't feel a fucking thing.

Oh God! is this actually happening again? Am I really getting so strung out on fucking prescriptions that even SEVENTY-FIVE MILLIGRAMS OF DEMEROL DOESN'T WORK?

▲ ▼ ▲

Two hours before the orthoscopic knee procedure, I said to the nurse on duty, "Would you please tell the anesthesiologist that I might be a little tolerant to the dose of narcotic he uses?"

She glared up from her desk and said, " I don't understand. Why would I tell him something like that?"

"I just want him to understand my case. I want him to know everything when he puts me under." She looked at me like I was visiting from Mars. "I've waited two months for this operation. My doctor has had me on Percodan for the pain. Sometimes I take two or three because one doesn't work anymore." She just continued to stare. "I just want the anesthesiologist to know I might be a little tolerant, that's all." She stared. Dejected, I said, "I thought it was important."

She looked me right in the eye. "If you're taking two Percodan at a time, you're abusing them," she said simply and went back to whatever she'd been doing before I had interrupted her.

She doesn't get it! I don't "abuse" Percodan. I've just grown tolerant, that's all. The doctor told me to take them for the pain and now it hurts so much I just take a little more than I'm supposed to. I don't "abuse" drugs. Stupid fucking. . . .

When the pharmacist confronted me later that day about filling so many prescriptions for Percodan, I said to him, "Yea, I know it's a lot, but I'm a big guy (indicating my size). One doesn't do anything. I have to take two before it gets rid of the pain." He shook his head and told me to take a good look at what I was doing.

So I looked.

But it didn't matter. It didn't matter what the pharmacist told me and it didn't matter what the nurse told me. It didn't matter what *anybody* told me.

In my mind there was a perfectly rational medical explanation for my increased need for narcotics. The Voices told me so. They said I'd simply been in pain for some time now and that I needed to treat it with narcotics; that all my pains were doctor-diagnosed, legitimate illnesses; and that now I was just a little tolerant to the standard dose, that's all.

What's so difficult to understand about that? Nurses and pharmacists just didn't get it.

At Suzanne's suggestion, we went to the clinic to examine the issue of my growing dependency on prescription pain relievers. They listened to my defense and said, "Adam, you need to go away for thirty days to a hospital and get some help."

Six professionals in the field of drug addiction and alcoholism sat there and told me I needed to go away for a problem I'd once beaten with my own will. Six professionals faced Suzanne and me, in a little office with a brick-face wall and a window that overlooked a chain-link fence out back, and said in effect: You're out of control. You need help.

In short, I told them to "fuck off." (This is called "denial" by the professionals. By junkies, it's called "surviving.")

I tried to run an old walk-in medical clinic for some cough syrup. At least I can still get away with this bit, I told myself.

I waited an hour in the examining room before the physician saw me. *Why's this guy taking so long? What's the problem? All I want is a little bottle of Hycodan for this cough I got.*

The nurse came in and took my temperature and blood pressure. My BP was something ridiculous like 240 over 180. She scolded, "You have to give up salt immediately! And stop smoking! Your blood pressure is dangerously high!"

And I thought, *Shut up, lady. I know my blood pressure's a little high. It's called withdrawal. And if I don't get some fucking Hycodan for this cough soon, it's gonna get even fucking higher!*

The doctor came in. "What's the problem?" he asked. He flung his clipboard, with my chart attached, onto the table behind him. He glared.

"It's this cough, doc." (*Hack! Hack!*) "I can't seem to shake it. I can't get to sleep when I lay down at night. I go into a coughing fit, my chest hurts, but I can't get anything up." (*Hack! Hack!*) "You think you can give me something to help me stop coughing?"

"Do you use cocaine?" he asked.

He caught me totally off guard.

I said, "Do I WHAT, doc? Do I use WHAT?"

"Cocaine," he said, not phased in the least by my defensiveness. "Do you use cocaine? You're blood pressure's extremely high for a man your age." He wasn't budging. He reached for my chart. "Do you need to get high? Are you addicted to the stuff?"

Oh Christ, doc. Gimmee a break, will ya? Cocaine won't produce withdrawal that gives a person high blood pressure. I need NARCOTICS! Why don't you ask me if I need to get high on Percodan or something, fool! Cocaine! You're even stupider than that fucking nurse who was just in here!

"No, doctor," I said flatly. "I don't use cocaine. I wouldn't touch that shit if you paid me."

"Are you sure?"

"Of course I'm sure! I used that crap when I was a kid! I haven't touched that shit in five years!"

"Then how do you explain your blood pressure? Your skin is wet too. You're clammy," the doctor observed.

"I dunno, doc. You don't think it could have anything to do with the fact that I might be sick, do you?"

"I doubt it," he muttered. The doctor examined me roughly with his stethoscope and pounded my chest a few times. He wrote out a prescription for an antibiotic.

"Here," he said. He handed me the prescription blank. I read it. "Take it as directed. It'll clear up your chest." He opened the door and started to leave.

"What about my cough, doc?" (HACK!) "Can you give

me something (Hack! HACK!) to ease it up a little?" (HACK!)

"No," he said coldly. "You don't need it." He signed the payment form and the nurse told me it was forty-five dollars.

For THAT? I handed her a gold credit card.

Assholes!

I took a handful of Valium when I reached my car.

▲ ▼ ▲

Everyone was on to my narcotic scams. The doctor who did the knee surgery, the nurse at the hospital, the family pharmacist, the toe doctor and the emergency room interns—they were all on to me. Even the doctor at the walk in clinic pulled my name up on his computer and the votes were in: This guy's been here twenty times in the last few years and each time he comes in for a problem, he walks out the door with a prescription for controlled substances.

I had to take a different tack.

I went to see the ear, nose and throat doctor who'd helped me with my nasal infection in past years. He was still giving me a little codeine now and again.

I said to him, "I'm having a problem with Percodan, doctor." I bowed my head. "I'm hooked on 'em, I think. Can you give me something to get me off? Please?"

"Sure," he said, smiling. He thought it was humorous. "I was wondering when you were going to start having a problem with that stuff. Just wait a minute. I want to look it up and see what I can give you." He went into his office and returned in a few moments after consulting the *PDR*. He wrote me out a prescription for thirty, one milligram Xanax tablets. "Here," he said, "take these four times a day. You won't be anxious, and the withdrawal will be easier. You'll be off the Percodan in a week or so."

"Thanks, doc," I said.

I walked out of his examining room with a script for the tranquilizers. On the way out, I borrowed a couple of sets of works. Just in case.

In a week, just like the doctor had said, I was off the narcotics. No more Percs. No more codeine. No nothing.

The Xanax worked like magic. I didn't have to run the doctors. I didn't need to have unnecessary surgery performed in order to get my Demerol and my Percodan. I didn't have to scam coughing fits at the walk-in clinic. And I didn't have to bust up bones in my feet and have x-ray series done on my toes. Nothing. I was off the dope.

But the tranqs alone didn't cut it for me. Sorry, but they just didn't do the trick. I needed something juicer. I looked at the two, three cc. syringes I'd taken from the ear, nose and throat doctor. I thought about the ex-junkie bit. I thought about what *It* had done to me at one time. I thought about the clinic.

"No . . . ," I said out loud. "No. . . . "

I pulled the protective orange cap off the needle point.

"Oh God, no. . . . "

I put the syringe back down. They began to talk to me. They started talking to me about the future of my life on Xanax and drinking Scotch alone.

Oh God . . .

I could taste the back of my throat freeze up from the cocaine. My tongue started to tingle. I touched the syringes again.

We're baaaaaack! They said.

Oh God. . . . You're not really going to go through with this are you? You're just kidding, right? Please tell me you're just kidding? PLEASE? Aren't you? Please don't do it? Don't get it all going again? Please don't start it all up all over again? Please?

PLEASE? PLEEEEEEEEEEEEEEASSSE???

The syringes said, *"It's time to pay the piper, Adam. . . ."*

Boot Hill was right where I'd left it five years earlier. The cars still stopped on the corner, the black and Hispanic and white boys still mingled in the street doing their dirty little deals. They still took your money, they still went into The Barbecue Palace, and people still got beat and ripped off; but if you knew how to play the game, you could still get the product.

Some of them had changed. Some of them had gone to jail or gone to treatment. Some of them had given it up on their own, and I suppose, some of them had died. But if you knew who to ask and how to play the game, you could still get a dime, or a quarter, or a piece of rock, or a bag of P-Dope. *If* you knew how to play the game.

And I still knew how to play fucking ball.

It had been a long time. I had put in a few years off the needle—drinking, controlling it, managing it, keeping that steel fist around Its throat as best I could—but I finally came home. It was too much for me to try and manage. I couldn't fight it any more. I bought a hundred dollars' worth of cocaine.

I was twenty-eight years old.

It's time to pay . . .

They'd all deserted me. The doctors, the hospitals, the pharmacists, the interns, the clinics. They'd all turned against me and left me no other option. No one would write any more prescriptions for my pain. No one would allow me to pass a phoney script, or phone in a bogus order, or run the late night doctor or scam the Indian physician at the walk-in clinic. No one.

. . . the piper, Adam.

All they'd left me to do was to take a few lousy Xanax. There was no more legal Percodan. No more hydrocodone bitartrate. No more surgical procedures. No more busted up backs. Nothing.

There was nothing left for me to do but go back to the streets . . . and back to the needle.

They just didn't leave me any other choice.

TWELVE

Voices, Graveyards, and Denial

Trying to hide the fact that you're swallowing way too many narcotics, getting strung out wicked bad, running the clinics and the ER's, and taking sets of works from the doctor's office so you can go home and whack some blow into your veins is like putting an elephant in the center of your living room and then saying to people, "What elephant? Where? What are you talking about, 'Elephants in the living room'?"

People have a hard time swallowing your lie that "there's nothing there."

But I think some people *want* to believe there's nothing in the living room. *My* denial was one thing, but those who were close to me—Suzanne, Steven, my family, even the family doctor and pharmacist and the guy who rents movies down at the video store--well, I don't think they wanted to entirely toss away the There's Really Nothing In His Living Room theory either! Believing that there isn't any elephant is much less painful than believing that this guy is strung out on thirty-plus Percodan a day and buying junk again in the ghetto. It's easier. Sometimes, the truth is hard to bear.

People who surround an active addict or an active alcoholic have Voices in their heads too. Their Voices say things to them like, "Yea, well, maybe. Okay, I'll buy that those holes and bruises I see along his forearm really are from the blood work-up he says he got from the doctor a couple of days ago. And what? The missing twenty dollars from my wallet? Oh, well, yea, I guess I have been a little forgetful lately. Maybe I *did* just misplace it. Or maybe I spent it even and just forgot! He's my fucking *husband*, for Christ's sake! Why would he take money from me?"

Why would he take money indeed. . . .

There is a direct relation between how intimate a person is with the active addict and/or alcoholic and how thick the involved person's denial will be. The nurse behind the counter takes one look at the fact that you're swallowing two and three Percodan at a time and knows you're a dopefiend. She doesn't even debate it. It's a fact.

But when that same dopefiend is your husband or your best friend of almost twenty years and he's swallowing handfuls of pain killers, well, that's another story entirely. To the latter, the Voices say things like, "But he's got a bad back. He's in a lot of pain! And he *is* under the doctor's care, you know. He's okay. He'll come around." Suzanne, Steven, and even my family in Arizona wanted so badly to believe I was all right.

No one wants to believe that an ex-addict is getting addicted all over again. No one. Least of all the addict himself. And the waters of denial run deep.

For a brief time, I managed a record store until the owners started missing more money than they should have from their nightly deposits. They quickly threw out the There's

Not Really An Elephant Sitting In His Living Room theory also.

Doing junk and cocaine again didn't mean a paltry bottle of Hycodan or a script of Percs here and there anymore. I wasn't about to start holding up liquor stores (yet!) to support my habit, but I needed to get some money fast. Steven, once again, came to my rescue. Steven had gotten himself a killer position managing one of the best nightclubs in the Northeast. The place was called Magnolia's. It was huge and had name-band entertainment nightly; there was a line out the door a hundred people deep from when Magnolia's opened at ten at night to when it closed at four in the morning. Magnolia's was the hottest thing to hit New England in years. The bartenders who were lucky enough to work under Steven waltzed out of the place at the end of the week with over a thousand dollars in their pockets. Cash. For three or four nights work.

Steven thought a good job would be healthy for me, get me feeling all right about myself again and get rid of some of the idle time I had on my hands—the devil's playground he called it. He asked me if I wanted to come and work for him at Magnolia's.

It was the busiest fucking rock and roll nightclub I'd ever seen. The bartending was so intense, and so fast, and so constant, that you couldn't even get time to take a piss during your shift. But the money made it worth holding your bladder.

"So, pal?" Steven asked one night when we were counting out the fifties, "How are you feeling now? Good honest work? Plenty of cash?" He thumbed through a stack of bills and said, "Kinda makes you feel good about yourself again, after all that surgery crap and not working bullshit you been through and all that Percodan and other garbage you been doing lately, doesn't it?" I smiled. "You're through with that shit, right?" I nodded and kept smiling. We toasted our good fortune with a bottle of the owner's Scotch.

Suzanne, too, was glad to see me back on my feet. The Voices in her head said, "See? We told you he'd be okay."

The owner of said nightclub pulled me aside one busy night and asked, "Adam, were you doing dope last night?" I frowned. He didn't budge. "You looked like you were nodding behind the bar. I gotta ask you, Adam: Were you doing heroin or something?" I told him absolutely not. "Okay," he said. "I just had to be sure. I know you gave that shit up a few years ago! But it fucking looked like you were high last night, man. Shit. Okay." I thanked him for being so up-front, so concerned. We shook hands.

I smiled.

And I excused myself for a moment to run out to my car, where I emptied a couple of twenty dollar bags of P-Dope onto the fold-down glove compartment door, sniffed them up, and went back inside the nightclub to finish my shift.

▲ ▼ ▲

Inside of four months of sticking a needle back into my arms I was doing two, three, sometimes even four hundred dollars worth of heroin and cocaine a day (or "a night," since my hours at Magnolia's ended at about five in the morning). This is what the experts call "progression." Progression is the factor at work for drug addicts and alcoholics by which the longer a person uses the particular chemical, the worse it gets. It's like cancer. It gets more and more painful, you need more and more of the chemical to achieve the same effect, and you get into more and more trouble as the result of your use. I couldn't get my paws on enough of the stuff. A thousand dollars a week and still it wasn't enough. I was losing it.

Fast.

When I ran out of money, I beat the street dealers. I went to Boot Hill at five in the morning one night, and parked my car. A dealer came up to my car door, leaned in the window and said, "You owe me a hundred dollars, mother fucker!" He was just a kid. He was a fourteen-year-old black kid selling heroin and cocaine on the street at five in the morning. I'd taken him off—stolen his dope without paying—a couple of days before.

"Fuck off, asshole!" I said. I turned up the stereo in my Firebird and looked around, trying to find another dealer. I rested my arm on the window opening and said, "I don't owe you *shit*, punk!" I turned away and adjusted the station.

"I'll hurt you, mother fucker!" he said. "I got fucking rocks in my hand! Gimmee my fucking money or I'll fucking hurt you, man! I swear to God I will!"

"Fuck off, 'home'!" I reached for the volume.

He backed up . . . and whipped a handful of rocks into my head.

No. Not rocks. Boulders maybe. At first, I thought he had cut me. I thought I was going to pass out. I stepped on the gas instinctively and took off. I put my hand up to the side of my face and it came back covered with blood. "Fucking son of a BITCH!" I yelled at the night.

I went home and ran a bit on Suzanne. I spoke to her Voices and explained that some unknown punks had broken my car window as I was innocently driving home from work, just minding my own business. They threw rocks at my car, I told her, and thus the reason for my bleeding head. *Lousy, rotten, disrespectful fucking kids!* An hour later, I sat in the police officer's patrol car and gave him the same bit. The officer didn't think he'd be able to catch the punks who did it, but he offered to send a car into the area just in case. I thanked him for his time at such a late hour. Suzanne went back to bed. I stayed up, and when I saw that the cop had left my driveway I shot up two bags of heroin left over from the afternoon.

Elephants.

Elephants in the middle of your living room.

Would you like to buy some swamp land in Florida?

I didn't go to work at the nightclub the following evening. I called Steven and told him I was sick. He didn't even bother asking what was wrong.

I took the Eleven Hundred down to Boot Hill and bought some cocaine. I didn't beat anybody for it, and nobody beat me. No rocks in my face this time. But I was running out of bits.

I drove around for a little while trying to figure out a good place where I could sit down and just get high in peace. Home was totally out of the question. Suzanne was there, and she'd had it up to her eyeballs! with my locking myself in the bathroom for hours on end. I had pulled that the previous Sunday; I had said I was "taking a bath."

FOR THREE HOURS?! she screamed.

When I finally came out from my "bath" after her banging on the door, she was crying. She wanted to know if it was another woman. She couldn't understand why, whenever we planned to spend time together, I was gone. Or locked in the bathroom. Or passed out. And when I told her there wasn't another woman, she cried even harder. I think because that left only one option for her: that the other woman was really just a tin foil packet from the hills of Colombia. So much for not believing in Elephants In The Living Room, Suzanne.

No. Home was totally out of the question as long as Su-

zanne was there. I drove around for a while on the Eleven
Hundred, looking.

*Now where can I go and get high? Where can I go, with the
bike, and not be disturbed? Where can I go and just have everyone
leave me alone? Just leave me alone so I can get high!*

I pulled the bike into the driveway of the cemetery
where my mother was buried. It was dark by this point. I'd
ridden until well past sunset. There wasn't anybody else in
the cemetery except me, my bike, and my dead mother.

The caretaker's house was burning a light on the front
porch, but I thought he'd let me be. I just wanted to pay
my respects to my mother. I pulled the bike onto the grassy
area where her grave was; there was a small bronze plaque
embedded in the earth. I turned off the bike, set it on its
kickstand, got my covered cup with the water in it, found
her gravesite and sat down with her.

It was so quiet.

Just me. And my mother.

I poured the cocaine into the cooker and added a little
water. I mixed it up and drew it into the syringe. *Tap, tap,
tap.* The moon was almost full. I put the needle point into
my vein. I pushed home the plunger. The cocaine went
into my brain and . . . there were a ton of stars in the sky.

Sssssssssssssssshhhhhhhhhhhhhhhhhhhh . . . •

When cocaine hydrochloride hits your mind in that kind
of stillness, all the little monsters that have been quiet for
so long come alive in your own private, little delusion. You
see men coming out of the bushes! over there! by that little
group of tombstones on the side! You see their flashlight
beams moving along the grass! Searching for you! making
skipping, jerking movements in the turf! But when you go
over there to check, they've all moved away. They're gone.
And when you come back to the grave and inject still more
cocaine hydrochloride you jump because small worms start

to crawl out of the dirt. They come up out of the damp earth you're sitting on! The moist, dewy death ground! They slither onto your lap and scare the shit out of you! You leap up, but when you brush them off... they're gone, too. Vanished. Your heart thuds. You sweat.

And all you hear is your breath rushing in... and out... in... and out... in...

It's like a typhoon in your chest.

And it's all you hear.

It's all you hear except for the twigs cracking under his feet behind that tree! Over there! But he's not really there either. No one is. Not even the police car you see pulling into the driveway to come and get you! The red and blue whirling lights that seem to be swallowing you alive! You hear their tires crunching on the gravel in back of you! And you RUN! But it's just the cocaine hydrochloride.

Nobody's there.

It's just the delusion in your mind. The psychosis.

And they all just leave you there. Alone, with your cocaine, and your water cup, and your syringe, and your cooker, and your motorcycle, and your insanity. And your dead mother's grave.

Sssssssshhhhhhhhhhh...

Such silent madness.

▲ ▼ ▲

I worked Wednesday, Thursday, Friday, and Saturday nights at the nightclub. Four nights. Seven in the evening until five or six in the morning. In the remaining hours of the day, when I wasn't injecting heroin and cocaine or swallowing handfuls of pills, I did projects around the house. I cut down trees in the back yard with my neighbor's chain saw; I re-painted the kitchen and one of the upstairs bedrooms; I re-surfaced the driveway, planted flowers in the front yard, seeded the lawn, and hung a door between the living room and the den in order to section it off as a home office. To work out of. At *what* I didn't know, but I made the room my home office nonetheless. I think perhaps I knew I wasn't going to last much longer in the bartending profession. (And fixing things around the house is just a manifestation of denial. It's a last ditch effort on the addict's part to make his life look like an Ozzie And Harriet episode when in reality his life is crumbling. *Look honey, see what I did with the trees out back that were obstructing our view, and the walls of the upstairs bathroom? See? I told you I was okay.*)

I was outside in the driveway one afternoon sanding white paint off the front door. The door was off its frame and on two sawhorses at the far end of the driveway. I was sanding it down with my Black and Decker electric sander and trying to keep from breathing in too much sawdust, when Suzanne pulled her Nissan into the driveway.

I looked up as she stepped out of the car and noticed she was wearing a black business suit, not her usual working attire.

"Hi, hon!" I said, turning off the sander. "How's it going?" I set the sander down on a corner of the door. "How was work, babe?"

"You're going into a hospital," she said. Cold.

She shut the door to her Nissan.

"What?" I blurted. It was my turn to play stupid.

She's been talking to somebody. Probably her stupid therapist, or one of her fucking know-it-all friends! Somebody put her up to this.

"What do you mean I'm 'going into a hospital'? What are you talking about, Suzanne?"

"Just what I said." She looked back into her car as

though she'd left something on the front seat. She turned back and glared. "You're going into a rehab. Tomorrow if possible."

She's so calm about this. So nonchalant.

Lemmee tell ya something here, Buck-O. This bitch doesn't understand jack shit about . . .

She said, "If you don't, I'm leaving." She raised her eyebrows, waited a moment and said, "Well?"

She stood next to her Nissan with one arm on the roof and the other arm propped against her waist, bent at the elbow, hand on hip. Her eyes were flat, and her face expressionless. She didn't smile. She didn't cry. And she didn't drum her fingers on the roof waiting for my reply. She simply stated her ultimatum and then stood there regarding me in the late afternoon sun.

"Shit, Suzanne . . . ," I mumbled.

I ran my fingers through my hair and wiped the sweat off the back of my neck. I took a deep breath, let it out, and slowly shook my head. The doctor scams, the prescription games, the surgical procedures, the broken bones, the doctors' examinations, the mounting bills I couldn't pay because I was spending my thousand dollars a week up on Boot Hill, my ridiculous facade for a marriage, my rotten prospects for getting any kind of work other than a lousy job tending bar till all hours of the morning, and the retched fact that when I tried to get myself *off* prescription narcotics, I wound up sticking a needle full of heroin and cocaine into my arm anyway! I had tried to give up the pills and I had wound up shooting dope again *anyway!*

I was the jack rabbit in the headlamps once again.

My mind screamed. *I BEAT THIS THING ONCE! I ALREADY DID THIS!*

What's wrong, Buck-O? You're still the best husband and . . .

I thought about my family, my friends, and I thought

about the counselors at the clinic who'd helped me to conquer this once and for all. I thought about the years of hard work and the effort I had put into pulling my life back together.

But I make a lot of MONEY! I married a NICE GIRL! My CREDIT! My CARS! What about all the HARD WORK I've been doing these last five years? WHAT THE FUCK WAS ALL THAT FOR? So I can wind up at twenty-eight years old with a needle hanging out of my vein again and have to go into AN-OTHER rehab? ANOTHER ONE? SIX YEARS LATER?

What's the matter, Buck-O? It's not like you're shooting dope or anything like that . . .

WHAT THE FUCK IS WRONG WITH ME.???

"All right, Suzanne," I said. "I'll go."

"How do you wanna work this thing?"

"C'mon," she said.

She put her arm around me. She led me up the stairs and into the house to work out the logistics for my second full-term hospitalization, and my *sixth* try, at freeing myself from this shit once and for all.

THIRTEEN

GOING UP THE RIVER

Spruce Park Rehabilitation Center is a chemical dependency treatment facility in the northwest corner of New York State. When I called the day before, the woman described it by saying they offered detoxification for narcotic addiction and a twenty-eight day in-patient program for treatment of my problem. She explained their program as consisting of patient groups, lectures by the staff, educational classes twice a day, individual counseling with a qualified drug and alcohol counselor, and support from twelve-step fellowships. During my free time, she explained, I would be welcome to use the olympic sized pool, the fully equipped gymnasium, the steam room, and the sauna, or I could walk around the beautiful thirty-five acres on which the Center was set. The woman on the phone told me the staff of caring professionals would do everything possible to help me overcome my problem. She told me to dress casually, to pack comfortable clothing like jeans and sweats and sneakers, to bring a bathing suit for the pool, and to bring any personal items I thought might enhance my stay. She told me not to bring anything suggestive of drugs or alcohol and definitely not to bring chemicals into the facility. Not only would my stay at the Center be terminated if I tried that stunt, she said, but also, they'd have my butt thrown into the nearest slammer. And after remembering Nick and his little episode years ago at Hallmarke, I didn't think hiding a couple of quarters of heroin in my suitcase a particularly bright idea.

I asked Suzanne for a hundred dollars the morning before we left.

"For what?" she asked.

"If I don't fix, Suzanne, I'm gonna get sick. You want me getting sick all over your car?"

She gave me the hundred dollars. And I fixed.

It was a five hour drive to Spruce Park. Suzanne gripped onto the wheel, alternating between looking like she wanted to cry and looking like she wanted to kill me. I just nodded from the six bags of dope.

The intake counselor saw us right away. Suzanne wrote out a check for two thousand dollars, presented it to the intake counselor along with the appropriate insurance forms, and signed the paper guaranteeing the balance of nine thousand dollars should the insurance company decide not to pay for my treatment. The intake counselor said, "Why don't you say goodbye to him now? We want to get him upstairs as soon as possible."

Suzanne sat in the chair next to me; we both sat at the desk, facing the intake counselor. Then Suzanne turned to face me and tried to say goodbye. She was crying. A month short of her first wedding anniversary and here she was writing out a two thousand dollar check for her husband so he could go into treatment for being a drug addict. I think she was on auto pilot.

How does a woman do that? How does a woman marry a man—a man she believes with all her heart is a good man, an honest man, a man with whom she's going to spend the rest of her life, hopefully happily—and less than a year later drive five hours to take him to a drug treatment center and write out a check for two thousand dollars when she gets there? How does a woman do something like that? I can only imagine what must have been going through Suzanne's mind then.

She cried and sniveled, but she kept her chin up. With a courageous expression, she said in effect, "Don't worry. You're going to be okay. We're going to get through this. I could fucking kill you for what you're doing to yourself and me, but we're going to make it."

Still, it was hard for her to face me.

Through the tears, Suzanne and I parted for twenty-eight days. She dried her eyes, kissed me goodbye, and gave me a hug, and I watched as she went through the door, got into her car, and started the five hour return trip home. Suzanne was a courageous woman, though at the time I was simply too stoned to see.

I'm sorry, Suzanne.

An intake counselor walked me up to the detoxification floor. I didn't get sick; I didn't go into withdrawal that day; I didn't get sick the following day. I was laughing, eating, and making friends with some of the others.

Maybe I'm gonna get over this time. Maybe my habit isn't really all that bad.

I went to dinner on my second night there, had a big meal, and then . . . I went into labor.

With the rats.

It's time to pay the piper, Adam.

On my second night at Spruce Park, just as I was starting to know I was going to get sick and not avoid the withdrawal symptoms, the evening nurse came in and said, "Adam, roll over." She nudged me gently. I had been nodding off, hoping I could get a little sleep before I got *really* sick. I looked up. She was standing over me with a three cc. syringe in her hand.

"Do WHAT?" I exclaimed.

"Roll over, Adam," she repeated. "I have to give you a vitamin booster. It's less painful if I give it to you in your butt." This was the supreme irony.

I said, "Why don't you just give the needle to me? Fifty bucks says I can hit the vein better than you."

She laughed. "Adam, it's only a vitamin B-12 booster. It's nothing you'd enjoy." She held the syringe over me. "Now where do you want it?" I rolled up the sleeve on my sweaty tee shirt. "It's going to hurt you more if I give it to you in your arm." I told her to do it there anyway. "Okay." she said.

"YEOWWW!" I screamed, "Wha'da you got in there? Borax?"

She laughed, maybe with a little glee that said *I told you so*! She said, "Awww, there, there widdle baby." She rubbed the site with an alcohol swab. "Adam? How come you junkies can stick yourselves over and over and over again with heroin and cocaine and junk like that, but when you have to get an eentsy weentsy vitamin booster you scream bloody murder? Why is that, Adam?"

"I don't know," I said, rubbing my shoulder and sticking out my lower lip. "I guess it just hurts less if you do it to yourself!"

We laughed together a little longer. She told me I was going to be all right.

And that was the most fun I had at Spruce Park.

I was in acute withdrawal for four days, and Spruce Park

doesn't believe in Methadone for withdrawing dopefiends. Well, maybe they believe in it—they just don't use it. Phenobarbital (a barbiturate) and clonodine (an anti-hypertensive) are used to ameliorate narcotic withdrawal symptoms, leaving the patient feeling as though his brain has been removed from his skull and replaced with three-month-old oatmeal. Sorry. But Spruce Park did not make it to my list of The Top Ten Most Cushy Detoxes.

▲ ▼ ▲

There is a critical difference between a *hospital* for chemical dependency and a *rehab* for chemical dependency. The former consists of things like group therapy with board certified psychiatrists, therapeutic volleyball tournaments, community grievance meetings between patients and staff, and long, long talks underneath the big oak in the front lawn with your therapist. The latter is more like to a twenty eight-day stint at Fort Bragg. Whatever happened to art therapy?

Wake-up for me was five-thirty each morning. My job was to make the coffee, feed the plants, open the window blinds, or anything else they could dream up to get me out of bed at that ungodly hour. I suppose I was special though: the other residents were allowed to sleep until six.

As patients at Spruce Park, we weren't allowed to so much as think of lying or sitting on our beds between the hours of 6:00 A.M. and 10:00 P.M. Taking a break or resting during the day was *verboten*. We were allowed to smoke only when the staff told us we could; we had to walk through the halls without talking; and we had to attend two lectures a day, one in the morning and one in the afternoon, on different aspects of our disease. We were ordered to bring a notebook and pencil to these lectures and to take notes. Attendance three times a week at some exercise related activity was mandatory (Spruce Park had a four man team of drill sergeants, er, *instructors*, for this). We had to go to Feelings Group, Medical Consequences Group, Fourth-Step Group, Recovering At Home Group, Confrontation Group, Men's And Women's Group (separately, of course), and we had to attend those stupid twelve-step meetings held in the auditorium. We were given a battery of psychological tests within our first week there, including my own personal favorite, the five hundred and sixty-six word Minnesota Multi-Phasic Personality Inventory.

Suzanne came back up the following weekend, as did the wives, husbands, sons, daughters, mothers, fathers, best friends, aunts and uncles of the other clients, for Family Weekend. It was a weekend of thrills and chills, lectures and therapy sessions, classes and group exercises designed to educate and inform the client *and* the family members that alcoholism and chemical dependency are *diseases*— chronic, progressive, and, if left untreated, *fatal* diseases.

Family Weekend was intense. The counselors packed as much information as they could into the forty-eight hours regarding the facts about substance abuse, twelve-step recovery for those with the disease, continued care following hospitalization, and the need for support systems at home. The staff tried to bash it through our thick skulls that although it was a tough disease to have, there was hope for the chemically dependent. That yes, it was a disease, like diabetes or cancer, and it was really a bitch, but that there was *hope*. With treatment, education, and support for the rest of our lives, they said, we could learn to be useful, happy people and live with our disease. It *is* possible, they told us. Even for the lowliest of dopefiends.

Suzanne stayed the entire weekend at a nearby hotel,

came to all the classes, lectures and exercises, and her hope
grew. She went home after Family Weekend smiling.

And if all this—Family Weekends and classes and lectures and taking notes and going to the gym and attending
meetings and making the coffee and watering the plants—
wasn't enough to occupy my time and keep my mind off
using drugs and alcohol during my stay at Spruce Park, I
had to meet with my caseworker three times a week. At *her*
convenience.

Catherine Burke was my caseworker. She was a short
woman, maybe five feet five if that, with light blonde curly
hair. She was somewhat wide in the glide, and walked
around the halls of Spruce Park in a manner that said if she
didn't reach her destination in the next three seconds the
orbit of the Earth would cease. Immediately. When Catherine Burke came into a hallway, the Red Sea parted.

"Adam?" she said, one morning after I'd been there a
little over a week. "Will you please come to my office at
three o'clock this afternoon?"

"Okay," I said, trembling. I was in deep shit this time.

▲ ▼ ▲

A psycho-social evaluation is the clinician's way of getting a
fairly complete history of his or her client. It covers areas of
family relationships, peer influences, sexual activity, education, legal involvement, and developmental milestones,
and it gives a fairly clear picture of the client's drug and alcohol involvement. It gives the clinician names, dates,
places, and other pertinent information, and it is generally
the first thing one does with a caseworker when one goes in
for treatment of chemical dependency.

"Let's get started here, Adam, shall we?" Catherine
Burke asked, opening her notebook and placing it on her

not so tiny lap. She took out a pen and began. "When were you born, Adam?" *Piece of cake.* "Brothers? Sisters? Hometown? Parent's names?" *This is a breeze.* "How long have you been married, Adam?"

"Almost a year," I told her.

"Are your parents still alive?"

I told Catherine Burke my mother had died four years previous of diabetic complications and coronary heart failure. She asked about my relationships with my mother, my father, and my two older brothers. I told her that my mother and I were extremely close, that I was her favorite, and that when she was alive we had a very warm and giving relationship. Her death was a blow to me, I said, but in time I'd come to accept it. My father currently lived in Arizona with one of my brothers, and I explained that even though we had our share of father-son, brother-brother crap, I thought our relationships were all right. I wasn't all that close with my eldest brother, but still, I told her, I supposed we could count on each other when the chips were down. All in all, I said, I thought my family was a pretty good one. Along with my wife, everyone was quite worried about how I was going to overcome my problem with heroin, cocaine, pills.

"What was it like for you when you were growing up, Adam? At home? Did you enjoy school? Did you make friends easily?"

"I guess it was okay, Cathy. I suppose I did all right in school when I was a kid. I liked to goof around though, you know, class clown stuff and all?" She wrote something down in her notebook. "I had a couple of friends. The usual. I remember my mom and dad would take us on vacation a couple of times a year. We went away to places like Washington, D.C. and Cape Kennedy, and they took us to a lot of plays, museums, concerts and stuff like that. I guess they wanted to introduce us to cultural things while we were kids. It was okay growing up I guess..." I stopped for a second. "But I always felt a little..."

"What, Adam?"

"Well, I don't know. I just felt a little...different. You know what I mean?"

"Yes," she said. "I know what you mean." She wrote something in her book again.

I didn't think I should bring up the thing I did when I was nine; I thought I'd save that for a later time in a group meeting when I didn't have anything better to talk about.

"Adam, when did you first begin to use drugs and alcohol?"

"I think I was about nine or ten, Cathy. Yea. I smoked my first joint when I was in the fifth grade."

"Then what happened, Adam?"

I almost burst out laughing. "Well, I don't know! I guess I just kept on using them! Know what I mean?"

"Yes, Adam, I know what you mean." She continued to ask me questions while she wrote notations in her black notebook. "So you continued to use marijuana into junior high school?" I nodded. "In school?" Yup. "What happened after that, Adam?"

"Well, I dunno, I guess I started messing around with other stuff, you know? Downs, hash, a little beer here and there, acid. You know, the usual stuff. But it never really did me any harm, Cath! I always managed to get good grades in school and keep up with things."

"I see," she said. "Go on, Adam."

"I used a lot of drugs in high school, but one day, I just stopped. I was in the tenth grade, I didn't like doing it anymore. I was too stoned all the time, so I gave it up. I kept drinking beer and stuff, but I stopped taking drugs. Then I went away to college and I did pretty well there too."

"I see." She wrote another note in the book. "When did you become sexually active, Adam?"

They always pry into this shit, don't they?

"Seventeen..." I said. "...with my high school sweetheart."

"I see," she said.

Again with the "I see's"! I wish somebody would show me!

"So you began to use drugs in elementary school. You experimented with different kinds including alcohol. Your family life and friendships were 'all right.' You stopped using drugs for a period of time in high school, but you kept on drinking. You became sexually active at seventeen. You consider yourself 'sexually normal.' And then you went off to college." I nodded. "When did you start using heroin and cocaine?"

Shit...

"Well," I began, "I was going to college at the time. I was really doing well there. I had a three-point-eight grade point average, but I messed up my back at some point. The doctors gave me pain killers for the pain...and...well, I dunno...I guess I just wanted something stronger, you know?"

"No," she said, "I don't know. What do you mean?"

Here we go...

"I was working as a mental health worker in a psychiatric hospital..." She wrote in her notebook again. *How many times have I told THIS story?* "...and I met a junkie there who taught me about shooting dope." Another notation. "I didn't think it was any big deal at first, but I guess it just got the better of me, you know? Before I knew it I got addicted to it and had to come home and get some help."

"So you never finished college?"

I shook my head. "I have ninety-four credits towards my B.A."

"Adam, you said you 'came home to get some help.' What kind of help?"

Christ. . . .

"I went to a hospital."

"When?"

"When I was twenty-two."

"A drug and alcohol hospital?"

"Yes."

She looked at me. "So you've been through this be-fore?"

"Uh huh."

"Adam, what's different for you this time?"

That was a tough one.

I said, "I dunno, Cath. I just fucked up. I quit this stuff before." She raised her eyebrows. "When I got out of that first hospital, I went back on drugs for another year or so. It really kicked my ass! I went to a clinic, cleaned up my act, and I didn't touch any drugs for almost two years, Cath! I don't know what happened to me! I was going along just fine, things were looking real good in my life and then BOOM! I got hit with a couple of injuries, I took a few pain killers, and before I knew what was happening I'm shoot-ing dope again!" I tossed my hands up in the air. "I just don't know what the fuck happened!"

"I see," she said again.

I wished I could!

"Do you drink a lot, Adam?" she asked.

I smiled. Through the grin I said, "Well yea, Cath. I drink. I don't know about "a lot" though. I mean, I work in a bar. Yea, I suppose I have a couple now and then."

She went to her book again. "What's 'a couple', Adam?"

I didn't follow her. "You know *a couple!* Two. Maybe three. I dunno, Cath."

She stopped writing, looked at me and said, "You say that a lot."

"What?"

"You say you 'don't know' a lot."

"Well I *don't*, Cath!"

"Okay, Adam." She took a moment to write some more.

"Look Cath, I'm not an alcoholic or anything like that! I just have a couple of drinks once in a while. It's not like I have a drinking problem, if that's what you're trying to get at."

"No?" she asked.

"No," I said. I was going to hold to my guns on this one. I said, "I drink when I want to. If I don't want to—I don't drink. I go out sometimes and I order soda, Cath! It's not like I have to drink!"

"No?" she asked innocently.

"What's the big deal? I have a couple of drinks when I want! I don't have any DWI's, and I don't get drunk all the time..."

Whoooooops! Slip of the tongue there, Buck-O?

"You get 'drunk,' Adam?" she asked.

"Well, yea, sometimes. But look Cath, I don't really care about a little drinking now and then. I don't have a problem with my drinking. Can we just..."

"You don't?" she asked.

"Huh? No! I don't! I'm not worried about my drinking! I've got much bigger..."

"Maybe you should be, Adam," she suggested. Then she dropped that particular line of questioning. I still didn't get what she was driving at.

She turned the page and asked, "Do you have any legal problems? Have you ever been arrested for possession or anything like that? Are you on probation?" I shook my head. "You've never been in jail then?"

"No. Nothing like that."

I said, "I got caught about five years ago for impersonating a physician, but they wiped my record clean. They have this accelerated probation thing where I live. My family got a lawyer, I got four months probation, and when it was done they erased it. It's like I never got arrested. My record's clean."

Catherine Burke shook her head. She said, "So all you have is a problem with heroin and cocaine, right Adam?" I nodded. "Can you think of anything else in your life that we can help you with while you're here?"

I had to think about that for a moment. I said, "I dunno. Maybe some more marriage counseling for me and my wife or something?"

"Is there anything else, Adam?" Do you have any other issues we can help you with?"

"I don't know, Cath. I've had a lot of therapy; I've been trying to get my shit together for a long time now. I've worked on a lot of my crap in the last few years."

"Okay, Adam," she said. She put the pen with which she'd been writing behind her ear, and she sat back in her chair. She folded her hands in her lap, smiled, and then asked me, "Adam, why did you come into treatment? What do you want out of this?" She opened up her palms like she was saying, "Go for it."

I took in a deep breath and slowly exhaled. I said, "Cath, you guys gotta help me. I just don't know what happened! I was doing pretty well there for a couple of years. Things looked good. I was doing all right, and the next thing I know I'm shooting dope again and I wind up here!" I shook my head. I could feel tears welling in my eyes. "I'm gonna lose my job. Suzanne's gonna leave me! All of a sudden everything's going right down the tubes, and I can't straighten out! I just can't seem to stop myself! I don't know what's wrong with me! All I know is I had to go away somewhere and get some help," I sniveled.

The room was quiet.

She moved a little closer to me, shuffling her chair along the floor. Catherine Burke smiled and nodded as though she understood.

She said, "You know something, Adam?" I looked at her through my teary eyes. She soothed me with her smile and nodded slowly. Warmly, she continued, "You're a nice guy." She passed me her box of Kleenex and I wiped my nose. "You know, I don't get it either." She shook her head in confusion. "I just don't get it. You come from a nice family. Your parents loved you. They did all they could to help you. You and your mother had a 'very special' relationship. I just don't understand it either, Adam."

Finally!

"You've always had plenty of money. You're college educated."

I began to smile again; the tears were drying.

"You've worked in this field before at a psychiatric hospital. You understand about drug addiction. You have a good job, where you make good money. You just married the girl of your dreams. Everybody loves you and wants to support you. I just don't get it either, Adam."

Thank you, thank you, thank you.

"You really are a nice guy." She paused.

And then there was deathly silence in her office. Catherine Burke stopped smiling. The air seemed to hang like it was made of concrete.

She dropped the smile she'd had on her face, moved to within two inches of mine and unloaded, "And you're a *fucking junkie?* You're a fucking junkie and a *drunk* to boot?"

Like a rock. Catherine Burke looked like she wanted to spit. Or vomit maybe.

She said, "You're a fucking mess, Adam! Look at yourself! You've been strung out on one thing or another since

you were nine years old." I was still trying to get out from
underneath the load of bricks she'd dropped. "They
should have locked you away a long time ago. You've never
been in jail? How did you manage that?"

Clever?

She said, "It's a miracle you're even still alive. You're
family and friends enable the shit out of you! Every time
you get into trouble somebody bails you out! You've been
getting over, getting around, avoiding any kind of conse-
quence for your chemical abuse for a long time, Adam, and
it's not going to last much longer!" She looked in amazement at me. "You forged your own prescriptions? That's a
fucking felony, Adam!"

"I . . ."

"Shut up, Adam. I don't wanna hear it. You think pretending you're a doctor is normal? You think everyone
walks around doing that? You think you're any different
from a junkie in the streets, just because you get doctors to
give you pills and you call in your own prescriptions?"

Well, as a matter of fact, I . . .

She waved me off. "Adam?" she said, "You're gonna
die. Do you hear me? If you don't cut this shit out *right now*,
you're just gonna die. Your wife? Your home? Your money?
Your job? You're gonna lose it all, Adam. And then you're
just gonna die." She sat back in her chair and caught her
breath. She looked out the office window for a few minutes, gaining composure. I said nothing.

"Adam? You're in a mess of shit." And she screamed,
"*WAKE THE FUCK UP!*" She threw her notebook onto
the desk. She threatened: "This is going to be really hard
for you. You're not going to like it here. You're so full of
fucking shit, Adam . . ." she trailed off in disgust. "But it's
not going to work here; you picked the wrong place to try
and run your con games." She leaned in for the *coup de*

grâce: "Now get the fuck out of my office," she said.

She offered something else about not wanting to look at my face, and I got out of the chair and left.

And all I could think about for the next twenty-eight days were jack rabbits, headlamps, and the lights that were screaming towards me from the on-coming Mack Truck.

▲ ▼ ▲

The question sometimes comes up, why do women get pregnant again after the first time? After the pain, the nausea, the swollen ankles, the backaches? Not to mention the actual pain of giving birth and trying to pass something the size of a basketball through an opening designed only to allow a golf ball? Why do women go through that all over again?

They forget.

They forget how much pain is involved. They forget their screams to the OB-GYN for another shot of Demerol, and they forget telling their husbands, *You're gonna rue the day you ever decided to do this to me you son of a bitch!*

Girls just forget. They want to have another baby. The first one is really cute, they forget how intense the pain was, and they go off the pill. Wanting the baby supersedes the pain that goes along with it.

It's the same thing with junkies. They forget how bad it really is out there. As soon as they start feeling the slightest bit better, as soon as the withdrawal passes and the vomiting stops, as soon as they're done with the sweats and the chills and the needing to wrap themselves with a comforter in August, they just forget. They want to get high again, and they forget that along with getting high comes *pain*.

That's how I could say to my caseworker, "I don't know what happened! All of a sudden I was. . . . "

I just forgot about the pain, that's all. And I couldn't re-member why the hell I ever thought shooting dope was such a bad idea in the first place.

FOURTEEN

SAY HELLO TO DEATH

I learned two things in Spruce Park Rehabilitation Center. First, I learned that for the last nine years of my life I had been paying too much for my heroin. New York Heroin costs ten dollars a bag. If you buy ten bags together, you get what's called a "bundle." A bundle comes wrapped up in a neat little package with a rubber band around the ten small bags. No deals. Just ten bucks a bag. Heroin in Connecticut is twenty dollars a bag. I learned that bit of information from another junkie at Spruce Park.

The second thing I learned at Spruce Park was that I really was a junkie. A full-blown, out of my fucking skull, junkie. And that I learned just by picking up the needle again. And it only took forty-eight hours after my release from the facility to figure that out. Two days.

I went back to Suzanne, and we had a homecoming. Suzanne took me out to dinner at a nice restaurant—neither one of us drank—and though it was tenuous and strained after not being together for twenty-eight days, we somehow managed to make conversation, say prayers for the prospects of a continued sober life, and make plans to get me back on my feet the following morning.

The next day I went out and got a job slicing meat in a local deli. The owner was an old friend, only too willing to help a down-and-out junkie fresh out of rehab.

And I swear to you when I left that deli after my second day of work, I had full intentions of going home to Suzanne, having dinner with her, telling her about my day at the job and going to a meeting afterwards. I swear to you that in my mind, that's exactly what I was going to go home and do.

But when I reached my car outside in the parking lot and got in to drive home, my brain had other ideas. Something up there broke! Somewhere between the front door to that deli and the door to my car, something gave way. It was like the rubber band that had held all the pieces of my mind together, keeping them secure, holding them together for so long, just popped apart—and my brain shattered into a million little disconnected synapses. Everything screamed around inside my skull, and the bones up there—the bones that were supposed to be holding my mind together and preventing my brains from leaking out my ears onto the floor shattered too. There was no movie projector. No Best Of Collection. All that was left was the bag. And my car went to Boot Hill, like it had a mind of its own. Trying to turn away would have been like attempting to stop an oncoming freight train by holding out my arm.

I lost it. Big time.

I got beat for a hundred dollars at The Barbecue Palace. Right after the sour deal, a black man came over and pulled me aside into a doorway. He looked around to make sure no one else was listening. It was Ted. He didn't talk directly at me, but whispered his offer to the air.

He said, "How come you don't go to New York, man? You spend too much money down here to let these assholes keep beating you like this." He faced me now and smiled.

So what the fuck are you being so generous for?

"You wanna take me down?" I asked.

"Sure, man. I'll go."

"What's in it for you?" I asked.

"I got nothin better to do," he said. "'Sides, I see you down here all the time. You spend a lot of money. I could get you good shit for your money in the Bronx, but I got no way of gettin down there. And I thought for the favor... you know... you'd gimmee a little something. Know what I mean?"

"Yea," I said. I pulled him by his coat collar and we headed for the Bronx. "I know what you mean."

If I had to go to a place where Colombians held an Uzi in my face while I bought my dope, or if I had to go to a neighborhood where junkies wound up dead in a dumpster out back from an overdose in the shooting gallery three floors up, so be it. The risk wasn't a factor anymore.

There were no "factors" anymore.

Where once I had been going to college, writing research papers, helping the professor with his research on the biogenic amine hypothesis of schizophrenia and giving lectures to the freshmen class, there was now only my single-minded determination for the bag of heroin. At any price.

Where once I'd been an ex-addict, working out in the gym and pumping up my body to its maximum potential, doing ten-hour shifts behind the bar and flexing my muscles for the admiring crowd, I was now only a corpse needing to feed. It wasn't a joke. The fun was gone. And the good times were gone too.

Now I was a junkie. Now it owned me. And all it took was one injection.

For twenty years drugs and alcohol had been my friends. They had been my lover, my companion, my confidant and my saving grace. They had shown me how to have a good time that day, how to enjoy life to the fullest, how to conquer my feelings and how to take the world by storm. But now they were going to show me how to die.

And Hunt's Point Avenue was the place to do it.

▲ ▼ ▲

Ted hadn't been down to The Avenue in a couple of years and it took him a little while to get his bearings. We drove around for a while looking, Ted spotted somebody, and we pulled over to a liquor store on the corner. Ted got out and asked a Puerto Rican guy if he knew where to get any dope. The Hispanic was about twenty-five years old, rather muscled and well built, and not really the kind I thought would be involved in the heroin trade. The Hispanic was just a guy shoveling snow on a November afternoon, but like I said before, junkies smell other junkies.

"He'll do it for us," Ted said. "But he's gonna want a couple of bags for the favor." I looked at the Puerto Rican. He smiled at me.

His teeth are incredibly white and straight for a junkie.

"That's okay," I said. Ted got into the back of the car and the Hispanic got into the passenger's seat in front.

"Just pull the car over here and wait," the Puerto Rican instructed. He pointed to a space on Hunt's Point Avenue in front of a video arcade, about halfway between two intersections. Ted and the Puerto Rican got out of the car and talked. The Puerto Rican looked at me through the open window and said, "You're not a cop or nothing, are you?"

"No," I said. "I ain't a cop."

"Good." And he continued to talk with Ted.

Ted opened the passenger's side door and got in with

me. The Puerto Rican went to the video arcade store and stood outside.

Ted said, "Whad'da you want, man? He's cool. We can trust him."

I gave Ted three hundred dollars. "Get me two bundles, and get me a hundred dollar piece of cocaine."

Ted got out of the car with my money.

I watched the two of them walk down the sidewalk, past the arcade, a deli, and a furniture store, and I watched them disappear around a corner and down a side street.

I sat in my Firebird and wondered if I was getting beat again.

If that son of a bitch takes me for my money, I'll kill him. I'll find out where he fucking lives, and I'll fucking kill him. I swear to God. I'll get a gun, and I'll just shoot him in his fucking face if he beats me for my three hundred dollars.

I waited.

Ten minutes. Twenty.

I watched the guys on the corner running their hustle, yelling at the people who drove by in their cars.

Half an hour.

If he beats me, I swear to fucking God I'll. . . .

I watched a group of punks standing next to a steel fence. I watched them take money and give money, and pass little things I couldn't see between their greasy hands. I watched a couple of hookers try and get their Johns; and I watched people pull up in new Chevrolet Camaros and Cadillac Sevilles, go into the building there on the corner, and come back out five or ten minutes later with just what they'd come down here for: heroin. Ten bucks a bag. Ten bags in a bundle.

Thirty-five minutes.

If he tries to beat me I'm gonna fucking. . . .

Ted came back to my car and got in on the passenger's side.

"How'd it go?" I asked him.

His breath was racing in and out of his chest like he'd been running from somebody. He held out his fist over my hand and dropped two small packages into my palm. In my hand were two little bundles, each with ten glassine envelopes of heroin wrapped up with a tiny blue rubber band. I curled my fingers around the packages. It felt like I held God Almighty in the palm of my hand.

"I gotta get the coke from another guy," Ted said. "I gotta go around the corner for it." His breath was still racing. "Gimmee a couple of bags for the Puerto Rican."

I peeled two envelopes out of the package. "Sure." I put two little envelopes that had ROMEO AND JULIET stamped in ink on them into Ted's hands (dope dealers always give names to their product: TANGO AND CASH, WILD SIDE, SIX BANGER, LUV STUFF), and I put the other eighteen into the inside pocket of my overcoat. "Make sure the coke is good," I told Ted.

He smiled. "It's *all* good down here," he said and got out of the car.

"Hey Ted!" I yelled. "Get me some works, too!"

"Yea. . . ."

And he went around another corner to get the cocaine.

Like a fucking department store. Just put in your order, pay the man over here, and pick up your merchandise over there at the counter. Like a fucking Caldor Department Store.

▲ ▼ ▲

Ted returned in less than ten minutes. In his hand he held four packages of aluminum foil. Each had been folded over lengthwise, and then again at the sides, the side folds being held together with staples. The packets each looked like they contained something roughly the size of a large marble. *Christ! This is how they sell cocaine down here?*

"How is it?" I asked.

"You wanna check it out, man?"

I nodded.

Ted put a finger nail underneath one of the staples and pried it off. He peeled apart the aluminum foil of one of the packages, opened the fold, and . . .

. . . and inside the foil was a goddamned golf ball of Peruvian rock cocaine. It was the biggest piece of cocaine I'd ever seen in my entire life.

"Let's get outta here," he said. I put the car in gear and we drove off down The Avenue.

My previous experience with cocaine had been a paltry amount of white powder in a little piece of tin foil from the fellas in my hometown. On Hunt's Point I had a fucking golf ball. In Connecticut, sometimes I got beat with baking soda, Mannitol (a diuretic), or Borax for my fifty dollars. On The Avenue the cocaine was on.

Ted got the cocaine from The Old Jew. The Old Jew sat in a beat up Ford on one of the side streets off Hunt's Point Avenue and sold cocaine all day. He was sixty or sixty-five years old and The Old Jew sat in his car all day selling cocaine from a brown paper bag he kept underneath the front seat. No one ever said "Boo!" to him. Ted went up to the car window and paid The Old Jew, who went into his brown paper bag and pulled out Ted's order.

"He's got the best shit down here," Ted muttered.

We snorted one packet on the highway driving home. In Connecticut, I gave Ted another one for him and his girlfriend. It seemed a small price to pay. I still had two packages left for the vein in my arm.

▲ ▼ ▲

I maxed-out all my credit cards, taking cash advances for thousands of dollars. I hocked everything I owned. I proba-

bly got together around twenty grand. And then I went to
Hunt's Point Avenue for the run of my life.

I went insane.

Ted and I went down every day or every other day, depending on our score. We never got beat. We never got bad
product. All we ever got were golf ball chunks of cocaine
and ten bag bundles of ROMEO AND JULIET.

In preceding years, I had maintained my habit in Connecticut on three or four bags of P-Dope a day. Now, with
Ted, I was injecting upwards of twenty and thirty bags a
day, as well as an eighth of an ounce of cocaine for the rush
(and an eighth of an ounce is a shit-load of blow).

I was seething.

I needed a wake-up now. I needed a syringe filled with
heroin waiting for me each morning when I awoke. My
body needed it. I prepared it the night before and left it for
the morning in the top drawer of my dresser next to the
bed. If I got stupid or greedy and I didn't leave myself the
shot, well, I just paid the price for being a junkie, that's all.

I quit my job at the deli after a week, giving Suzanne
some bullshit excuse about how I'd go look for another one.
I got up in the mornings, like a good little husband, and
pretended. As soon as she was out of sight and in the bathroom getting ready, I reached over to my nightstand and
did the shot before I got out of bed. Fuck the tourniquet.
Fuck cooking it up. I just shot it.

If she hung around a little longer than usual and I had to
get off, I just went into the bathroom before she did. No
big deal. I'd shoot up on the toilet with the door locked behind me, and then I'd shower, dress, and go to Ted's.

She never saw me shoot up. She never knew I was dope
sick. And if she ever asked me anything, I just told her it
was nerves, Honey.

She wanted so badly to believe Spruce Park had
worked.

I went to Ted's apartment in the ghetto each morning and sat in his living room with his girlfriend and their five-year-old daughter, while Ted got dressed in the bedroom. "Wheel Of Fortune" blared on the television set. Ted's daughter sat glued to it, holding her dolly between her legs, rocking, while Ted's girlfriend and I discussed the different ways we did our cocaine.

"I ain't never done it wit a needle," she said. "I'm too scared o' that. The coke's you'z gives to Teddy he 'jus cooks up in the kitchen 'an we'ez smokes it together. He shares it wit me. I don't think he's never done it wit a needle neither. We'ez both too scared for that!"

Whatever floats your fucking boat.

I could smell the food behind the garbage pail in the kitchen, the food tucked way up underneath the bottoms of the cabinets. It smelled like it had been there too long. It smelled old, dying. Vanna White turned around another vowel on the tube.

"Ted! C'mon, man! We gotta go!" I yelled over the television's volume.

"I'm coming, man!" He came into the living room with his construction boots in his hands. He sat down into the ratty chair, put the boots on, and laced them up. He looked over at his girlfriend.

"We'll be back in a couple of hours," he said. "The baby need anything?"

"Can you git some milk? And can you git me a pack of Salems?" Ted nodded. He finished lacing his boots. His girlfriend looked at both of us and asked, "You won't forgit about me, will ya?"

Ted looked at me. I nodded. A chunk of cocaine wasn't too much to ask. If Ted wanted to share it with his girlfriend, what the hell did I care. It was *his* business.

My business was with Ted every morning. Seven days a week. Before anything else in my life.

My relationship with Ted, his girlfriend, and their five-year-old daughter ended abruptly two months later when I came down to get Ted one morning and he wasn't there.

"Well, where the fuck is he?" I demanded.

She shrank away from me. "He's off on a job some-where," she said. "He'll be back in a couple of hours. You wanna wait for him inside?"

"No."

"You sure?" she asked. She offered to let me watch some Vanna White with their five year old.

"NO!" I told her again. "Where's he working? Did he say? Did he say where I can get him?"

"Uh uh." She shook her head.

Shit! Now what?

I told her to have Ted give me a call the minute he came home. But I was too sick to wait around.

I went down to The Avenue alone.

The Puerto Rican who'd been copping for Ted was right were we'd left him the previous day. He was standing on the corner with some of his buddies, waiting. I saw him and I pulled my Firebird over to the side and parked. I shut the car down. I jumped out of the car, crossed the street, and walked towards him. He looked a little frightened of me at first. Startled. I wonder what he saw?

"Hey," I said. The Puerto Rican backed up a step. I walked a little slower. "I'm Ted's friend, man." He recognized me. "Can you help me out?"

He smiled and put out his hand. "Oh yea, man! Sure! I can *always* help *you* out!" We both relaxed a little.

"C'mon, man," he said. "Let's talk." And we moved down the block, away from the others where we could be alone and "talk" in private. "What can I do for you?" he asked.

I went all out: "Listen, man, I come down here all the

time. I got a lot of money. If you beat me, it's all you get. You'll be fucked." He shook his head and squinted at me, not understanding. "Get my shit for me and we can work out a deal." His smile returned. I said, "I want three bundles. I'll take care of you when you come back with it." I put three hundred dollars into his hand. "Don't fucking beat me, man!"

He made a contorted face, not understanding my apprehension. He said, "I won't beat you, man! You're a good customer! I'll take care of you anytime. Just come see me." He nodded at the other guys down the block and said, "But don't deal with nobody else down here, all right? They might try and take you off." He pointed across the street at a small, Puerto Rican family store. "You go wait in that deli over there. Go in and make like you're buying a soda or something." He stuffed the money into his pocket. I asked him if the deli was safe. He smiled. "They're cool, man! You just go over there and wait for me. They know what's going down."

He stopped. "Be cool. It's going to take a few minutes to chill out here." He pointed down the street behind us, where two cops were putting a man into the back seat of their cruiser. I must have looked scared because the Puerto Rican got a big grin on his face.

He said, "You worry too much, amigo! Beats. Arrests. It's cool here, man!"

He said "*conjo!*" which translates roughly to "Christ! You white boys can be real fucking assholes when you're out of your element."

He said, "They gotta do that once in a while. They gotta bust *someone!* Gotta make it look good!" He seemed amused. He pointed at the brick tenement on our left. "Ain't nobody gonna hurt The Man inside. He's doing a half a million dollars a day in there! Five Oh (street euphemism for Police Force) ain't gonna touch him! He pays 'em too much!" I nodded. I understood the game. He cautioned, "The cops ain't gonna arrest you, and I ain't gonna beat you. Okay amigo?" I nodded. "You just be cool. Go over there and get a soda, and I'll meet you in a couple of minutes."

"Can you get some coke in there too?" I reached into my pants to get another couple of hundred.

He held out his arm and stopped me. "Lemme get this first," he said. "Then we can talk about the jae-yo."

Ten minutes later, I put thirty envelopes of heroin into my coat pocket right next to my wallet and my credit cards. I bought a soda, paid the man with the contemptuous eyes behind the deli's counter, and I walked back to my car. I gave the Puerto Rican five packets of heroin—sort of as a tip—so he'd know what a good customer I'd be in the future. He got me some "jae-yo" and thanked me for choosing him as my connection.

"I'm out here all the time after eleven," the Puerto Rican said. "You come see me any time, amigo. I always take care of you!" We shook hands on the deal. "I'll see you tomorrow," he said as I was leaving.

Yea, you will see me tomorrow. And every fucking day from now on.

I took my twenty, thirty bag a day habit and my cocaine to boot. . . and I stuck the needle point into my arm.

And for the next two months, I never took it out. Not to breath. Not to eat.

The only time I pulled the syringe out of my vein in the next two months was to reload it.

But trust me on this one: that was the only time.

FIFTEEN

SUICIDE SAL, WHERE ARE YOU NOW?

To Suzanne, Steven, and the dwindling circle of friends who still took the trouble to bother with me, I said nothing of my adventures in the south Bronx. I lied. I led them all to believe that Spruce Park had saved me, that I was sober, that my problems were over, and that pretty soon I'd find a job and be back on my feet. When Suzanne or Steven asked if I was okay, I said "Yes." If they asked, "Are you sure? You're looking kind of funny, Adam," I told them, "Yea. I'm okay. Really."

On Christmas Day, six weeks after my discharge from Spruce Park, I left my house early in the morning telling Suzanne I'd be back in a couple of hours and then we'd open up our presents. I told her I was going to the local soup kitchen where I was going to volunteer a few hours of my time for the homeless in our town, and that as soon as my services were through, I'd be home. Around noon, I said. She told me that was a nice thing to do on Christmas morning, how "unselfish," she thought. She said she'd be waiting for my return and that she'd get Christmas Dinner going while I was out. She gave me a kiss, saying how sweet and noble she thought the idea was.

That night I overdosed—Merry Christmas, everyone— and there was nò more pretending. There was no more trying to tell people I was fine or that I was all right or that I was sober and working with the homeless on Christmas morning. I wasn't, and they knew it. In frustration, they said to me, "Fine, Adam. If you want to kill yourself, go right ahead. If that's really what you want to do, we're not going to try to stop you anymore."

I did thirty bags that day.

At 6:00 P.M. I was already high as a kite. Suzanne made turkey, stuffing, potatoes, beans, gravy, and a cherry pie (my favorite) for desert, and my face almost fell in the plate from the nod.

"What's the matter, honey?" she asked.

"Nothing, babe," I said. "I'm just tired."

At seven o'clock she said she was going out for a while to a meeting (for wives and relatives of addicted people) and that she'd be home around ten.

I told her I was going to a meeting (for the *addicted* people) also.

"Okay," she said, "I'll see you in a couple of hours."

"Okay, honey."

When she closed the door behind her, I cooked up another six bags. I loaded the syringe, tied off my arm, and began to push home the plunger. That's the last thing I remembered.

Suzanne told me later she thought I was dead. She came home a little after nine to find me lying on the couch in the living room. She said she couldn't tell whether or not I was still breathing.

On the coffee table in front of me were the empty heroin bags, the cooker, the butane lighter. The syringe was on the floor, and my brown leather belt was still around the upper part of my biceps. She tried shaking me, pulling me, hitting me, slapping me, picking me up and throwing me back on the sofa, screaming in my ears. Nothing worked. I just lay there. In panic, Suzanne dialed 911. A paramedic said they'd be right over, and told Suzanne to squeeze my ear like she was trying to twist it off my head. It's close to a nerve in the brain, he told her, and sometimes it can rouse a person who's in an overdose.

I guess that's what she finally did, because the first thing I remember when I opened my eyes was a feeling like someone was stabbing a serrated knife into the side of my head.

"Whaaa?!" I screamed.

I could make out Suzanne's silhouette swaying in front of me. The world was cloudy and gray. I knew I was still in the living room. I saw all my garbage on the coffee table, but everything else was fuzzy, blurred. At first, I had no idea what was wrong. It was like time had momentarily frozen. Then it started moving again.

"Looks like we're having a bit of a problem here," Suzanne began, nodding at the coffee table. She folded her arms over her breasts. There was no compassion left.

"Oh, Christ..." I slobbered. It was like watching things through water.

"I called an ambulance," she said calmly. "They'll be here any minute."

"You did *WHAT?!*" I yelped. I tried to stand up and fell onto the coffee table; it splintered apart on my back and I fell onto the floor behind it. *Jack rabbits....Headlamps....* "Oh shit, Suzanne. Wha'd you call an ambulance for? Suzanne! Call them back and tell them I'm all right! Tell them you don't need them to come anymore!" I tried to stand up again and fell down again.

"C'mon, Suzanne, call them. I don't need an ambulance. I'm all right. Look!" I waited a moment, got a grip, and was able to stand up this time around.

Suzanne sat down on a stereo speaker and glared at me. Time. She was just waiting out the time till somebody got there. She looked tired and fed-up, like my words didn't mean anything anymore. I sat back down on the sofa. Suzanne didn't say anything else.

The rescue unit arrived with the red and blue flashing strobes, and the neighbors came out their front doors to see what the hell was happening across the street on Christmas night. The paramedics, the neighbors, Suzanne's best friend—they all came. They all came to see if the junkie had died this time.

The paramedic asked, "Are you all right"? He looked into my eyes with one of those pen lights, waving it across my face.

"I'm all right," I told him.

He then picked up my syringe and put a cork on the needle point. He stuffed it into a plastic bag.

That belongs to ME, mother fucker! You can't just take it like that! This is my HOUSE!

"You got any more heroin here?" he asked.

"No," I said, "that's it." There were ten more bags upstairs.

The paramedic said, "C'mon, we're going down to the emergency room and have you checked out."

"I'm okay, really. I just shot too much dope. I'll be all right."

"You either come with us," he offered, "or you can come with the police." He raised an eye waiting for my decision.

It wasn't a difficult call to make.

I went to the emergency room and let the doctor check me out. I lay on the stretcher for two hours until the doctor looked me over and made the decision that he wasn't going to need a freezer tonight for another dead junkie. Not tonight at least.

At midnight, the nurse came in and told me I could go home. She also told me to get some help with my problem. "Sure," I said to her. Suzanne spent the night with her best friend.

Good, now I can get high in fucking peace!

She came home the following night, methodically hung her coat over the banister, and walked upstairs to the bedroom. She didn't say "Hi." She only glanced at me and then turned away seemingly unmoved by my presence and went upstairs to our room. She came back down fifteen minutes later, suitcase in hand.

"What are you doing?" I asked, as though it were any great surprise.

"I'm leaving for a while. I'm going to stay with friends." The words came out of her mouth so very matter-of-factly, like she'd been rehearsing them over and over and over in her mind all day. She said, "You're just really crazy right now. I can't be around you." She was calm. She spoke rationally, peacefully, and she said the words very clearly: *You're just really crazy right now.* There wasn't any emotion behind it. It was a simple statement of fact. *You're just really crazy.*

But she looked tense, frightened. She had a look that said, *I've got to get away from you right away! You're dangerous to yourself, and now you're becoming dangerous to me! I can't be near you.*

I'll never forget the look on her face that night, standing at the bottom of the stairs and carrying her suitcase. For as long as I live, I'll never forget the expression my wife had on her face.

And now, I was alone.

▲ ▼ ▲

In the next two months, I saw that same look on many people's faces. Some of them were close to me, some were just acquaintances; but I could see it in their eyes. I could *smell* it if I got close, and I could *feel* it coming off their bodies in waves. It was an animal scent, a protection, on their part. It was as though if they could have spoken about it, they would have said, *Get away from me! You scare me! Don't come any closer, Adam!*

During those final weeks I was to come to know Death intimately. I was to come so close to Him that I could put my face next to His and kiss Him on the lips. I went to bed with Him. I slept with Him. And when I woke up each morning, He was right there next to me. Right where I'd left Him the night before. I spend my days with Him. And my nights. And when I injected heroin and cocaine, He kissed me. Over. And over. And over again. His lips. On mine.

Come to me, He said. *Come. . . .*

These were the hours, and the minutes, and the seconds of each day that ticked by when I wanted to die. When I lay in my bed curled into a shivering ball, too scared or too sick to answer the phone, or to see who it was at the front door when the bell rang. These were the mornings when the very moment I opened my eyes and realized that I'd made it though another night alive—that I had to exist like this for another day—I would have turned a gun on myself if it had been on the nightstand next to me. These were my numbered days in Hell.

I pulled the blinds down and taped the shades closed where any sunlight poked through. I took the phone off the hook. If I didn't leave myself a wake-up dose of heroin for the morning, I drank two bottles of Nyquil or a half a fifth of vodka instead—or sometimes a ten-year-old bottle of Manachewitz cherry wine from the musty liquor cabinet downstairs. If there weren't any tranquilizers around, I swallowed over-the-counter antihistamines. Or Unisom. Or Sominex tablets. Then I shivered in my bed and sweat. Alone. With *Him*. Until I could get up, go out, run another scam, and score my dope. So I could come back to Hell.

Again.

▲ ▼ ▲

You reach a point with chemicals where they cease to work. After a while, the drugs lose their ability to do what they've always done for you, and what's left is something just short of madness. They don't take away the pain any longer. As a matter of fact, they add to it. A thousand fold.

I couldn't work. The twenty grand from the credit card bit was gone in a matter of weeks. Hunt's Point Avenue had nabbed most of that. So, I began to pass bad checks, steal, and hock anything and everything from my house in a vain attempt to get whatever money I could from the pawn broker, the antique dealer, the camera shop, the stereo store...

...or the music dealer. I had promised myself I'd *never!* get so bad that I'd sell my guitar for dope! Anything else! but never the guitar!

My mother bought it for me when I was still in college. It was a Guild D-40, and she paid nearly a thousand dollars for it. It had appreciated to well over that in the eight years I had owned it.

I thought about the songs I wrote on that guitar. I thought about the afternoons I spent in the den of my family's home, singing and playing for my mother while she suffered with her diabetic condition and in all probability was close to dying, watching the happiness light on her face as she listened with so much delight to her boy. I thought about how she used to close her eyes and listen. I thought about how peaceful she looked back then.

No! Not my guitar!

I thought about my friends of three or four years ago. How they had supported me at the gigs, how they had come to the bars where I sang and sat at the front tables, how they stayed for all three sets, and how they applauded and cheered after every song. I thought about the demo tape I had cut one summer with a friend. Ten of the best songs I'd ever written. What I had planned to *do* with that demo tape!

NOT MY GUITAR!

I thought about my dreams. I thought about my hopes. I thought about my mother's dying face, the way she used to smile while I sang to her.

NOOOOOOOOOOOOOOOOOOOOOO!

"I can give you a hundred bucks for it," the guy behind the counter at the music store told me.

"That's it?" I asked.

He nodded.

"All right."

He handed me the cash.

I walked out the door. I didn't want him to see me bawling.

▲ ▼ ▲

I tried to pass a check with the manager of a record store where I'd worked a few months previously. I considered him a friend. He had always honored my checks in the past, and even if the check bounced he would let me put the balance onto one of my credit cards instead of making a stink about the bounced check. But he looked at me now and said, "Sorry, Adam. I just can't do it this time." He shook his head. "I'm sorry."

I didn't press him. I knew I'd just done it one too many times. But it was the way he looked at me that told me not to press him any further. He seemed to put his arms out in front of him, like he would push me away if I tried to come any closer to him, like he was afraid to catch something from me, something deadly. That if I came any closer, I might infect him. He didn't have to say anything. I just smelled it. Like he thought I was diseased!

I'M DYING! my minded screamed, *AND I CAN'T STOP!*

Steven tried to help. He came over to talk one afternoon before he went to work. He came to my home when I was high enough on my day's fix so that I could sit and listen to what he had to say.

"You look like shit," he said. I could hear tears catching in his throat as he tried to talk. "You gotta do something, Adam. Somehow, you gotta STOP!" He said he was afraid I was going to die. He asked what the hell was wrong with me. I thought for a moment about the jack rabbit, but couldn't offer any explanations.

Steven said he'd bring me to a meeting the following day. "Maybe they can help you there," he said. I agreed.

The next morning I bought a shit-load of cocaine on Hunt's Point Avenue. I was out of control. I prepared the cocaine for injection and wanted to see how far I could take it. I wanted to see if I could really do it after all. I loaded a three cc. syringe, and I just kept pressing, and pressing, and pressing down on the plunger. I couldn't stop. I felt myself seizing but I couldn't stop my finger. I just kept watching the lines along the barrel. I watched the gradations click off into my vein. One...two...three...

five...TEN....More, and more, and more. My finger wouldn't stop.

I dropped onto the bed. A seizure came over me like a tornado. The needle hung out of my vein like it was part of me. I couldn't move my body. I just lay there and shook. I thought I was going to die.

The seizure slowed. And I did it again.

And again. And again. And again. The world turned into a fucking jet turbine. Screaming. It ripped through my mind, white. Insane. My pulse hammered against my temples and neck, and my eyeballs flipped around in their sockets. All the while my index finger kept pressing down on the plunger.

Just a little bit more. Just one, more, notch. Maybe this time. Just one more little black line on the barrel, and maybe, just maybe, this time I'll do it....

Steven pulled into the driveway. I heard his car door slam. He rang the front bell.

Please make him go away? Please God? PLEASE JUST MAKE HIM GO AWAY?

He rang the bell again. He pounded the door with his fist. "I know you're home!" he screamed. "Lemme in, Adam! I know you're in there!" He kept banging on the front door.

I shook. I couldn't move from the bed. My head twisted back and I began to dry-vomit. It was two hundred degrees in my bedroom! Nothing in my field of vision made sense: it was all just white, lightening. Electricity. My eyeballs flipped and the world went mad. The only sound was the screaming in my mind and the hammering on the front door.

PLEASE GOD?

Steven moved into the front yard underneath my bedroom window and yelled up, "C'mon, Adam! I know you're in there! I know you're in your bedroom!"

The seizure started to slow.

I crawled off the bed and onto the floor, just underneath the window sill. I stuck one, glassed eye to the window, between the shade and the frame. I saw Steven standing there.

Please God? PLEASE? Make him go away? Make them ALL go away? Please God? PLEASE? JUST MAKE IT ALL DISAPPEAR? PLEEEEEEEEEEEASE???

I curled down underneath the window sill and shook. The sweat poured off me, and I clutched my knees to my chest, praying to God for the world to disappear.

PLEASE JUST MAKE IT ALL GO AWAY?

Steven got into his car and drove off. After a few minutes, he just gave up. He figured out he wasn't going to be able to help me today.

I crawled back to the bed.

I only wanted to die. I injected my last eight bags of heroin.

▲ ▼ ▲

The world went away and what became real was my own, little delusion. No one else lived there. No one entered into it. It's called insanity, and it's all that was left.

I broke a needle tip off in my ankle. It was getting harder and harder to hit the veins in my arms; they were too traumatized from continuous cocaine and heroin injections. My forearms were red, and black and blue, and were scarring badly. I was using the veins of my ankle when one morning I broke the needle point off in one of the veins. I pulled it out. Useless. I didn't have another syringe in my house.

I drove to a pharmacy and asked the pharmacist if he'd

give me a needle. "I'm an addict," I told him. "I don't have a needle and I need to fix."

He wouldn't do it. "It's against the law to sell needles without a prescription. Sorry," he said and went back to filling his prescriptions behind the counter. Not another glance.

I went to the Department Of Health.

"I'm addicted to heroin," I told the girl at the desk. "I don't want to use a dirty needle and I'm sick. I'm gonna fix one way or the other, so would you please give me a clean needle?"

She looked at me like the pharmacist did. "I'm sorry," she told me. "I can't do that. It's against the law to hand out needles to addicts. I'm sorry." And then, "Why don't you go to the clinic downtown and get some help?" She started to look them up in the phone directory. "Here's their number . . . "

"I don't want help. I want a *needle!* If I've got to use a dirty one, I will. But I'm going to inject my heroin one way or another." I turned around and started for the door. "*I'm* the one who's sorry," I said.

"Wait a minute," she said. She looked up and down the corridor to make sure no one was around. She held one finger up and said, "Just hold on a second." She walked through the swinging doors behind her and disappeared. In a moment, she reappeared and handed me a brown paper bag the size of a lunch bag. "Here," she said. "Take this."

She was young, in her early twenties, and she didn't seem like she belonged in the Department Of Health, where sometimes you became distant, almost immune to the things you saw, like disease and death and sick infants and junkies coming in and asking for clean needles so they could fix. She wasn't hardened. For a moment, I saw something in her eyes. Something like concern. Or pity maybe.

She said, "They'd *kill* me if they found out I was doing this for you." She didn't seem frightened of me anymore. "Here. It's clean," she said. "Please don't use a dirty needle? Okay?"

"Thank you," I said.

She looked at me and said, "At least *think* about getting some help for yourself, okay?"

"Maybe," I said and skulked back to my car outside in the rain.

▲ ▼ ▲

They weren't as compassionate three nights later when I went to the emergency room at three o'clock in the morning and told them I was a diabetic visiting from another state and I'd run out of my insulin syringes. The nurse told me to sit in one of the examining rooms and wait for the doctor. "He'll have to check your blood sugar level and give you the injection himself." I went into the room and sat on the stretcher.

On the counter in the examining room was a red plastic container. A big one. It was marked INFECTED WASTE in large, bold, capital letters. It also had other words printed onto he label, like CAUTION and WARNING and DANGEROUS and SHARP.

I reached my hand into the container to get some syringes. I reached past a plastic guard that was cut in such a way that things were meant to go into the container, but not out. The plastic around the top was cut into sharp points and bent downward.

I felt around the bottom of the container, got stuck a couple of times, grabbed a couple of sets and stuffed the syringes into my gym sock. I walked out of the emergency room.

The nurse at the station looked at me, confused.

"The hell with it," I said disgusted, like their service wasn't good enough for me. "I'll call my own doctor in the morning."

She knew.

"Suit yourself," she shrugged.

I did.

▲ ▼ ▲

When you've got a ten thousand dollar line of credit on your Gold VISA card, I suppose, and when you hold down a job and can at least bring home a check on Friday afternoons, people are willing to cut you some slack. But when you're a junkie in the rain, begging for needles and stealing your works from the INFECTED WASTE container at your hospital, no one cuts you any slack. Doctors turn off their taps, friends refuse to lend you any more money, businesses don't cash checks for you, and your family says, "Uh, uh," when you call and ask them to bail you out of jail.

No. Nobody cuts any slack for a begging junkie. Everybody is suddenly "sorry." Old doctors who once treated you with compassion, good friends who once shared a glass or two of wine with you, your family that once gave you chance after chance after goddamned chance, and the girlfriends and wives you once bought dinners and diamond rings for, they all just look at you now and say they're "sorry."

A sad look comes over their face. It looks like it hurts them to say it, but they say it anyway. "We're sorry, Adam," they say.

Even the boys on Boot Hill become "sorry." I had always been able to get credit with them. I could always get a couple of bags to tide me over when times were good and they knew the money would be following tomorrow.

But when a junkie is reduced to stealing his works from the infected waste container at the local hospital emergency room, even the boys on Boot Hill stop understanding. Even they don't cut you slack. Now they look at you and say, "Sorry, amigo. I can't get you no credit today. Nobody giving credit to you!"

That's when being a junkie gets real hard, real fast.

SIXTEEN

DELUSIONS AND INSANITY

Hunt's Point Avenue is different at night. The red and orange and yellow lights blink from the arcades and delis and liquor stores, and they twist the darkness, making it breathe, making it come alive somehow. The rats and the gutters and the rain in the sewers whisper. They become one with the breathing. At the same time there's something dead in the air. People are shadows. They move in and out of the tenement doorways, the storefront overhangs, and down the alleyways; there isn't as much noise down here at night as there is during the day. There's less movement. Fewer people. Not as many cars. All you hear is that breathing, the shadows moving around in the doorways, and the rats crawling in the in the sewer.

It's dead, and at the same time alive.

It was 11:00 P.M. on a Friday night when I went down to Hunt's Point Avenue to buy forty dollars' worth of cocaine. I parked my car beneath a streetlamp, got out, and locked the car door. I walked across The Avenue towards the building where I knew they sold cocaine. I was almost to the other side of the street when he came up to me and asked, "You going to get some coke?"

He was about my age, in his late twenties or early thirties, white, and I would have though him a fairly handsome man: dark eyes, dark hair, an angular jaw, and a growth of beard maybe a day or two old. He reminded me of Don Johnson. He wore a baseball cap, and he had his hands stuffed into the side pockets of his leather flight jacket, an expensive leather flight jacket.

What's this all about?

"You buying coke?" he asked again. I stared at him with a *What the fuck do you want from me?* expression, and he halted. He said, "Hey! You're not a cop or nothing, are you?"

I didn't answer. I kept walking to the corner and out of the way of the few cars that came down the street.

He came up to my side again. "You're getting coke, right?" I walked a little faster. He kept up with me. "Look," he started, "do me a favor? If you tell that guy over there we're together when you buy your coke, and if I can get another guy to do me the same, I can get my bag for seven dollars."

What the hell is this routine? It felt like he was going to grab my arm and start begging.

He said, "C'mon, man. Just do me the favor, huh?"

I gave him another *Get away from me!* look, wanting him just to leave me the fuck alone, and again he asked, "Hey! You're not a cop or nothing, are you?" I still didn't answer. He came up to me again.

"Whatever." I muttered.

"Good," he said and left my side. He crossed to the opposite corner of the side street and stood there. He looked like he was watching out for someone. Or some*thing*.

I walked over to the black man who stood on the steps of the cocaine building. I handed him forty dollars and told him I wanted two rocks. He went up the steps, through the front door and disappeared for a moment, giving the cash to the man inside. The black man came back down the steps and told me it would be a minute or two. I stood fifteen feet away in a doorway. The black cocaine man waited on the steps of the cocaine building. The Do Me A Favor? guy stood on the corner across the street. Watching. Looking nervous.

In a couple of minutes, the black cocaine man went back up the steps of the building, disappeared again, and came out with an aluminum foil package. I took it and slipped it into the outside pocket of my overcoat. I started to walk up the side street to the corner and cross Hunt's Point Avenue to my car.

The Do Me A Favor? guy came from the opposite corner and started walking towards me. I walked onto The Avenue.

"Hey!" he yelled. "Did you tell him?"

I ignored him.

"Yo! Man!" he yelled again. "Did you tell him you and me were together? Did you tell him I was with you?"

I kept walking towards my car. I was halfway across Hunt's Point Avenue.

"Hey, man," he said, "You're not a fucking cop or nothing, are you?"

I reached the door to my Firebird.

I snapped: *"NO, I'm not a fucking cop! What the FUCK do you want???"*

"Good!" he said. "Cause I *am!"* and pulled a New York City detective's badge from his back pocket. "You're under arrest, asshole! Get against the fucking car!"

I put the cocaine into my mouth and tried to swallow it,

but the package was too big. I spit it out and kicked it underneath my car.

"Where's your fucking keys?!" he yelled. He pushed me against my car, reached into the pockets of my overcoat, and grabbed my keys. He was behind me now; he held a hand on the back of my neck, mashing my face onto the car's top. He pinned me like that and kicked my feet apart. "Where's your fucking..."

He saw the aluminum foil package on the ground. He reached down to pick it up and he said, "Move and you're dead, asshole!" He pressed something small and very hard into the back of my rib cage. He picked up the package of cocaine.

"It's fucking WET!" he screamed. "What the fuck are you trying to do?" He pulled my head off the roof of the car. "Get in the fucking car!" he ordered, shoving me into the back seat and putting the package of cocaine into his jacket.

When I looked at him I could see what he'd stuck into my ribs a couple of seconds before.

Another cop came to the driver's side door; the first cop tossed him my keys. He got in the driver's seat, while the first cop sat in the back with me. He held the gun in his right hand. "Let's get out of here," he said to his partner.

The detective in front started the car and put it in gear. It stalled. He tried again. It jerked and stalled again. "C'mon!" the cop with me yelled. "Let's *go!*" The driver finally got the feel for the car's clutch and pulled away from the curb. He made a U-turn on Hunt's Point Avenue and headed down to the highway.

The cop in back looked at me. "Where's the rest of your coke?" I told him that was all I had. "Bullshit! You gotta have more than this!" He patted my pockets to feel for more bags, and then reached inside my coat with his left hand and hit my chest. He kept the gun in his right hand. Pointed at me. "Where's the rest of it?!" he yelled.

"That's all I got!"

"BULLSHIT!"

"That's all I got!" I screamed.

The cop took my wallet from inside my overcoat. It was empty.

"Where's your money then?" he asked. He kept patting down my pockets. "Where's the rest of your fucking money, asshole?!"

"I got no more money, man! All I got was that package you got there!" I nodded to the packet he stuffed in his pocket. "It's all the coke and all the money I had! I swear!"

The driver looked at us in the rearview mirror. "Maybe he ain't got nothing," he said.

"BULLSHIT!" the first cop screamed. He hit my chest again and went inside my coat. "Where the fuck is it?"

"I told you, man! That's all I fucking got!"

The cop in back put his gun underneath my chin and pressed it into my throat. I felt my bladder let go. Softly, and very slowly, he said, "We saw you go to that building back there and buy cocaine. We watched you. If you don't give it all up to us now, me and my partner here are gonna take you down to the station and lock up your ass for a long fucking time." He nodded his head to emphasize the word "long." "It's up to you, asshole. Now give us your dope."

"Look," I started, "all I had on me was forty lousy dollars. I gave you all I had! I swear to God! It's all I fucking got!"

The one driving said to his partner. "Wha'do you wanna do with him?" The cop in back shot me a look. He was pissed. He took the gun out from underneath my chin and holstered it back underneath his leather jacket. He leaned back against the car door. He smiled.

"Let's take him down and lock his ass up," he said.

And then it was quiet.

They let it sink in.

▲ ▼ ▲

We drove around for about twenty minutes, and by this point I had no idea where in the south Bronx I was; everything was unfamiliar. All I could see were dark streets, black alleys, highway overpasses, and a run-down corner bar with a dumpster outside. All my bearings from Hunt's Point Avenue and the roads leading to and from it were gone.

They parked my car. The driver turned off the engine. The cop in back turned to face me. He said, "Listen kid, I been thinking. Me and my partner don't really want to take you down and bust you for this lousy rock." He held the foil packet between his fingers in front of my face. "How about we go back there and you do a buy for us?" I didn't understand what he meant. He explained. "You go back, buy some more coke, and you lead us to the big guy. We don't want you—you're a punk. We want the dealer. We want the guy who deals the quantity in that building. He's the one we're really after." He let me chew it around for a second. "You go back and buy a bunch of coke from him, and we'll bust him instead of you." I told them again I didn't have any more money. "Can you get some?" he asked.

"I don't know," I said.

The driver burst in and said, "Let's lock his ass up and..."

"Wait a second!" the first one shouted. He studied me. He said, "Listen, we're gonna give you a break. You get me and my partner a hundred bucks each and we'll let you go. Forget the fucking buy. It's too much bullshit paper-work for us. Just get us a hundred bucks each and we'll let you go. Can you do that?"

I looked at my checkbook and wallet the cop had taken from my coat pocket. "I can cash a check," I said.

The one in back said, "All right, this is how it goes." He tore a check from my checkbook and handed it to me. "I'm giving you *one* check," he said. "You get two hundred dollars, see? And you meet me and my partner back here in an hour with the fucking money or we're locking your fuck-ing ass up in jail! Got it?" I nodded. "Can you be back in an hour?" I nodded again. He looked at his watch. "All right. We'll meet you back here at one o'clock." Then he said, "What else you got?" I didn't know what he meant. He screamed, "What else you got? For collateral! You don't think we're just gonna let you take off and fuck us, do you? C'mon now, what else you got?"

He took my checkbook, my wallet, my credit cards, my watch, and my wedding band for collateral.

"Good," he said. "Now we're gonna hold this stuff till you come back with the money. If you don't show we'll send a squad car to Connecticut to get you. You under-stand?" I nodded again.

They gave me directions on how to meet them later. They gave me back the keys to my car and warned me that if my ass wasn't back there in an hour, my butt was gonna be in one, enormous, mess of shit. Then they got out of the car.

"One hour, asshole!" one of them said looking back at me. "One hour!" And they walked out of sight.

I put the key into the ignition and started my car. I looked down at my pants. There was a dark stain growing where I'd lost control of myself.

▲ ▼ ▲

I left the Bronx that night to cash that one check for two hundred dollars, come back to the Bronx in an hour, meet those two cops, and pay them off. And if my buddy's bar had been open that night instead of Closed For Remodeling, I might have gotten the OK from him to cash one check; I might have gotten two hundred dollars together; and I might have gone back down to the south Bronx, paid the two cops off, gone to bed that night, and slept soundly, knowing that my ass wasn't going to be locked up in The Tombs or on Riker's Island. If my buddy's bar had been open that night I might have done exactly that.

But I didn't.

I walked into an all-night video store and told the seventeen year old behind the counter that if he didn't give me all of his fucking money right now, I was going to bash his fucking brains into the fucking wall behind his fucking head.

I got the two hundred dollars.

But I went to Boot Hill instead of the south Bronx.

▲ ▼ ▲

That seventeen-year-old kid's face will be etched onto my memory forever.

I wouldn't have hurt him. If the kid had said "no," I would have just walked away and tried somewhere else. But the terror I saw in that kid's eyes, the fear he saw when some insane, desperate, lunatic junkie took him for all his money—the thoughts for his *life* that must have whipped through his head that night at one o'clock in the morning— I'll just never be able to forget.

Sometimes I still see him. Sometimes, it's like it was just last night. I see him shaking, I smell his fear, I see his eyes, and I still see the way he moved—how he jerked, and jumped, and put the money into my hand in two seconds flat. *Just anything! Anything! Please mister? But just don't hurt me! Please?*

And I still hear the screams inside my own skull yelling, *What in God's name are you fucking DOING?*

I still have nightmares.

"Mom's" was open for business up on Boot Hill. Twenty-four hours a day, seven days a week, I could always get cocaine at Mom's. I never met her. I don't know what she looked like. I don't even know if she really was a mother or not—I had never met any of her "children." But Mom was always open for the cocaine business if you knew the right person. And I did.

I got three grams, and I went home to blow my brains out. Just one more time. Just one last time to see if I could really do it. Just one . . . last . . . time. . . .

The telephone rang in my kitchen at two o'clock in the morning, just as I was loosening the brown belt around my biceps and just as the freight train was starting to rip my ass through the tunnel. I let the answering machine take the call.

It was the two cops from the south Bronx. The wanted to know where I was. They wanted to know where their *fucking money* was. They wanted to tell me that if I didn't show in the next hour, a car would be dispatched to my home in Connecticut and that my ass wasn't going to be worth dog shit!

I whacked another load of cocaine.

I called Steven at three-thirty and told him everything. I was crying. I told him what had happened to me in the

Bronx, I told him what I had done at the video store, and I told him about "Mom" and what I was doing now. He said he'd be right over.

He came in through the front door about half an hour later and stopped dead in the hallway, staring at me.

Steven walked into the kitchen and his eyes flashed around the room. He saw the syringe on the kitchen table, the cooker, the empty foil packets of cocaine, the belt and the glass of water I used for the injections. He saw the blood.

He saw the blood on the floor, on my arms, on my jeans and on my shirt. He saw it on the kitchen table and on the chairs. Steven saw the blood on the walls, on the counter where the vial of Valium was, and he saw the bloody hand print on the white metal door of the refrigerator.

"Jesus Christ!" he yelled. "What the fuck are you do-ing to yourself??!!" His hands were making fists. Open... close... open... close. His breath was racing in and out of his chest in gusts. "You're TRYING to kill yourself! You WANNA die!" he screamed. He looked around the kitchen. "WHAT THE FUCK IS WRONG WITH YOU??" I could only look at the floor. "Get on the phone!" he ordered.

"But Steven..."

"Get on the fucking phone NOW! I don't give a fuck WHO you call, but call SOMEBODY! NOW!" He threw the phone directory on the kitchen table. "Jesus Christ! Adam, you gotta get help!"

I picked up the phone. Steven kept looking around the kitchen. His breath began to slow as I picked up the tele-phone and dialed. I called the names in the book, the ones under Drug Addiction and Alcoholism. I left messages for help on their answering machines. Messages that I was dy-ing.

Steven picked up the syringe and flung it into the refrigerator. It snapped apart. The plunger bounced a couple
of times on its rubber tip across the kitchen floor. He said,
"What's WRONG with you?"

"I don't know, Steven," I said. "I don't know anymore." I leaned over the table and put my head into my
hands. I couldn't hold back my tears any longer. Steven
came over and put his arms around me. He said, "Hang on,
Adam. C'mon, just hang on. It's gonna be all right." I
couldn't stop bawling. "Listen, Adam," he began. He was
trying to stay calm. "We'll get you into a place, all right.
We'll find you a place to go. Tomorrow! Those people will
call back! You're gonna be all right, Adam!"

I was still shaking, but his words were taking some of
the horror from the air. He wasn't yelling anymore; he was
my friend again, only wanting his best friend not to die. He
said, almost joking now, "You're outta your fucking mind;
you know that, don't you?" I nodded.

"What the fuck am I doing, Steven? What about those
cops in the Bronx? What the fuck am I gonna do about
those two cops?"

He smiled and laughed. "Where's their car?" he asked.
I looked at him; I didn't understand his question. "So
where's their big, bad police cruiser they were gonna send
to get you? Huh?" It still made no sense. I was too whacked
from the cocaine. He said, "They weren't cops, asshole.
They were just junkies like you. They had a better scam,
that's all." Then warmly, "God! you're so fucking out of
your mind. You gotta go away and get some help."

Steven kneeled down in front of me so our faces were
level. I wanted it all to end. He said, "Adam, they were
just two guys who wanted to take your dope and your
money." He started shaking his head again. "Look at yourself. You're crazy! You're almost getting killed in the

Bronx? You're sticking up kids in the street?" He looked around the kitchen. "And *this?*" I hung my head. Steven ordered, "You're going away. You're putting yourself away before you die—or before someone kills you!"

I began to cry again.

Steven asked, "You want me to stay here with you? You want me to stay tonight?"

I sniveled, "No. I'll be okay." Then I put my face into my hands and screamed, "I am so fucking scared!"

"I know, I know," he said. He held me. "Tomorrow." He asked, "You gonna be able to sleep?"

I nodded at the Valium prescription on the window ledge. He smiled. Somehow, I guess it relieved a little of the tension, the absurdity of the whole scene.

"You're an asshole," he said warmly. "You never *stopped* being an asshole!" He was almost laughing now at this cruel joke. And then in the next instant, he was almost crying. "You sure you're gonna be all right?"

"Yea, Steven, I'll be okay. I'll just eat some Valium and I'll be able to sleep."

He folded his arms on his chest. "Don't overdose yourself again, asshole!"

I wanted to laugh too. *Who me?*

"I'll be over tomorrow," he said. "I'm gonna go home and get some sleep now, but we'll take you somewhere tomorrow. Don't worry." And then seriously, "Don't be an asshole! Don't go getting fucking arrested or killing yourself or something!" I shook my head. "It's gonna be all right," he reassured. "We're gonna come outta this one all right, okay? We've both been through worse, huh?" I started smiling. "It's gonna be all right. Don't worry." And with that, he left.

I watched him pull his car out of my driveway. I shut

the front door to my house and threw the bolt. I went up to my bedroom, injected the last two bags of heroin I had left in the house, swallowed a handful of Valium, and lay down to go to sleep.

For me, it was almost over.

SEVENTEEN

A STEEL CAGE AND A HOSPITAL BED

The telephone rang early the next morning. The counselor on the other end had said he was returning my call from the previous night. If I could come to his office Monday morning, he had said, he would try to give me some help. He had said I sounded pretty banged up. That was Saturday morning.

The night before, I had hid my car around the corner from my house hoping that if the two "cops" from the Bronx came to arrest me, they'd see my car wasn't in the driveway and they'd leave me alone. When I got off the phone with the counselor, I went out to find it, but I couldn't remember where I had parked it. Then I thought Steven might have taken it away in an attempt to keep me from killing myself, so I took my motorcycle out instead. In January.

There was one clear thought in my mind that morning, one singular, solitary, all-consuming thought: that if I didn't get high, I would die. It had become that simple in the end. If I didn't get high, I would just go mad and die.

I had found some antique dishes in the attic, put them in a box, lashed the box onto the back of the bike and took off. The roads were frozen with ice and I shivered while I rode the motorcycle. I couldn't go faster than fifteen or twenty miles an hour.

The guy at the pawn shop gave me twenty bucks for the dishes.

My dope!

I left the pawn shop and headed for Boot Hill.

I've gotta get . . .

It was so cold that morning. The roads were slick. Icy. I was shaking.

My dope!

I twisted the throttle.

I've gotta get . . .

All I could see was the bag. I flew on the bike, faster and faster and . . .

MY DOPE!

The wind bit my face. I could see the guy putting the bags of dope into my hands.

I WANT . . .

I could feel the needle going into my vein and the rush as the sickness left my body. Faster.

I gotta . . .

Just turn three more roads and then downtown. FASTER!

Wait!

I gotta have my dope!

WAIT! STOP!

The front wheel of the bike started to tremble and slip on the ice.

SLOW DOWN!

The corner was coming up on me way too fast.

I'm not going to make it!

I hit the brake and the rear wheel just slid.

Oh God! I'm not going to make it!

Then the front wheel locked. I smashed the bike into a tree in somebody's front yard at forty miles an hour. I lay there. I was conscious, but I couldn't breathe. Then slowly, I felt my body. I felt my hands, my legs, my arms, and I felt myself breathing. *My dope.* I gradually sat up in the snow and took off my helmet. Nothing was broken. A little blood. My leather and my pants were torn, but I hadn't broken anything. *I gotta get my DOPE!* Somehow, I stood up. I was dazed. But there was only one thing in my mind.

I leaned over the Eleven Hundred and got the bike up. And I got both the bike and myself down to Boot Hill for a lousy ten dollar bag of cocaine. In January. In the snow. With nothing left to my mind but the need for the rush.

I got to The Hill, bought a dime of cocaine. And I was glad when I got arrested.

I didn't fight. I didn't run away. When the undercover detectives came toward me from their cars, I lamely tossed the package of cocaine to the ground and kept on walking. *Maybe they won't even care.*

They picked it up, grabbed me by my jacket, cuffed me, and put me into the back of their unmarked car. I didn't have the energy to protest.

My hand was swelling badly by this point from the accident. The detective sat with me in the back seat of the cruiser and asked, "What's wrong with your hand?"

"I think it's broken," I whimpered.

"Whad'you do?" he asked.

"I smashed it when I cracked up my motorcycle this morning."

The detective looked at me like I was crazy. "You were riding a fucking motorcycle this morning?" he exclaimed. "It's below zero out there!"

I hung my head.

He took the key from his key chain and undid the hand-
cuff a notch or two. He offered something about how fucking sick I must be to go out motorcycle riding in the middle
of fucking January.

They brought me to the station and left me to sit on the
concrete ledge of the Bull Pen (the room where you wait for
a cell assignment). They took the cuffs off, processed the
arrest, and in about an hour said, "C'mon, the Director of
the Narcotics Division wants to ask you a couple of questions." They took me to his office.

The Director wanted to know about the Hill. He
wanted names of dealers, where they lived, where they
dealt. He wanted to know if I knew about any of the higher
ups.

I couldn't answer his questions. Not because I didn't
have the information he wanted, but because I couldn't
stop bawling like a baby. I was so fucking sick, hurt, and
beat-the-fuck-up from the past days and weeks and
months, that it all came out on the detective and I couldn't
stop blubbering. I couldn't control myself. I just couldn't
do anything by cry.

I told him I bought my crap down there from anybody
and everybody who sold it. I had to, I said. I was strung-
out. I was sick, and if I didn't get to a hospital soon, I
thought I was going to die. I told him I didn't know how
much longer I could last. And then I just sat there crying.

He passed me the box of tissues.

I looked up at the Director of the Narcotics Division,
and for a split second I saw something in his eye. He
looked like he might have had a sixteen-year-old daughter,
a little girl who maybe got knocked up by her stupid boy-
friend and didn't know what to do now about the preg-
nancy. Or maybe he had a son, a son who just got all
screwed up one night drinking beer with the fellas and

thought tearing up the neighbor's lawn with their cars might be a whole lot of fun. Or maybe he just had a fucked-up punk of a kid like me, who was all kinds of screwed up, really sick, and who just needed one more break.

We locked eyes for that one second—me, who was sick and sniveling and crying like a five year old who has just shat his pants, and the Director of the Narcotics Division, who saw just another whining junkie (and how many does this one make today?)—and in that split second I saw something in that man's eyes. I saw compassion. It was as though the Director thought to himself: *Maybe I can cut this one some slack. Maybe if I cut him some slack I won't be peeling him up off the sidewalk with a bullet in his head. Maybe. Just maybe.* And he left me alone.

He locked me in a cage. He charged me with another felony. But he gave me a break the only way he knew how. He kept me in a cage, locked away from myself and from the needle, and when he was relatively sure I'd had enough and that I'd make it to a counselor's office, he let me out of jail. On Sunday night.

And because of that Narcotics Division Director—as well as Steven, my oldest brother, and a counselor I went to see the morning after they let me out of the jail—I went straight into a hospital. Into detox and off the street.

I'll never know if I could have made it another day out there.

I doubt it.

And now I was sitting in the visitor's lounge, on the seventh floor of the hospital, with my oldest brother, Mike, and Doctor Oscar Lebrecht. They were giving me the deal, straight up: My house was gone, my money was gone, and my wife was gone. There was no job left, and the freebies, the motorcycles, the shrinks, the clinics, the credit cards and the bouncing of the checks, were all gone. The understanding, the cushy detoxes, the Methadone with LuvLee, the doctors and the work-out gyms were all in the shitter, and for that matter, so were the paid lawyers who always got me out of trouble.

All that was left, they said, was heroin and NyQuil bottles, syringes and empty Scotch bottles, cocaine psychoses and robbing seventeen-year-olds in the middle of the night. From there, it could only be courtroom after courtroom, jail cell after jail cell. If I wanted to, Mike and Doctor Lebrecht said, I could detoxify here in the hospital for seven days, go to a drug and alcohol hospital for another six to eight weeks after that, and then go to a long-term facility or a half-way house if I had any hopes of wanting to live.

"Or," they offered, "you can leave here now and you'll probably die."

The choice was up to me.

▲ ▼ ▲

Oscar Lebrecht, hung a sign on the door of my hospital room that said NO VISITORS. More than preventing anyone from smuggling in drugs or a quart of Scotch, the sign made sure I was left alone. It was metaphor for my madness, a move on Doctor Lebrecht's part that said, *Leave him alone. Leave him be with his insanity, and let him SEE what this garbage has done to him in the last twenty years. Just let him lay in there and rot for a while.*

And so I lay there for seven days, shivering and sweating and staring out a small window. I looked out past the buildings and the streets, and I could see the waters of the Long Island Sound far away in the distance. When I looked down I could see the tops of the buildings beneath my seventh floor room. I could see the tar they used to paper the roofs and the blacktop on the streets as they wound in and out between the buildings. I could see little people walking on the sidewalk below.

I wondered what it would be like to fly. I wondered what it would be like if I could squeeze my body through the window and fly out, just fly down onto the top of one of those buildings or maybe, all the way down to the pavement below. Just put out my arms and soar. No more pain. No more madness. Just the wind in my ears, as I spread out my arms and went floating down through the air. How peaceful, I thought. How quiet.

Oscar Lebrecht used Methadone to detoxify me. He started my dose with twenty milligrams. (I'd been started on eighty milligrams that summer in Hallmarke.) "Six days," he said. "Then I want you completely off for a day so we can observe you before you go to the rehabilitation hospital."

On the seventh day, not only did they discover how I chose to augment my Methadone detoxification, but they also found out how mad I'd really become.

The first afternoon in detox I took a three cc. syringe from the portable med cart. When the nurse brought in my dose of Methadone in the afternoon, I crushed up the pills in a paper cup in the bathroom, added some hot water, and injected the dose into my arm. (Unlike Halmarke's biscuits of Methadone which can't injected, hospital Methadone is water soluble and easily injected.) When the Methadone wasn't enough, I followed the nurse—and her med cart— around the floor of the hospital. I waited. When she entered a patient's room to administer medication, I opened up the plastic drawers on the sides of the cart and removed any clear, glass vials I could find that looked like they might do something to me. I stole heart medications, blood pressure medicines, anti-nauseants, and anti-emetics. I really didn't care what I took. I broke the tips off the ampoules, drew the injections up into the syringe, and shot them into my bloodstream. I figured two things would happen: either the drugs would get me high or they would kill me. Both, were acceptable options.

In addition to a doctor, a general internist, and a charge nurse, I was assigned a social worker, Stephanie.

When the Voices in my head told me *I was nothing but the biggest bag of shit on the face of the earth and that I had no right to go on living and that everyone would be a whole lot better off if I would just off and kill myself*, Stephanie said, "You're gonna be all right, Adam. We're sending you to a hospital. We're taking care of it for you, and you're going to be all right." Stephanie held my hand, wiped the sweat from my brow, fed me, and did her best to comfort me during the pain from this thing I'd done to myself for the better part of twenty years.

And when they found me stealing the ampoules from the med cart, Stephanie stood behind me. She *understood* how crazy I'd become.

It was the morning of my discharge when the medication nurse caught me taking the ampoules. She caught the crazy man. She heard some noise coming from the hall and came out to see what the hell I was doing out of bed.

"Gimmee that!" she screamed. I backed up from the cart and stuffed the ampoules into the back pocket of my jeans. "Gimmee that RIGHT NOW!" she ordered. "Give me what you just put into your pocket!"

I put three glass vials into her palm.

"What's WRONG with you?!" she screamed in amazement. "What the hell is THE MATTER with you? Do you have any idea what this stuff can do to you?"

I was the jack rabbit in the headlamps for the last time. She called the charge nurse and they all came: the head nurse, the medication nurse, my brother Mike, and Stephanie. They all came.

They all came to find out what the hell was WRONG with the fucking junkie. What in God's name would make a person want to inject himself with blood pressure medicines, anti-nauseants, heart medications, and Lord only know's what else?

"We thought you wanted to stop?!" they screamed and scolded. "We thought you wanted to HELP yourself?" The charge nurse held out the ampoules in her hand. "YOU CALL THIS TRYING TO STOP?"

I could only wait to be run over by the Mack.

Stephanie stayed behind when the others went to the nurse's station to document the incident and to shake their heads in disbelief together over what the junkie had done. "Just give me a couple of minutes alone with him," Stephanie said. She was upset.

I looked up from the floor and cried, "I can't stop, Stephanie! I just can't stop!" I was heaving and rattling all over. I wanted to rip my brains out of my head and throw them onto the fucking wall. All I could do was scream and cry and yell, "What's wrong with me, Stephanie?! What the fuck is WRONG with me?"

She grabbed my hands away from my face. She held them tight. She said simply, "Adam, listen to me. You're sick. But you're going to be all right."

I looked away. How many times had I heard that lie before? How many more times would I listen to that shit that I was going to be okay?

She said, "You're going to go to a hospital in Vermont. They're going to help."

Noooooo! I don't wanna hear this shit anymore!

I tried to pull away. She lifted my chin with her hand and made me look her in the eye.

"Do you hear me?" she said. "Do you hear what I'm saying? You're going to be all right!"

Noooo! I hate it! I hate myself and I hate what I've become

and I hate everything about me! Why don't you just leave me the
fuck alone and let me kill myself? JUST LET ME DIE! I
wanted to scream in her face.

But I nodded my head.

"Good," she said. And she held me in her arms. She
just let me sob, and she held me.

I don't remember how long we stayed like that.

▲ ▼ ▲

My oldest brother came back to the hospital room in a little
while and said, "Let's go." He didn't smile. He didn't add
any other sentiments. He just spoke the words, *Let's go* like
he'd say *Pass the salt.* I have absolutely no idea what he
must have thought or felt about taking his little brother to
treatment again, and were I to even take a guess at it, my
guesses probably wouldn't even come close. My family had
been going through this shit for nine years. In and out. Off
and on. Okay. Not okay. And still, my oldest brother was
here to take me to Vermont. For one last shot. He carried
my bags for me and helped me down the steps and into his
car. We left the city, got onto Interstate 91, and began the
four hour ride to the hospital in Vermont.

I heard words coming from him. I tried to make conversation but I really wanted to just open up the passenger's
side door, slide out, and slip underneath the tires of one of
those eighteen wheelers that kept passing us. I was just so
fucking sick of it all. I didn't think it would hurt all that
much. Just fast, quick. And nothing would matter anymore. But something kept me in my brother's car.

We got to Vermont about an hour ahead of my intake
appointment. My brother liked the state. He came here often to ski, he said, and he didn't want to sit around the hospital waiting for them to take me, so he drove the car
around for a while and showed me the scenery.

I remember the snow. I remember it being freezing cold outside—it was the middle of January—and I remember wishing I had a pair of sunglasses because the sun's reflection off the snow was making my eyes hurt. The sky was blue, there weren't many clouds, and I just remember having to squint my eyes the whole time because I couldn't open them fully to the light. It was like I'd never seen the sun so bright before.

You can see The Vermont Retreat from the highway. It's a huge, old complex; I think it's almost two hundred years old. They've been treating drug addicts and alcoholics there since the nineteenth century.

I'm going to rest now. God! I'm so fucking tired.

My brother turned the car into the parking lot, shut off the engine, and came around the side of the car to help me out.

My brother took my bags and helped me through the doors of my—God willing—last hospital for drug and alcohol dependency.

God willing, I left my twenty-year career of drinking, taking tranquilizers, shooting heroin and cocaine, stealing and being a junkie to the brink of madness and almost death, on the front steps of The Vermont Retreat.

And God willing, that's were it will remain.

Forever.

EIGHTEEN

A Place
for Us

For reading these pages and for sharing my experiences, thank you. If you walk away from reading this book and take with you only one thing, please let it be this: There is hope.

Whether rich or poor, black or white, young or old, fat or thin, smart or dumb (and personally, I think the smarter you are, the more difficult it is to get sober!), there is hope. Whether you live on Park Avenue or on 125th Street in Harlem, whether you graduated from Yale University or never made it past the second grade, or whether you drive a shiny new Buick or you've already totaled out fifteen of them, there is hope. Whether your family still loves you or they've all deserted you, whether you have a good paying job or you just got fired, or whether you've never gotten a speeding ticket in your entire life or you've got felony arrests out your ying yang, there is hope. There is hope for anyone and everyone who suffers with the pains of drug addiction, alcoholism, chemical dependency, or whatever you prefer to call this problem. Anyone. The words "hopeless" and "incorrigible" are a lie. I know too many people, who were a whole lot worse off than I when they began to get sober, who today are happy, free, and leading useful, purposeful lives.

My story is nothing special; there are millions of people in the world today with the same. Only the names, the places, and perhaps a few of the events, are different. But our stories are always the same. They are stories of pain, of torment, of guilt and remorse; they are stories of despair and what we thought was hopelessness. And today we are recovering. I am not any brighter, any richer, any better looking, any stronger of will, or of any higher moral fiber than any other addict, alcoholic, or person who is chemically dependent.

What I *am* and what I *was* four years ago is someone who has been completely and absolutely beaten by the awesome devastation that this disease can wreck. What this disease has the power to do to a human being and the amount of pain and anguish, despair and helplessness that it produces in a person's life and in everything he or she touches, is nothing short of awesome. In the beginning of my recovery process, this disease scared the living shit out of me. I was terrified of what it had to power to do to me. Now, I only respect it.

Chemical dependency kills.

And it does so almost without effort.

Although I almost died numerous times seizing and overdosing and driving a motor vehicle blind, and though I should have died numerous times from some of the places I went and from some of the people I met in those places (does a drug deal gone sour strike a familiar note?), there was still a faint spark of hope inside me. However small. However minuscule. I believe that spark is God. And God does not forsake any of us, not even lowly scumbag junkies like me who stick broken bottles up their asses, who rob seventeen-year-old kids in video stores, and who would rip the gold fillings from their mother's mouth and hock them at the pawn shop for a daily fix. No, God forsakes no one.

I surrendered to this disease. I gave up, I quit trying to run the whole bit myself, and I stopped that idiotic thinking that somehow, someway, I'd find a way to control my dopefiend ways and be able to abuse drugs and alcohol like a normal person. I couldn't. I can't. I'll never be able to. I gave up the whole stupid notion. I asked for help. And for that, I needed something much stronger than I. When I was ready—when I'd been through enough, when I had been beaten to a pulp, and when I couldn't take it any longer—I asked for help. And I got it. In spades!

From a support group, I got (and continue to get today) the love, the nurturing, and the guidance to live my life a day at a time without having to stick needles in my arms, or swallow handfuls of pharmaceuticals, or drink bottles of NyQuil to get out of bed in the morning.

Without the drugs and the booze, my life today is nothing short of miraculous. I see beauty in people where before there was nothing but bitterness. I am alive to my feelings (and sometimes, I'm even pretty much in tune with them); fellowship has replaced loneliness, and that feeling of isolation, of being different from everybody else, has been replaced by a common bond with my fellows.

There is love again, where, for years, there was nothing but hatred. Giving something to others has replaced always take, take, take and gimmee, gimmee, gimmee. And slowly, quite slowly indeed, I am learning that life is a series of good times and bad, of joys and sorrows, of proverbial "ups" and "downs," and that hard as I might try and as much as I might want it the Big Brass Ring does not exist.

There is only being *human*. The rush is a lie. It always was. I just had to chase it for twenty years to find that out.

And with the help I find in those "stupid meetings" (and no, they're not "stupid" at all; those meetings saved my life, and I love them and the people who go to them, dearly), I am learning to love being alive. Each day. Every day.

I am learning that there is happiness, there is joy, there is a purpose in this world even for dopefiends like me, and there is growth. There is opportunity to make amends for the damage I did during my chemical use, to make amends to the people I hurt. And I'm learning that there really are people who love me just for who I am. They just need to be given the chance, that's all. "It's a good thing," as a friend of mine always says.

An aside: If you've never listened to the song from which a few words were stolen to title this chapter, do yourself a favor. Listen to "Somewhere." It is one of the most beautiful songs ever written about hope, and faith, and the courage to keep on keeping on, and God—the things I believe essential to living sober. I cry almost every time I listen to it.

Yes, it is a good thing.

▲ ▼ ▲

I suppose you want to know what happened, right? Well, I spent six weeks in that last hospital in Vermont, and I began to get sober there. The reason that I got sober in Vermont is that I finally allowed people in. I finally admitted I was really sick from the years and years of messing with the stuff; I admitted I had no idea of how to help myself. I just opened my heart for those around me and allowed them to reach inside. Also, I was out of my denial phase—that had pretty much been kicked to shit and tossed out the window by Catherine Burke a few months before at Spruce Park. Thanks, Cathy.

There was a funny alcohol and drug counselor in my final hospital named Jack. Jack was a raving lunatic. Like me, he had been an intravenous cocaine addict. He was four years sober at the time that I knew him, but still he was a nut case. Jack used to come onto the unit for his morning presentation, with all of us patients gathered in a circle around the center of the room, and Jack would step inside that circle and start screaming at us with a huge grin on his face, "YOU'RE ALL SICK! YOU'RE ALL A BUNCH OF SICK FUCKING DOPEFIENDS!" Then he'd wait to see our reactions.

After we had shrunk away in stark terror from this lunatic who was pretending to be a counselor, he'd soften up. He'd get real caring and concerned. He would look like he loved each and every one of us, and he would say, "So why don't you just allow yourselves be sick? Why don't you just relax, admit that you're really a bunch of desperately sick units, and let us help you? Huh? Why don't you just let us help?"

Jack made a lot of sense to me that winter in Vermont. It all became so simple for me in the end: I had been beaten to a pulp and had no idea how to get better. I needed people to put me back together. I thought, *I give up. I'm gonna let someone else do this. I can't figure it out, but these people here seem to know something I don't.*

There was another woman, a social worker at that hospital, who used to sit me in her office and motion with her fingers as though she was pulling the strings of a marionette. She used to say, "This is you, Adam," and she'd pull the strings of her imaginary marionette and make it dance about before her.

This is you, Adam.

She was right.

For years, I had been a proverbial puppet on a string, performing, doing for others, keeping up that false image, pretending, and my social worker was the first person who ever told me I didn't have to live the rest of my life doing that. I could, she said, learn to be true to myself. I still talk with her today. I love you, Phyllis. Thanks.

The other reason I began to get well in Vermont was because I started going to meetings there. I went to my support group every day, and when I'd been at the hospital long enough (after about five weeks), I started going twice a day. Like the dope, I just couldn't get enough. Trust me on this one: it works.

From the hospital, I went to a halfway house where I stayed until the end of the summer. I got a job scooping ice cream and worked there for a year. (I had trouble tying my shoes in those days, so don't laugh because I could barely figure out, *uh, was that vanilla you just asked for?*) I kept on going to my support group, and I moved into a small apartment where I spent the next two years.

But that first year sober was the most glorious year of my life. For the first time, I had friends. I went dancing without being drunk. I had people to call when I was lonely. I went to sober parties. I went to the beach and swam and laid out in the sun for the first time since I was a kid. I knew people really cared about me. My boss at the ice cream parlor trusted me (he made me a manager after only a couple of months), and he honestly liked me, too. Also for the first time in my life, I paid my own rent, my own utilities, and my own food bills without having to ask mommy, or daddy, or my wife, or any one else because I was too stoned and too sick and too messed up to go out and earn a buck myself. It was one of the greatest feelings.

I worked with children in a drug and alcohol treatment facility for a while during my second year, and honestly it broke my heart. Can you imagine a twelve-year-old girl strung out on crack? Or a fifteen-year-old guy who learned how to shoot heroin from his father? And now the *kid* is strung out? I lasted less than a year in that job.

I began to write in the halfway house and have continued since. I write poems, and stories, and letters to the editor of our local paper. And somewhere along the line, over the course of the following couple of years, I put together this book. It has been good for me and my recovery process. But I think most of all I wrote it because I have the hope that someone out there might pick it up, read it, and say something to himself or herself like, *Shit! If this guy can get sober, well...maybe....Heck, I'm gonna give this thing a try.*

You know, if someone had told me when I was using chemicals that I would enjoy being alive as much as I do today, I just don't know if I would have believed them. I never would have thought it was possible. Well, I want to say it is possible. When I tell you that I'm sober, I'm happy, and the best thing I ever did in my life was to give up chemicals and go to a support group, I mean it with all my heart. The journey so far, has been absolutely incredible.

My editor asked me to include what I do today for excitement, now that I'm not taking drugs anymore, and to that, I can only reply that sometimes just getting up in the morning and showing up to see what life has in store for me is about all the excitement this dopefiend can handle! Life, all by itself, has proved to be all the challenge and excitement I need.

Was anything difficult? Yes. As a matter of fact, sometimes being sober is not so picture perfect. You see, when you start using chemicals, you stop growing emotionally. In other words, when I got sober, I was like a nine- or ten-year-old kid on the inside. I had the social skills of a boy entering puberty. Not the most ideal set of circumstances to have when you're walking around with a body that's supposed to be twenty-nine.

It's painful. It's hard to grow up. It hurts, and sometimes you have to kick and scream a little because it really does get that uncomfortable. But for me at least, all those nights spent crying on my living room floor—confused, not understanding a thing about what was happening around me, but knowing only that I wouldn't get high or drink over it—were (and still are) worth it. The growth I experience, even though it hurts, is worth any price.

Suzanne and I divorced shortly after I got sober, but you expected that, didn't you? Sometimes, people just have to stay angry and hurt. And to be quite frank, when I first got sober, I was in no condition to be intimately involved with anyone: I was a basket case for the first couple of years.

I didn't have a car for my first three years because I couldn't afford one. I went bankrupt. My name is listed with a federal bank agency, and as such, I am not allowed to have a bank account for five years (and that's for an overdrawn account which I never covered); I'll probably be paying people back the money I owe on old debts till the day I die. I have two felonies on my record (which make things like getting a job and voting sometimes difficult). I was on probation for the first couple of years. But I guess, really, about the worst thing I have to show for my years as a dopefiend (besides the emotional twisting I incurred) is a two-inch scar on the vein of my left forearm, right where it meets the elbow. It's sort of a constant reminder of my days on The Avenue.

On the flip side, I've been graced with many gifts, aside from those already mentioned. Today I have a car. I'm going back to college to finish my degree (finally). I have a nice apartment, a good job, and I live with an incredibly understanding and tolerant woman. And I have been given the opportunity, on a daily basis, to try and help someone who is still suffering with this disease. It's a small effort, sometimes it's just a phone call or talking over a cup of coffee, but it makes me feel good. I like to do it. I speak when I'm asked to, I try to make myself available for others, and I'm active in service work. It's kind of like giving back a little for the incredible gift which has been given me. I'm a very fortunate man.

My best friend Steven and I are still close and probably will be till the day one of us dies. My family and I are still trying. That one I'll probably go to the grave with also. Families are a biggie. I think the toughest of all. Still, we try. A day at a time.

All in all, when I think about the friends I've lost, when I think about the people I know who can't or don't want to get out from under their particular addictions, and when I think about how lucky I was and how I should have got a bullet through my head out there, I just thank God.

And maybe, that's about all a recovering dopefiend like me can do.

▲ ▼ ▲

Just a few more things and then I'll take my leave. If you're strung out or if you know someone who is, don't give up. If you want help, open your phone book. In it, you'll find a myriad of counselors, clergy, twelve-step fellowships, clinics, hospitals, rehabs, shrinks, doctors, social workers, civic organizations, and quite possibly, even the Director of the

Narcotics Division himself, all of whom are more than willing to help. Don't even try to do this thing alone! It's impossible. Ask for help. You'll get it. (I have left numbers and addresses at the end of this chapter.)

No one need be destined to a life of misery, chained to this disease. There are simply too many people willing to help. But you have to ask.

And finally, I'm going to get up on my soapbox and make my plea. It goes something like this: As a society, if we are going to have any hopes whatsoever of coming to terms with our current drug and alcohol problems, we need to stop passing the buck. This problem does not belong to the police, the government, the Drug Enforcement Administration, nor does it belong to the cartels in Colombia or the manufacturers in Marseilles. The former tries to clean up the mess, the latter just makes money from the mess. Neither of which matters much to the problem itself.

The problem is with us. That means you, and that means me. It's our problem. It belongs to mothers, it belongs to fathers, it belongs to brothers and sisters, and it belongs to anyone whose duty it is to love another human being.

To turn your back when a child needs you, is a crime. To say there isn't a problem, is arrogance. And to say it's not my fault, is ignorance. Running away from the problem and trying to pass it off on someone else is fear. People fear what they don't understand. People are ignorant, because they simply haven't been provided the knowledge.

Solving the problem of drug and alcohol abuse is not the responsibility of the high school principle whose students deal drugs any more than it is the responsibility of the ambulance driver who pulls you out of the auto wreckage because you got drunk and smashed the car. They're just putting Band-Aids on the problem.

The problem began a long time ago. With our children.

In our living rooms. In our bedrooms. Yours. And mine. This is where we will find our answers. So, what do we do? We spend time with our children, we give them our love, our attention, and we try and instill values in them by being good models ourselves. We show them that there are other ways of dealing with the problems that arise in their lives than turning to booze and drugs. It's really tough to tell kids to Just Say No To Drugs while you're sucking down a Budweiser. (And I'm sorry, but if they're not learning it from us, well then from whom are they learning it?) We stop being so damned selfish and give a little more to them. We show our children how to talk, how to communicate effectively, how to care, how to acknowledge their feelings, how to fight fair, and how to accept their own uniqueness, their own humanness, and most importantly that they are loved. By us. By others. And by God.

We do it at home, we do it in the schools, we do it in the churches, and we do it on the playgrounds. We do it anywhere and everywhere we can. We have to. It's our obligation. If we don't begin to do these things for our young, we're going to keep churning out kids that get high, kids that get into car wrecks because they got drunk, and kids that have to go to rehab when they're fifteen years old. If that's a gloomy forecast, well I'm sorry. But that's the way we're headed. Just look around.

If we can't reach the children when they're young, we get to them when their older. And that means treatment. We put our time, our money and our efforts into helping people when they're hurt. We treat the sick. And treatment is nothing more than having places for people to go: hospitals, rehabs, clinics, and halfway houses. It's not a terribly complicated concept. We just need more of them, that's all. They're the only two ways to deal with the problem. education and treatment.

Trying to stop the flow of illicit drugs into the country,

or asking the police force "remove" the drug dealers from your city, or pouring our money into lining our shores with interceptor helicopters and high-speed, drug-chasing, kill-em-if-they-open-fire Coast Guard cruisers, is like trying to get rid of cockroaches in your apartment: When you light a bug bomb in the kitchen they leave the kitchen...only to move to the bathroom. Same thing with drugs. It's supply and demand. (We tried this once with Prohibition, didn't we?)

So instead of trying to stop the supply, why don't we try and do something about the demand? All of us. You. And me.

▲ ▼ ▲

One more thing, and then I swear I'm going. I'd like to pass on something someone said to me during the last couple of months of my active chemical addiction. At the time, I was trying desperately to get sober. I couldn't. But it didn't stop me from wanting. I went to see an old friend of mine, a recovering junkie. Before he got sober we had shot a lot of dope together.

I went to see him one day when I was really down and out, and we sat in the living room of his apartment. It was nice: clean, well-kept, neat, new furniture and thick pile carpeting, and in a really good area of town. He was doing all right for himself. I looked around at the television, the stereo, the couches and chairs, the art work on his walls. His wife was in the kitchen making coffee; they were expecting their first child. Both of them were sober. He was four years sober, she was ten. And dare I say that before then both of them were two of the sickest dopefiends I had ever known!

Anyway, what they had was great. I wanted what they

had, what they were doing, the way they were living their lives. I wanted the nice apartment, the television, the wife in the kitchen expecting a first child, the good job, living each day without having to shoot heroin. It seemed like an impossibility. Something other people could get, but not me. I thought I was the one God had singled out to rot in a living hell and to die a stinking junkie. But I asked him how he had done it nevertheless.

"D.J.?" I asked, "How the hell do you do it? How the hell did you ever get out of this and stop shooting dope?"

D.J. turned to me and smiled. I think he may have even laughed a little, sort of like, *Adam? When are you just gonna get this through your thick fucking skull?* He said, "Adam, when I get up in the morning, I get down on my knees and I ask, and then at night I get down on my knees again and I say 'thank you'. It ain't all that complicated."

A few months later, I found myself in jail and tried his advice. It worked.

So I do it every day now. Been doing it for four years. And you know what? It's never failed me. I haven't had to shoot dope in four years. And all I do is say, "please" and "thank you." Once in the morning, once at night. Sometimes it seems so damn simple and easy. (Mind you: I'm saying *sometimes!*)

▲ ▼ ▲

So that's my spiel. I hope you don't feel so alone now.
God loves you. So do I.
And please, don't give up. I know it's hard.
But you just don't have to do that crap anymore.
If you need help, if someone you know needs help, it is no further than your telephone directory. In the city where I live I found forty-seven listings under ALCOHOLISM

and another twenty-five under DRUG ADDICTION. (I didn't even bother checking the COUNSELING heading.)

Nationwide, you will find phone numbers for A.A. (Alcoholics Anonymous), C.A. (Cocaine Anonymous), and N.A. (Narcotics Anonymous) in your telephone directory or from directory assistance. These fellowships are free and there is no requirement for attendance or membership other than a desire to be free from the pains of alcoholism and/or drug addiction. (Most will even give you a lift if you have no means of transportation to get to one of their meetings.)

If you are affected by someone else's chemical use, there are Al-Anon (for family members and friends of alcoholics), Ala-Teen (for teenagers affected by an alcoholic), Coc-Anon (for friends and families of cocaine abusers), and Nar-Anon (for those affected by a person abusing narcotics and other pharmaceuticals). There are support groups for Children Of Alcoholics (COA), Adult Children Of Alcoholics (ACOA), and people who identify themselves as CoDependent (CODAP). ("CoDependency" is a term for those "addicted" to a person who is chemically addicted.)

All these support groups cost nothing, they are all nationwide (some are even worldwide). At these groups you will find others who share your fears and your feelings, your questions and your frustrations; you will find the answers, hope, and strength to deal with your particular aspect of this disease.

Please call.

▲ ▼ ▲

FOR THOSE AFFECTED IN ANY WAY BY COCAINE dial:
1-800-COCAINE

FOR A LISTING OF ADULT AND ADOLESCENT TREATMENT
PROGRAMS dial:
1-800-854-0318 (anywhere but California)
1-800-442-4427 (in Northern California)
1-800-422-4143 (in Southern California)

or call
THE NATIONAL COUNCIL ON ALCOHOLISM
at
1-800-622-2255

▲ ▼ ▲

Or call or write the following:
ALCOHOLICS ANONYMOUS WORLD SERVICES
P.O. Box 459
Grand Central Station
New York, NY 10016   (212) 686-1100

AL-ANON FAMILY GROUP HEADQUARTERS
P.O. Box 862
Midtown Station
New York, NY 10018   (212) 302-7240 or 1-800-356-9996

CHILDREN OF ALCOHOLICS FOUNDATION
200 Park Avenue, 31st Floor
New York, NY 10166   (212) 351-2680

COCAINE ANONYMOUS WORLD SERVICES
3740 Overland Avenue, Suite 6
Los Angeles, CA 90034   (213) 559-5833

DRUG-ANON FOCUS (a support group for families of drug
addicts)
Park West Station
P.O. Box 20806
New York, NY 10025   (212) 888-5671

DRUGS ANONYMOUS
P.O. Box 473
Ansonia Station
New York, NY 10023   (212) 874-0700

GAY AA
84 Broadway
New Haven, CT 06511   (203) 865-6354

NARCOTICS ANONYMOUS
P.O. Box 9999
Van Nuys, CA 91409   (818) 780-3951

NATIONAL ASSOCIATION FOR CHILDREN OF ALCOHOLICS
31582 Coast Highway, Suite B
South Laguna, CA 92677   (714) 499-3889

THE NATIONAL ASSOCIATION OF DRUG ABUSE PROBLEMS
(a referral service)
355 Lexington Avenue
New York, NY 10017   (212) 986-1170

NATIONAL ASSOCIATION OF LESBIAN/GAY ALCOHOLISM
PROFESSIONALS
204 West 20th Street
New York, NY 10011   (212) 713-5074

NATIONAL BLACK ALCOHOLISM COUNCIL
53 West Jackson, #828
Chicago, IL 60604   (312) 663-5780

NATIONAL CATHOLIC COUNCIL ON ALCOHOLISM AND RE-
LATED DRUG PROBLEMS (for affected clergy)
1200 Varnum Street N.E.
Washington, DC 20017   (202) 832-2811

POTSMOKERS ANONYMOUS
316 E Third Street
New York, NY 10009   (212) 254-1777

ALATEEN (Can usually reached through AL-ANON)

Good Luck!
And God Keep you . . .